**W9-CPE-281**

PENGUIN BOOKS

SMALL FORTUNES

Ed Zuckerman has written for *Esquire*, *Rolling Stone*, *Outside*, *Spy*, and *The New York Times Magazine*. The author of *The Day After World War III* (Viking), he lives in New York City.

# SMALL FORTUNES

## Two Guys in Pursuit of the American Dream

### EDWARD ZUCKERMAN

PENGUIN BOOKS

PENGUIN BOOKS
Published by the Penguin Group
Viking Penguin, a division of Penguin Books USA Inc.,
375 Hudson Street, New York, New York 10014, U.S.A.
Penguin Books Ltd, 27 Wrights Lane,
London W8 5TZ, England
Penguin Books Australia Ltd, Ringwood,
Victoria, Australia
Penguin Books Canada Ltd, 10 Alcorn Avenue, Suite 300,
Toronto, Ontario, Canada M4V 3B2
Penguin Books (N.Z.) Ltd, 182–190 Wairau Road,
Auckland 10, New Zealand

Penguin Books Ltd, Registered Offices:
Harmondsworth, Middlesex, England

First published in the United States of America by
Viking Penguin, a division of
Penguin Books USA Inc., 1991
Published in Penguin Books 1992

1  3  5  7  9  10  8  6  4  2

In the interest of protecting the privacy of individuals whose
identities are not central to the true story told here, certain names
and other descriptive details have been altered in several instances.

THE LIBRARY OF CONGRESS HAS CATALOGUED THE HARDCOVER AS FOLLOWS:
Zuckerman, Edward.
Small fortunes / Edward Zuckerman.
p.   cm.
ISBN 0-670-81644-2 (hc.)
ISBN 0 14 01.0006 7 (pbk.)
1. Success in business   I. Title.
HF5386.Z83   1990
650.1–dc20      90–50007

Printed in the United States of America
Set in Primer
Designed by Bernard Schleifer

To The Team of Central Park

# Contents

# PROLOGUE

I WAS IN BUSINESS once myself.

In 1977, a magazine dispatched me to South America to write an article about the infamous killer bees, and I came home with a seven-thousand-word story and a great idea: why not import and market genuine killer bee honey as a gourmet/gift/novelty item? I found a partner, and he and I located a source of killer bee honey, arranged for its transportation to the United States, rented a warehouse, bought bottles, bought bottle caps, designed labels and boxes, hired a beekeeper to put the honey in the bottles, hired a woman from Iceland to put the bottles in the boxes, and met several times with a business consultant who told us over and over to remember that we were "selling the sizzle, not the steak." Whichever, we began to sell the stuff. The press loved it (except for one food critic who wrote that Killer Bee Honey tasted like "silage or hay in a country barn," which I took to be a negative review). *The New York Times* ran a big article about us with a picture of the jar. *Vegetarian Times* gave us a nice writeup, too. *Genesis* ran a photo of a half-naked woman, mock bee stripes painted on her breasts, sampling the product. I made personal appearances in Bloomingdale's and Jordan Marsh, dressed in a beekeeper costume, dispensing free tastes on crackers. My dentist wrote me a congratulatory letter lamenting that he hadn't invested in the enterprise (I had mentioned it to him once while he was scaling my gums). We sold thousands of jars. That wasn't enough. The business failed.

I went back to writing, where I belonged.

My specialty was writing amusing magazine articles. I visited the deposed king of Albania, and the world's greatest life insurance salesman, and a sign-language-speaking gorilla ("I love you," she signed to me. "Come tickle me") and then went home and sat in my room and wrote about them. This was a pretty good way to make a living—I didn't have to get up at 7:00 a.m. or wear a tie or work outdoors in the rain—but I was occasionally troubled, as writers sometimes are, by the feeling that I was experiencing life at second hand.

When I visited the deposed king of Albania, he was training a small army in his backyard to overthrow the Communist Albanian regime. The world's greatest life insurance salesman was selling life insurance and getting rich. The gorilla didn't seem to have much on her mind beside tickling, but her trainer was trying to push back the frontiers of science by breaking down the barriers between species. I was putting words on paper about all these ventures. My venture was composing a string of sentences.

Was this a fit occupation for a man? Shouldn't I be clearing the prairies or something?

My doubts were exacerbated by the fact that I had been living for several years in New York City, which is not exactly what you would call a regular place. I suspected I was missing something of the essence of American life. Not only was I not experiencing it directly, I couldn't even see it from my window. Many a man in my position would have been stirred by these thoughts to do something really stupid, but I had already had my experience with Killer Bee Honey and didn't need another one. So I just stewed.

I was stewing still on a hot summer afternoon in the mid-1980s as I sat reading a newspaper in a café on the main street of Navasota, Texas.

I had come to Navasota to see a man about the killer bees. The killer bees were at that time several years away from flying into Texas from Mexico, and, my expertise in the field having been well established, a magazine editor in New York City had dispatched me to write an article about how America's front-line beekeepers were preparing for the invasion. I had spent the day with Binford Weaver, whose family ran an immense bee enterprise that employed the labor of 150 million bees. The Weavers sold honey, queen bees, and packages of bees (a three-pound pack containing ten thousand live worker bees and one queen cost $29.40, plus postage). The Weavers' bees were gentle, and the Weavers wanted to keep them that way, so they were considering how they might prevent their queens from mating with wild killer bee drones. An entomologist had suggested that instead of letting their virgin queens fly free on their once-in-a-lifetime mating flights, the Weavers confine them to a large enclosed space where the only males admitted would be gentle, non-killer drones. For this to work, however, the queens would have to be fooled into thinking they were flying off great distances as usual, so the scheme would require equipping the enclosed space with wind machines and video screens with images of Texas scenery whizzing by. "Like in the Space Museum," Weaver explained to me.

I wrote in my notebook: "Like Disneyland for bees."

This was good material. It was going to be an amusing article. Another amusing article. Another deposed king of Albania.

I looked around the café.

I ordered a slice of pie.

I turned back to the newspaper I had laid beside my plate—it was the *Navasota Examiner*—and skimmed the column of social notes from the town of Bedias ("Mr. and Mrs. Roy Isbell of Iola recently visited the Strands and brought watermelon and cantaloupe"). Then my eye was caught by a page with the headline "City Police Report." This was a long and detailed roundup of recent law-enforcement activity in Navasota. Some of it was recognizable to me as such—a hit-and-run accident, a wife seeking protection from an estranged husband—but then there were these accounts:

A woman on Willie Street complained to officers Wednesday that her brother's girlfriend was wearing her blue jeans and would not return them. The woman said she would handle the matter personally, however.

A minor accident was reported to officers Saturday at a West Washington Street address, but there were no drivers in the area when the officers arrived. Lawmen learned the accident involved two vehicles bumping together in a private driveway with no damage and no injuries.

Officers responded to reports of a theft at a Montgomery Street location where a horse and saddle was missing. The two items were found in possession of another man, who claimed he had been given permission by a third party to ride the horse away. The investigation is continuing.

Reports of a suspicious vehicle parked at an East Washington Avenue business address drew a police investigation Wednesday. Officers said the driver ran a stop sign and failed to produce a driver's license when confronted. He did have a loud mouth, lawmen said, and was jailed on a complaint charging him with disorderly conduct.

Officers, on Friday, stopped a vehicle on Sycamore Street and questioned the driver who had been reported running as if fleeing someone prior to the arrival of officers. Lawmen found the man was running to catch his ride to a local industry.

I found this news uncommonly interesting. There were very few horse thefts in New York City, and the police there didn't have much time for investigating auto accidents with no damage and no injuries. In New York City, none of this would have been news at all. I felt like I was reading a newspaper from Mars. During a visit to Mars. Everywhere I'd gone in Texas, strangers had said "Howdy" to me and addressed me as "Sir." I wasn't used to being treated like this. People moved with a deliberate calm, and they said things—slowly, with accents—that it took me several seconds to realize were very witty, although I wasn't always sure. That line in the newspaper, "He did have a loud mouth," and that business about handling the blue jean matter "personally" were clearly written with humorous intent. Weren't they?

As it happened, I was in no hurry to get back to New York. My most pressing business there was a complex and futile dispute with my landlord about my rights as a subtenant in a rent-stabilized apartment. That was how people in New York City spent their time.

In Texas I had, by chance, two standing invitations from people I had recently met. One lived near College Station; we had met in the U.S. Virgin Islands, where he was buying cattle. The other lived in Austin; we had met in New York, where he was selling T-shirts. Both had invited me to drop by and say howdy if I was ever in the area.

I sat in the Navasota café for a while and thought about things.

I decided to drive up to College Station and see what was happening there.


From the rough patio behind the cinder-block house, we could see the red cattle that were going to make Pete Binion's fortune, he hoped. Pete talked about them as he fired up the barbecue and laid several enormous steaks on the grill. He spoke with the excitement of a happy man. His cattle were looking good. He loved his wife. He had three rambunctious (but polite) young children. He was about to eat a large piece of beef. And his business project—his dream for the red cattle, a rare breed called Senepol—was exhilarating. Not only would it assure the security of his family, it would also benefit American agriculture. It would transform ranching throughout Texas and the southern United States and in foreign countries as well. It would improve the nation's balance of payments. It would be a boon to meat-eating consumers. It was a grand undertaking, and Pete was confident it was going to succeed.

The patio was shaded by a large oak tree. Beyond it, a lawn ran down a slope, spotted with more trees, to an electrified fence and a pen where a cow with a suckling calf and two larger weaned calves were munching on a bale of hay. Beyond the pen was a hay meadow of a lush greenness that was surprising in the Texas summer heat. It was prize-winning hay, proclaimed grand champion of the 1984 Brazos County Hay Show, a heartening omen for Pete and his family; that had been their first year on this ranch, Hopes Creek Ranch. Winning the hay trophy had made Pete feel proud, made him feel that everything was going to work out fine.

Pete's wife, Becky, a big-boned blonde, came out on the patio with a tray of frozen strawberry daiquiris she had whipped up from a powdered mix in her blender. As daiquiris go, they were on the chewy side; the blender hadn't ground the ice very fine. Becky handed them out and went back into the house, passing through the dining area on her way to the kitchen. The diningroom table was cluttered with business papers piled around an Apple II computer, but work was done for the day. Out on the patio, everything was slow and peaceful. I sat back in my chair, soaking up the unfamiliar calm, listening as Keith Newbill, a slightly built, dapper young man who was Pete's ranch manager, told stories about Meg, his New Zealand eye dog. Meg could apparently herd cattle with near-supernatural ability. All Keith had to do was whistle or say the right word and Meg would move any cow anywhere Keith wanted that cow to go. "She can pick out a cow and bring her right in," Keith was saying. "She can move 'em through a gate, or keep 'em from moving through a gate. She can take the place of at least two cowboys, on a *bad* day. She can move so slow you don't see her move. She can do everything but read and write." She couldn't *drive* either, Keith admitted, but there was a reason for that. "She can't hit the clutch, because her legs aren't long enough. . . ."

Pete didn't care much for cow dogs—he thought they got cattle too excited—but he listened politely as he tended the steaks. A red bull snorted in a pasture around the side of the house. Becky brought out more drinks. The cattle in the pen chewed on their championship hay. We chewed on our daiquiris. The cattle and the trees and the fence and the meadow all glowed prettily in the precise soft clarity of the light in the hour before sunset.

When the steaks were done, Bryan Pratt, Becky's brother

and a hand on the ranch, came out and took one and began to eat without saying a word. I thought he was surly; Pete told me later he had been born with brain damage and was shy about talking in front of strangers for fear he would make a mistake.

Wendell Binion, Pete's half brother and the other ranch hand, had no aversion to conversation whatsoever. But now he just listened to Keith and ate his meal and watched the shadows of the oaks lengthen across the meadow. He enjoyed this part of the day. He was twenty-five years old and had lived most of his life in Houston before moving to the ranch with his girlfriend Aleta six months earlier. He had met Aleta while they were both working as exterminators in the city. They were assigned to the same crew one day; a couple of weeks later Wendell invited Aleta to his birthday party, and they had been together ever since. They lost their exterminating jobs when the company folded up, and there wasn't much work in Houston just then— the Texas economy was in near-depression—so they'd moved out to Hopes Creek Ranch. Wendell was a competent cowhand. Aleta cleaned the house and cooked.

From where we sat, the ranch went back as far as we could see. There were woods behind the hay meadow, and they were part of the ranch, too. It was an historic piece of property. James Hope, one of the settlers led into Texas by Stephen Austin, had been, in 1824, the first Anglo-American to receive a land grant in what is now Brazos County. That grant included this ranch. The creek that ran through the back was Hopes Creek.

The ranch was on a dirt road where few cars ever passed. Pete's red cattle were scattered around in pastures and pens. There were only a few dozen of them, and they were the only Senepol cattle in the entire state of Texas, where there were fourteen million head of cattle.

Pete saw his opportunity in this. He had a vision: someday he would drive across Texas and everywhere he looked he would see herds of red cattle. He thought this was realistic, and he was doing everything he could to make it come true. It was painful to think what would happen if he failed. He was thirty-six years old and had invested everything he had in the Senepol, and everything Becky and Bryan had, too. More than once he said, on that night and other nights, "I'm staking my family's future on this."

Keith started telling stories about some time he'd spent working in the Australian Outback, where the flies were so thick the cowboys couldn't open their mouths to talk, and the nearest town was 150 miles away, on a dirt road. "You didn't run down to the Seven-Eleven to get a six-pack," Keith was saying.

We nodded at his stories and ate our steaks and drank our daiquiris and listened to the crickets, droning ferociously, as the sky turned very slowly from blue to red to black.

Two nights later, I stood on another Texas patio 120 miles from Hopes Creek Ranch. This patio, an elaborate wood deck, was built on two levels around a swimming pool perched on a bluff above Lake Austin. Leaning over the rail, I could see prosperous young Austinites playing in their speedboats. Turning around, I saw the high roof of Jim Teal's house. This was Jim's backyard.

Jim had designed the house himself. It was a bachelor's dream. You walked through the front door to find a single immense room with a lofty peaked ceiling. If you walked straight ahead, you would bump into a crap table. To the right was a polished brass bar and a full-sized pool table. Leather couches in a sunken conversation pit faced a freestanding fireplace and a large-screen projection TV. The TV swiveled toward a bedroom alcove with a king-sized bed. The bathroom complex included a weight room and a sauna. A wall of glass doors led to the patio and the swimming pool. And a hot tub. And an artificial waterfall.

Jim had been raised in a working-class home in Columbus, Ohio, dreaming of luxury like this. At the age of eighteen, he had begun his career as a dollar-an-hour chicken breader at a Kentucky Fried Chicken store. By the time he was thirty, he was a fast-food millionaire. Then he had left the fast-food business for other ventures, and his fortune had waxed and waned. His male stripper bars had done well. His hot tub rental business had failed. "People paid twenty dollars an hour to rent private hot tubs with their girlfriends and fuck," he explained. "Business was good until *Newsweek* and *Time* started running articles about herpes and AIDS every week." Now Jim was in the T-shirt business. He and his partner licensed the rights to put popular comic-strip characters on T-shirts, and they appeared to be on the verge of making it big.

Jim was relaxing this evening, having a couple of drinks at his house with a friend and me. After a while, we drove to an outdoor restaurant where a Hawaiian theme party was under way. We arrived a little late. Most of the luau had been consumed, and a lot of the guests were wandering around drunk in their flowered shirts. Jim was wearing a red shirt with pictures of surfers on it, but he was clearly not drunk. For one thing, he was recognizable. According to Jim's own theory, which he had explained to me, being drunk distorts one's features. He cited as evidence an occasion at the Club Med in Martinique when he had overindulged at a picnic and had to be carried off a nude beach by eight men using a surfboard as a stretcher. After he came to, he showered and dressed and went down to a pavilion where other vacationers were looking at Polaroid pictures of the picnic, including shots of Jim being hauled away. "Look at that asshole," somebody said. "He ripped my top off, the shit," said somebody else. Jim nodded and said, "Yeah, what an asshole." Nobody recognized him, confirming his theory.

A lot of people recognized Jim at the Hawaiian party. He had been in Austin for nine years by then. He was a big man, friendly and witty and outgoing. He greeted many people, and they seemed glad to see him.

One of them was Diane, a clerk at a store Jim frequented, who was sitting at the bar. Jim gave her a friendly hello and bought her a drink. They talked for a while—Diane, no great beauty, enjoyed Jim's attention—and they moved to a table. They talked some more, and then Jim removed Diane's brassiere without removing her blouse. Diane giggled.

The four of us—Diane, Jim, Jim's friend, and I—left the bar together, and I drove us all, in my rented car, to the house of another friend of Jim's, where there was supposed to be a party.

When we got there, my three passengers went upstairs. I walked to the back of the house and joined some people by the pool. Another patio.

The conversation there was a little stiff, owing largely to the presence of two prim sisters from Oklahoma somebody had brought along from the luau. We were talking about movies we had seen lately when flashbulbs started to go off in an upstairs bedroom window.

Jim's friends were amused. They knew what this meant. Jim's friend was photographing Jim and Diane in sexual acts. Soon the two men would switch places. Jim's friends on the patio explained this to all of us sitting by the pool, including the Oklahoma sisters, as the flashbulbs continued to pop in the second-story window, flickering over the patio like a small lightning storm.


Back in New York, I couldn't get Texas out of my mind. I found myself telling friends about Keith's dog, Pete's dream, Jim's casual approach to dating, Jim's consummate entrepreneurship, and the wonderful calm I had felt watching the sun set from Pete's patio.

Nobody got it. A couple of women declared that Jim sounded gross; nothing else elicited any reaction at all.

But my thoughts kept returning to Austin and College Station. I'd had glimpses of a land unlike my own, a land of wild behavior and great peace and audacious ambition. The place I was used to certainly had orgies and ambitions (if not peacefulness), but even the most elemental behaviors of the people I knew were mediated by self-consciousness and overlaid with nervous protocols.

For a year I didn't see Jim or Pete again, and then I began to shadow them. I wanted to see what became of them. I wanted to enter their worlds.

One of the first things that had become clear to me was that we were not of two different worlds but three. We were all American males born in 1948 or 1949. We all spoke English, liked beer, remembered Kennedy, and sometimes watched

David Letterman, yet the gaps between us were as wide as the Panhandle. Pete was a Texan of the old school; Jim was a typical modern Texan—from Ohio. Pete had been in combat in Vietnam and ridden wild bucking bulls, the most dangerous thing you can do in a rodeo, but when I mentioned to him that I play softball in Central Park on summer Saturdays, he was amazed at my foolish courage. "What do you do," he asked me, "all march in together holding your bats?" On two consecutive visits to College Station I automatically locked the door on getting out of Pete's car—forgetting that he never locked it and didn't even have a key—and we had to call for help to get it open. Jim has never met Pete but, based on the little he'd heard from me, once described him to a friend like this: "He lives out in the country. He doesn't have air conditioning. He's trying to be a cattle baron. He doesn't have cable. He never does cocaine."

For two and a half years I regularly visited Pete and Jim to chronicle the strange land into which I had stumbled. Since that land was America (or Texas, which is America but more so), the chronicle became in large part a business story. Pete's dreams were rooted in his business venture; he was scrambling to make it succeed. Jim's enjoyment of life derived from his early success in business; now he needed to succeed again to preserve what he had gained. Both Jim and Pete had emerged from modest backgrounds to invent their own lives; entrepreneurship was the door that would open on the lives they wanted.

Their quests carried them to livestock shows, to toy shows, to a topless golf tournament, to an Aggie football game, to Wall Street, to Guatemala City, to Parris Island, to Paris. They encountered investment bankers, Pulitzer Prize-winning cartoonists, Times Square drug dealers, U.S. Marine Corps officers, the nephew of a dead dictator, the man who invented "Dirty Words," and a legendary basketball star (who turned out to be a lousy sailor). The variety of American life is astounding. Pete and Jim led me on one hell of a tour.

# I. GETTING STARTED

# A Wedding

A T THIRTY-SEVEN, Jim tired of the bachelor life. He had enjoyed it immensely—certainly more than most people—but the appeal of casual sex had diminished. He found himself enjoying quiet evenings at home. And he had met Frances.

He walked into a jewelry store one day with a friend and saw her working behind the counter. She was a pretty blonde with long pale hair and long red nails. She knew who *he* was; she'd heard he was a pervert. He struck up a conversation and they talked for a while. They talked a few times after that and when he asked her out she accepted.

He sent a dozen roses the day of their first date. Soon they were spending a lot of time together. She often stayed at his house. Alone there one weekend while Jim was out of town, she found a briefcase filled with photographs of Jim in sexual acts with dozens of women. In the cabinet beneath the large-screen TV she found the videos. She burned the photographs in the fireplace. She ripped up the tapes and threw them in the swimming pool. Then she called Jim and told him what she'd done. Afterward, he said that this had clarified his feelings toward her: "I figured it must be love, because I wasn't real pissed."

The wedding was set for June 28. Frances was three months pregnant.

---

The organization of the bachelor party was taken on by Gary Shuster, Jim's childhood friend and current business partner. They had met, Gary often said, when they were seated together, because of the alphabetical proximity of their last names, in the third grade at Linden Elementary School in Columbus, Ohio. This history was the basis of the name of their company—Lin-Tex Marketing, Lin for Linden, Tex for Texas—and Gary enjoyed telling the story. He told it to customers, suppliers, salesmen, investors, friends, waitresses, taxi drivers, women in bars, and many other people. Jim had probably heard it a thousand times. He rolled his eyes whenever Gary started to tell it again, because, in fact, he had no memory of Gary before the seventh grade, when they did sit together and became good friends. Under intense questioning on one occasion, Gary confessed that he and Jim had not been in the same third-grade class. "But it makes a nice story."

Gary was a born-again bachelor himself. He had been married young, back in Ohio, and had three children to whom he was a devoted father. But he had not been a model husband. Toward the end of his marriage, he was spending only Sunday nights at home, and came home Sunday only because that was bowling night and he and his wife were on a coed team that was headed toward winning the league championship. Now, in Austin, he was living with an attractive young woman named Dayna who worked as a travel agent and had recently been featured in a *Playboy* pictorial on "The Girls of Texas": "Dayna Parsons (below right) is a travel consultant in Austin. She recently played a groupie in *Songwriter,* with Kris Kristofferson and Willie Nelson. Now we see why they've spent so much time in Texas."

The plan for Jim's bachelor party, Gary announced several weeks before the wedding, was to tell Frances the party was in San Antonio, load all the guests onto a chartered bus, and then drive to Houston for three days of "golf and fucking."

As it turned out, there was golf.

Two days before the bachelor party, Jim and Gary were "celebrity waiters" at an American Heart Association fundraising luncheon. They invited eight guests to the meal and then demanded "tips" for laying out place settings and bringing each course. They raised $1300 for charity this way. Then they drove out to their new country club, loaded up a cart with clubs and liquor, and lost several hundred dollars making stupid bets against the pro. Gary went home to take a nap. Jim headed to the airport in his Mercedes convertible to pick up his first out-of-town guest, and the two of them went out for a few drinks. As they drove around town, Jim used the car phone several times to call Frances and explain why he was late getting home. "Don't pay the ransom," he told her. "I've escaped."

Bright and early the next afternoon, Jim was at the airport again with the "Banana," a shining yellow GMC motor home, equipped with a bar, two TVs and a VCR, that was owned by Lin-Tex Marketing and was to be the mobile bachelor party headquarters. Jim was wearing a golf shirt and shorts, his standard summer attire for play and work, and had come to meet his friend Larry Jaffe, a jeweler from Dayton who was flying down with the rings. Larry arrived looking elegant in a pink shirt, pale linen jacket, and coordinated silk tie and handkerchief. "Where's Frankie?" Jim asked him. "He couldn't make it," said Larry. "He has a backgammon injury. He was playing in a bar and threw double fives to win a game. So he threw up his arms and cut his hand on a Tiffany lamp. He's suing."

"I don't think he wanted to come anyway," said Jim.

On the ride to the Lin-Tex office, Larry fixed himself a drink, and he and Jim reminisced about old times in Ohio, like the night they threw all the furniture in Larry's apartment off the balcony. Jim recalled another night when they'd been out late drinking and, driving them home, "I fell asleep in the middle of making a left turn." He was awakened by the car's landing in a ditch. A policeman who had witnessed the incident approached and inquired if Jim was able to drive. Jim allowed that maybe he wasn't. Can *he* drive? asked the cop, pointing to Larry. "Shit no," said Jim. "He's too drunk."

Unaccountably, the policeman did not arrest Jim but sat with him for a while until he appeared to be a little bit sober. Then the policeman followed as Jim drove to Larry's house. Larry got out, and Jim was supposed to stop there, too, but after the cop was gone Jim decided he felt much better and might as well carry on to his brother Duane's house, where he was staying. He took off again in the car, a Mazda RX-7 that belonged to Duane, and immediately started to feel drunk again. He figured the safest thing to do was to get to Duane's as quickly as possible, before he felt too drunk to drive, so he speeded up. Going ninety-five, he hit a snow-covered divider in the middle of the road and bounced off. The car felt like it had a flat tire, but Duane's was nearby, so Jim pressed on. He pulled into the driveway, threw off his clothes in the living room, and climbed upstairs for a few hours sleep. He had to be up early.

At 7:00 a.m., he stumbled downstairs naked to find his brother and sister-in-law unexpectedly returned from a trip. They seemed to be upset about the car. "What's the big deal?" asked Jim. "It has a flat tire."

Duane pointed out the window and Jim saw, for the first time, that his collision with the divider had not flattened a tire; it had sheared off the left front wheel. He had driven home on three tires and an axle end.

"Never mind that now," said Jim, still naked. He turned to his sister-in-law, who was not a big fan of his to begin with. "Give me your car keys. I've got to get to the club."

Larry smiled at the memory and poured another drink as the Banana arrived at the Lin-Tex office.

Inside Jim and Gary's private office—furnished in wood and leather and marble—other friends had gathered, and there were more stories and more refreshments. Jim's attention wandered between the gathering and "Jeopardy!" on his office TV (he was a big fan of "Jeopardy!"). "Who was *Lassie*?" he shouted at the screen as one of his guests stooped to scoop up some white powder from the floor. "This is the only office in Texas," the guest said, "where you can pick up lint off the carpet and. . . ." He snorted it through a rolled-up twenty.

Gary was watching. "He just snorted drywall," Gary said. (The office was undergoing construction.) The guest ran to the sink in the office bar and threw water in his nose.

———

The official bachelor party began the next day with a golf outing, after which all the guests gathered at a bar in a shopping center. They were mostly in their thirties and forties and mostly in business. Some were golfing buddies of Jim and Gary; some knew them from Austin charitable and civic organizations. Several were in real estate, although it was difficult to determine from a casual conversation exactly what they did with it. "Jim and Gary are very expensive friends," said a short bald man named Sam. "I went to Vail with them last winter and ended up buying a two hundred and fifty thousand-dollar ranch from a cab driver."

Between drinks, Sam was reading an article in that day's paper about the troubles of the Interfirst Corporation, a Texas bank holding company that had just announced it would lose $260 million in the quarter. Sam pointed it out to Jim, who had already read it. "It's not a loss yet," Jim said. "It's a reserve against bad loans."

Sam nodded. Everyone in Austin knew about bad loans. The decline in the price of oil had punctured the Texas economy like a big red balloon. Real estate developers across the state had borrowed billions of dollars from banks and savings and loans for projects nobody could afford to rent or buy and the developers couldn't afford to finish. One Austin builder had just announced an auction of brand-new condos; all bids would be accepted and a four-wheel-drive Suzuki was being given away as a door prize to lure people to the sale.

"I own more stock in that company than any other," Sam said of the Interfirst Corporation. But he didn't seem too upset by the company's bad news. He was soon involved in a long discussion with the bartender about how to make a drink called the Mexican Flag, which was supposed to *look* like the Mexican flag. Sam finally decided it needed tequila, grenadine, crème de menthe, and 151-proof rum to get the colors right. He ordered a round for the party.

Gary announced that it was time to move on, and the celebrants, several clutching their Mexican Flags, headed out to the Banana. As they were boarding, an out-of-town guest named Mel showed up with his date for the weekend, a woman named Leslie, who was not his wife. He had left his wife home. Mel and Leslie had skipped the golf outing to spend the day in Mel's hotel room and now, for the benefit of his friends, Mel made conspicuous gestures of exhaustion. Leslie looked around uncomfortably. "Is this a bachelor party?" she asked. Mel had told her it was a party for out-of-town wedding guests. She was wearing a black cocktail dress.

Gary admitted that it was a bachelor party, and that the next stop was a strip bar.

"I don't think I should go," Leslie said.

Mel, Gary, and several men she had never seen before in her life urged her to come. "It's okay," Gary assured her. "It's nothing but tits."

Wavering, Leslie was led onto the Banana, where she was offered a drink but otherwise ignored as the group chugged along to the Yellow Rose, a topless bar in another shopping center. The men cascaded in. Leslie hesitated in the entryway next to a sign that warned, "You may not touch, handle or fondle the dancers. If so, she will be fired immediately and you will be banned from the club."

The manager came out to greet the group and took over the task of reassuring Leslie. "You'll be comfortable," he told her. "Lots of women come here."

Leslie started to cry. The manager led her into his office.

Mel, meanwhile, was already deep into the club, an enormous room lit by colored lights and filled with dozens of tables and hundreds of men and lots of near-naked women, all of them young and most of them good-looking. Stripped down to G-strings, they were dancing on four separate runways and stages. One woman near the back of the room was turning somersaults on her stage. One was shinnying up a pole. Another was standing on her head. Still others, also stripped, were dancing on the floor next to customers' tables. Some were dancing *on* the tables. Naked legs and breasts were everywhere.

The men of the bachelor party seized a large table, and the women began to come by. "Is he going to want a table dance?" a brunette with an unbuttoned blouse asked Larry. She gestured to Jim, who she'd heard was the guest of honor. Table dances cost ten dollars plus whatever tips spectators were moved to offer. Some of the dancers had so many dollar bills stuck in the waistbands of their G-strings that they appeared to be wearing very short grass skirts.

One member of the party was already tipping, entranced by a woman shaking very large breasts just inches from his face. He never flinched. At the other end of the table, several men developed a keen interest in an intelligent-looking blonde wearing heavy black-framed glasses—the lady-librarian stripper look—who was dancing on one of the stages. After she finished her act, they hailed her as she walked by and handed her ten dollars for a table dance. She climbed up and started to move, stepping nimbly over ashtrays and drinks in her high heels. Her audience's enthusiasm was dimmed only by the realization that they had hired the wrong spectacled blonde (apparently a popular stripper look that season). This one wasn't as pretty as the one they had admired from across the room. When she finished her dance, they found the right one and got her up on the table.

Two hours later, the Banana rolled into the driveway of Gary's rented condo. His girlfriend was out for the evening, but four other women were on hand. While the bachelor partyers helped themselves to drinks and settled on couches in Gary's immaculately neat living room, the women started to strip. Three of them got down to G-strings and started to dance. The fourth, a tall, thin blonde with a butterfly tattooed on her breast, wore a black negligée and danced less gracefully than the others. Her designated function for the evening was to have sex with the groom, an honor Jim declined.

The women danced in front of Gary's large-screen TV, where an X-rated movie was playing. Genitals were exposed on the screen but not in the living room. The dancers approached individual men, shimmying for tips, and tips were offered in the hope that they would inspire total nudity. But they did not. Gary finally proposed an end to individual tipping, which his guests were beginning to find annoying. He collected twenty-five dollars a man and distributed it to the dancers. But they still didn't take off their G-strings.

Jim was disgusted. Not that he was particularly eager to see a professional stripper's private parts; it was the principle of the thing. "Did you know your nipple is exposed?" he asked in mock shock as one of the dancers walked by. She had actually put some of her clothes back *on*.

"Can I ask you something?" Gary said to the dancers as they took a drink break next to the television set. They nodded warily. He could *ask*. "I don't want to get rings on here," he said, running his hand along the top of the TV cabinet. "Could you keep your drinks off it?"

They said sure.

Somebody sent out for pizza and the party moved into the kitchen. "Pretend that I have clothes on," said Suzanne, one of the dancers, as she bit into a slice of mushroom and pepperoni and chatted with one of the guests. She made a token effort to cover her small breasts with an elbow. "I feel funny meeting you and I'm half-naked."

At 2:00 a.m., Gary abruptly announced that the party was over. Most of the men dribbled out. Leslie, who had arrived on the Banana and then secluded herself in an upstairs bedroom, emerged with a member of the bachelor party (not Mel) and left with him. She was never seen again.

Staying behind were Jim, Gary, two of their friends, and the four dancers. Everyone sat in the living room and passed around a joint. Three of the women had put some clothes on, but not Stella, a strikingly pretty nineteen-year-old with a perfect body. The joint came to her and she inhaled. Then, without a word, she put the lighted end in her mouth, grabbed the man next to her, pulled his face close to hers, and exhaled so that smoke streamed out the exposed end of the joint. He was supposed to inhale at precisely that moment, but, hopelessly distracted by being pulled toward Stella's naked body, he missed his cue.

Stella shrugged. She turned to the blonde with the butterfly on her breast and said, "It's funny. Do you find yourself doing things like your parents?"

"Oh yeah!" said the blonde.

"You mean that's the way your parents smoke joints?" asked the man next to Stella.

"My mom," she said.

"How old's your mom?"

"Forty," said Stella. "That's the way she blows dope."

Jim, who did not find this conversation interesting, spoke up with a suggestion. "Gee, look," he said, "there's eight of us here, four boys and four girls. You know what? We could split up. Maybe we could split up in pairs: boy-boy, girl-girl, boy-boy, girl-girl. Or we could split up boy-boy-boy-boy, girl-girl-girl-girl. Or—I've got it!—we could split up boy-girl, boy-girl, boy-girl, boy-girl."

The boys looked interested in this. The girls ignored Jim completely.

Eventually, most of the group did get in Gary's hot tub. The men stripped naked. The women never took off their G-strings.

Two days later, Jim greeted early-arriving wedding guests wearing a bathing suit, dripping wet, and holding a tiny, hyperventilating dog in his arms. The dog was Frances's Pomeranian, Ashley. "This dog has emphysema or something," Jim said. "All these people are getting her so excited she can't breathe." The wedding was called for 6:00 p.m. at Jim's house. It was five, and he had just finished his afternoon swim. Elaborately wrapped gifts were stacked on the crap table. Giant grilled shrimp and caviar were laid out on the pool table. The caviar was going fast.

Gary was having a drink at the bar. He was dressed in formal wear above the waist and white shorts below. His girlfriend, Dayna, a petite brunette, was plucking at the elasticized top of her strapless dress. "My enormous breasts keep popping out," she explained facetiously. In fact, the top was threatening to slip down over her less-than-enormous breasts. She had lost weight since her *Playboy* photo; Gary had promised to give her a thousand dollars if she got back up to a hundred pounds.

"I try to quit drinking," the man next to Dayna was saying. He was overweight and recently divorced. "I only go to bars to meet girls. Then I drink because I feel silly being in a bar and not drinking. Then I get too drunk to pick up girls." He took a drink. "Actually, I never fool around. I'm trying to preserve the sanctity of divorce." He was still in love with his ex-wife, who had once shot up their house with a .357 Magnum, and everybody knew it.

Larry Jaffe was at the pool table, scooping up the last of the caviar, and Jim's brothers Duane and Dave had also arrived from Ohio. Dave stood quietly in a corner, eyeing the company with interest. Duane looked like he might still be pissed off about the Mazda.

The happiest man in the room was Howard McNamara, a Baptist minister who was going to conduct the ceremony. Jim attended no church. He'd asked Howard to do the job because they played basketball together. "Jim is very considerate of others," Howard was telling a guest. "He takes an interest when he doesn't have to. . . . Now that Jim and Frances are having a family, they may be interested in getting involved with a church."

"Don't get carried away, Howard," said Jim, passing by with a drink in his hand. "If I join any church, it'll be that one on the corner where the minister drives a Ferrari."

Howard kept smiling.

The phone rang and Jim picked it up. "You're two hours late, Frances," he said, "and I'm getting pissed. You're missing the party." He grunted and hung up. "She says she's so nervous she's sick," he reported.

Howard smiled.

A seventeen-piece mariachi band suddenly marched into the living room, shouting, hooting, and playing trumpets. This put a damper on conversation. A fat fiddle player wearing an enormous sombrero tripped and fell on her face.

At the bar, a friend of Gary's greeted Dayna and shouted, "I hear you've got a new Mustang convertible. I bet you'll look cute in it."

Dayna plucked at the top of her dress. "I *already* look cute in it," she shouted.

The mariachi band marched out to the patio, the guests mingled and drank, and, eventually, Frances arrived, looking lovely if nervous in a lacy peach maternity wedding gown. Mel and the fat divorced man cornered her at the bar. "Dump Teal and come to Vegas with me," said the fat man.

Frances smiled politely.

"Come with *me*," said Mel. "I can get a bigger suite."

The wedding convened by the swimming pool, in front of the waterfall. Jim had changed into a gray suit and black cowboy boots. Frances looked calmer now in her voluminous dress. Howard smiled and began with a little speech. "One function of marriage," he said, "is to make a life complete. . . ."

He was interrupted by heckling. "We all know Jim was incomplete!" one of the guests shouted from the other side of the pool.

Howard continued without further interruption until he got to the vows. "Do you, Jim Teal, take this woman to be your lawful wedded wife, to have and to hold, for richer or poorer. . . ."

"Hopefully it won't be poorer," said Jim.

When the ceremony was finished, Jim, Frances, and Howard formed a line to receive the guests. Jim joked with his friends. The men kissed Frances. Howard stood a little apart and spoke to no one in particular. "It's a miracle," he said. "It's a miracle."

# Limited Partnership

**T**WO DAYS AFTER Jim Teal's wedding, while Jim and Frances were en route to Alaska on a luxury cruise, Pete Binion drove from his ranch to Houston in search of money. Pete was a little in awe of the world of money. He wasn't used to having much himself. Now his fundraising efforts occasionally brought him in contact with people who had a great deal of money. He looked at them and tried to figure out what separated them from people who didn't have money; how had they gotten from here to there? Observing their fluency in dealmaking and the language of dealmaking, it almost seemed to Pete as if they were in possession of magic words or keys that opened the world of money to them.

Whatever it was that brought money, it certainly wasn't something Pete was born with. He spent most of his childhood on a succession of ranches and farms outside small Texas towns— Quemado, Azle, Cleburne, Eagle Mountain Lake. His stepfather Binion (Pete's real dad died when Pete was four) generally worked as a draftsman in town while attempting, usually without much success, to make a go of agriculture at the same time. Pete had to work from the moment he got off the school bus until dark, and weekends too, irrigating fields, hoeing tomatoes and onions, picking corn, tending livestock. Meals often consisted of bean sandwiches with onions or tomatoes from the fields if they were ripe. Pete was very close to his five brothers and sisters, but he felt cut off from the rest of the world. When his friends from school were playing baseball, he was working. When his friends were starting to hang around with girls, he was working.

Pete graduated from high school in 1967 and went to a junior college for half a semester before enlisting in the Marines. He was sent to Vietnam, where he served on a tank crew and saw a lot of combat. Afterward, he rarely talked about what he had done in Vietnam although he occasionally alluded to "horrible" things he had seen there. Pete learned to drink in Vietnam, a pastime he practiced with great enthusiasm for several years after his return to Texas. He also took up riding bulls in weekend rodeos. The thrill of hanging on to wildly bucking 1500-pound animals with ferocious strength and deadly sharp horns took his mind off Vietnam.

Pete's normal physical condition during his bull-riding years included dislocated fingers and badly bruised legs. Once a bull stomped on his foot and broke several bones. Pete hobbled out of the arena, drove to a veterinary clinic where he worked part time, climbed up on a table and X-rayed the foot, and then went out and rented a pair of crutches. He never saw a doctor. Without missing a week, he continued to ride in the rodeo, wearing a Marine boot on his injured foot (it was too swollen for his cowboy boot), taping a spur to the substitute boot, and using his rented crutches to get to and from the bulls.

His best ride ever was on a bull called Ringeye, which had gored a rider to death the week before. Pete drew Ringeye because nobody else wanted to ride him, and he won first place and the prize that went with it—$120.

Another week Pete found himself wandering around a rodeo arena with no memory of who he was or what he was doing. Later, he figured out that he had probably been riding a horse bareback and fallen off and been kicked in the head. But, wandering in the arena, he knew nothing. His mind contained only a telephone number. He called it. A woman answered who turned out to be his sister Mollie. Pete asked her, "What's my situation? Am I working? Am I going to school? Where am I supposed to be going?" Mollie said, "Don't move," and came and got him.

Pete was going to school at the time, at Texas A&M University in College Station, where he earned a bachelor's degree in animal science. After graduation, he got a job with a Hereford breeder in Colorado, working seven days a week for $500 a month. After six months of that, he got a better job, managing a ranch near Burnet, in the Texas hill country. One of the most interesting things about his new job, from Pete's point of view, was that the ranch was one of the first in the area to employ a new technique called embryo transfers in breeding its best animals.

The old natural way, a superior cow could produce only one calf a year. With embryo transfers, she could produce dozens. First, she was injected with drugs to stimulate her reproductive system to produce multiple eggs. Then those eggs were fertilized with semen from a top-ranked bull. Then a specially trained rancher or veterinarian extracted the fertilized eggs and placed them, one by one, in the wombs of lower-grade "recipient" cows. Nine and a half months later, as many as ten identical sons or daughters of the superior cow and bull would be born. And the transplanting process could be repeated six or seven times a year.

Pete found this technology fascinating. After leaving the job in Burnet, he went to work at an industrial job in Houston until he'd saved enough money to return to Texas A&M for graduate study in animal breeding. Soon after getting back in school, Pete decided to start a company to put into practice some of the things he was learning. He named the company Universal Embryonics, after rejecting "World Embryonics" as too limited. "A lot of the things we were going to be doing were going to be kind of earth-shaking," he said later, "things like embryo transfers, gene injections, DNA. . . ." Universal Embryonics was going to operate on the cutting edge of cattle reproduction technology, for the combined benefit of world agriculture and Pete Binion and his family.

Meanwhile, for his master's thesis, Pete had been assigned to write about a Red Brangus operation in central Texas. The Red Brangus is a breed that was developed by crossing Angus cattle, known for their tasty beef, with Brahman cattle, a hardy breed that does well in hot climates. Pete thought the Red Brangus was an excellent animal. He had, in fact, already scraped together a few dollars to assemble a low-budget micro-herd of his own. It included two seemingly unpromising animals—a cow that was crippled and one that had failed to produce a calf the previous year—but Pete had palpated both animals, that is, he had examined their reproductive organs by inserting his arm, and concluded they were sound. He got them cheap.

Pete probably would have gone ahead and written his paper on the Red Brangus and never even heard of Senepol cattle, let alone staked his financial future on them, if his father-in-law, Billie Pratt, hadn't made an indiscreet business proposition at the ranch that was to be the subject of Pete's study. Billie was a country lawyer from Burnet who saw no reason to let any potential business connection slip away out of shyness. When Pete went to visit the Red Brangus operation, Billie went along for the ride. The ranch, which was owned by a wealthy man, impressed them both. A long paved driveway that led to the house doubled as a private airplane runway. The cows were implanted with mechanical devices that registered whether or not the animals were in heat. While a ranch manager was showing Pete and Billie around, Billie mentioned offhandedly that Pete was in the Red Brangus business, too, and that maybe he and the ranch could do something together. A few days later, a representative of the ranch called Texas A&M and demanded the return of some breeding data Pete had been given, on the grounds that he was a potential competitor. Pete was incredulous. "I had six cows. They had computers in their cows' backs." But he was assigned to a different research project.

The new project involved the Senepol, an obscure breed of cattle developed on the Caribbean island of St. Croix. Pete had never heard of the Senepol before—probably not one rancher in a thousand had—but he was so impressed by what he learned about them that he never did complete his master's thesis. He got sidetracked by his effort to be the first rancher to bring Senepol cattle into Texas.

Pete's first stop in Houston on the hot June day he drove down from the ranch was a medical clinic near the oil refineries on the Houston Ship Channel. He pulled into the parking lot in his bronze Chevy Blazer wagon, walked inside, and told a nurse he was there. So were a lot of other people. They were sitting in the waiting room and navigating a warren of examination rooms, shepherded by a flying squad of nurses. The scene, as always, reminded Pete of a cattle-herding operation.

The presiding physician, a short, trim man named Joe McCall, emerged from one of the examination rooms, instructed a nurse to hold up the flow for a few minutes, and ushered Pete into his large and quiet private office. Pete sat down, and he and the doctor started to talk about cows.

Pete had met Dr. McCall a couple of years before, shortly after he became interested in the Senepol. At the time, Dr. McCall was looking for a little relaxation. His medical practice, which consisted largely of workers whose employers had contracted with Dr. McCall's clinic for their health care, was exhausting. He rose at five-thirty every morning and routinely saw as many as eighty patients a day. His ambition was to retire from medicine entirely in fifteen years, when he would be fifty.

In the meantime, Dr. McCall and his wife Jackie had purchased a ranch in Fayette County, ninety-five miles from Houston, as a weekend retreat. They wanted some cattle for their ranch; Jackie wanted red ones, because she thought they would look nice against the green background. Looking for advice, Dr. McCall turned to a veterinarian he knew. The veterinarian referred him to his former part-time employee, Pete.

Dr. McCall and Pete had a meeting, and they hit it off, and Pete told Dr. McCall about the Senepol—how it appeared to be a superior beef animal for a climate like that of Texas, where it was unknown; how money might be made by introducing it to Texas ranchers; how it was red. Despite Jackie McCall's misgivings—"I just wanted cattle for relaxation," she said later—Dr. McCall joined Pete in the Senepol business.

It was Dr. McCall who suggested that they finance the importation of Senepols by organizing a limited partnership. As a physician with a good income, Dr. McCall had often been approached about investing in limited partnerships in the past, and he had often done so. The primary appeal of such ventures to people with large incomes was the tax advantages they offered. The deals were usually structured in such a way that investors (the "limited partners") were able to take paper losses that substantially reduced their tax bills, at least in a limited partnership's early years. Limited partners were often so focused on short-term tax savings, however, that they failed to notice that, as businesses, many limited partnerships stank. They produced little if any real profits over the long term and were commonly tilted in favor of the "general partners" who organized the ventures. When Dr. McCall and Pete became general partners themselves and set up MB (for McCall Binion) Universal Programs I, Dr. McCall vowed that it would be a fair deal.

Universal I got off to an inauspicious start when a tree fell on Pete. He was in the midst of methodically drafting the financial and legal documents that would launch the partnership when he took a break from paperwork one day to head into the back acres of Hopes Creek Ranch and cut some wood. He needed fence posts, and it was cheaper to cut them himself than to buy them from somebody else.

Using a chainsaw, Pete cut down a large tree that fell into the fork of a smaller tree and lodged there. He walked over to cut down the small tree, but, before he got to it, it buckled under the weight of the large tree, and the large tree fell on Pete. It knocked him in the head and landed hard on his right hip and left arm. Pete's brother-in-law Bryan, a powerfully built young man, ran over and managed to lift the tree off Pete. Then he grabbed Pete's injured arm to pull him up. Pete screamed. Bryan ran off to get help. Fearing that he might go into shock and die, Pete struggled to elevate his uninjured leg, and he prayed he wasn't lying on a fire-ant nest. Bryan returned with some others, and they got Pete to a hospital, where doctors set his hip, which was broken, and reconstructed his shattered arm with metal plates.

But Universal I worked out fine. Dr. McCall and Pete quickly sold all the shares, several of them to doctors Dr. McCall knew, and raised $270,000, which they used to establish a small herd of Senepols and recipient cows for Senepol embryos on Hopes Creek Ranch. Almost immediately, Pete and Dr. McCall began planning for MB Universal Programs II, a much larger limited partnership that would raise $1.8 million for a major herd expansion via extensive use of embryo transfers. For Pete, Universal II was going to be a big payoff. As a general partner and operator of the ranch where the Universal II herd would be based, he would receive a variety of fees from the partnership. There would be an administrative fee, and an allocation for operating expenses, and an annual cow maintenance fee of $400 an animal. Finally, all of the embryo transfer work for the program was to be performed by Universal Embryonics for a fee of $1000 per embryo.

Not all of this money would go in Pete's pocket. He was going to incur considerable expenses caring for the Universal II herd. And he was probably going to have to hire someone else to do the embryo transfers, since the arm injured by the falling tree was the arm he had always used to reach inside cows; he had a lower rate of successfully implanted pregnancies with his other arm. Nevertheless, the income generated by Universal II would put Hopes Creek Ranch, which had been operating in the red, solidly into the black.

The new limited partnership got off to a fast start when four wealthy Houston businessmen expressed interest in buying the whole program themselves. The deal appeared to be all but set when one of the investors was found dead of a shotgun blast in his Cadillac. Pete and Dr. McCall were back to square one, looking for $1.8 million.

That's where things stood on the day Pete stopped at the clinic. While patients stacked up outside Dr. McCall's office, the general partners sat and discussed the status of Universal II. Then Pete said goodbye and walked back out to the parking lot and the glaring sun and heavy humidity of the Houston summer. Pete was wearing jeans, boots, and a long-sleeved white shirt. He paused in the middle of the parking lot, lifted his right foot, and set it on a bumper. He took a tie out of his briefcase, wrapped it around his thigh, and tied a Windsor knot. Then he transferred the tie from his leg to his collar and pulled it half tight.

It was time to dress up. He was on his way to see the investment banker.


Pete had found his investment banker in the Yellow Pages. He had turned to "Investment Bankers" and started dialing numbers. Half the people he called wouldn't even listen to his story, but he finally reached a lawyer who referred him to Charles Lundelius.

Lundelius, with his wife Patricia, ran a small investment firm from posh offices near the Houston Galleria shopping mall. He had worked as a consultant to the Granada Corporation, a big Texas agricultural company that had launched dozens of cattle limited partnerships, so he knew the business. He was young, just thirty, and ambitious. The first time he met Pete, he was impressed by Pete's knowledge of cattle and his scrupulous honesty. He became convinced that Pete had a good thing in the Senepol, and that he and Universal Programs could make money together.

Pete and Lundelius made an odd pair. Pete was tall and thick with muscle. His accent was heavy Texas, and he talked slowly. His rancher's sideburns and mustache were his only manifestations of style. His tie *looked* like it had been tied on his thigh in a parking lot.

Lundelius was pear-shaped. He wore expensive suits and was a confident talker. He respected Pete's abilities—when they first met he had been amazed at the complexity of a herd growth model Pete had worked out with pencil and paper (Lundelius promptly reworked it on a computer)—but he had fought to smooth off some of the rough edges in Pete's operation. He had insisted that Pete hire a secretary so there would be someone to answer the ranch phone at all times during business hours. It would shake investor confidence if their calls to Hopes Creek Ranch went unanswered, he explained. Pete hired the secretary—she sat in the little office he'd set up in the hay barn—but he balked at hiring the securities lawyer Lundelius urged upon him. The lawyer would have cost $30,000, which Pete thought was ridiculous. He figured he could do the paperwork himself, with some help from his father-in-law, Billie Pratt, for free.

As for the touches of altruism that marked Pete's ventures, Lundelius was amused. The prospectus for Universal II, written by Pete, said that one goal of MB Universal Programs was "to make American agriculture competitive with foreign imports." Asked about that, Lundelius replied, "I didn't write that section." And he mimicked: " 'And then we're going to end world hunger. Then we'll send cows into space. . . . ' "

Pete had had a few laughs of his own. When Lundelius and several of his brokers came out to Hopes Creek Ranch for a tour,

Pete showed them around, then served up an afternoon snack he identified as chicken nuggets. After the brokers dug in, he announced that these nuggets had never seen the inside of a chicken. They were actually the western delicacy known as mountain oysters—fried calf testicles. Some of the brokers spat, some turned green, and some did both. When Lundelius got home that night, his wife wouldn't kiss him until he brushed his teeth.

But Pete and Lundelius were relying on each other for the success of Universal II. Lundelius needed Pete to manage the program. Pete needed Lundelius to sell it. Having his fate in someone else's hands made Pete anxious, but Lundelius assured him that everything would work out fine.

"There should be strong interest," he said to Pete as they sat on leather chairs in his office. "We're going to market the shares through a network of brokerage firms. If we need to, we can bring in firms from California to the East Coast."

"If I can be of use," Pete offered, "if there's anyone I can see and talk to. . . ."

"We'll certainly let you know," said Lundelius.

Pete shifted forward in his chair. "When do you expect to start selling?"

"Mid-July is a safe bet."

Pete still looked nervous, but he was as satisfied as he could be for the moment. He wanted the program out on the market. He wanted the partnership shares sold. He had gone out on a personal financial limb in anticipation of its success. He had bought additional Senepol cattle and hay to feed them. He was paying salaries to Keith Newbill, his "cattle operations manager," and to the secretary he had hired at Lundelius's insistence. He was paying for health insurance and running several vehicles. Money was going out all over the place.

Universal II would turn that stream around. "If we had Universal II sold," he said, "that's all we need to make our operation cash-flow and work." He liked Lundelius's confidence, but he couldn't quite believe in it. "It's almost too good to be true," he said. "I'm just as nervous as a calf."

# "Against the Rules of Kentucky Fried Chicken"

**D**RIVING THROUGH COLUMBUS to the Ohio State Fair, Jim Teal and his brother Dave were talking about the Lemonade Shake-Up stands. The stands were fixtures at the annual fair and did a booming business in the August heat. "The guy gets a buck a glass," Jim said, "and there's nothing in there but sugar, water, and a little lemon."

Dave nodded.

"And then there's Dave's iced tea," Jim said. Dave, a Columbus restaurateur, operated a chain of iced-tea stands at the fair. One of them had taken in $2000 this year in a single day.

"And we don't bother with the lemon," Dave said.

"Did you ever think," Jim asked his brother, "that you might get to Heaven, and God will say, 'Dave, you fucked them on the iced tea. Your wife went to church every Sunday and prayed for you. You led a pretty decent life. But you fucked 'em on the tea.' "

Dave thought about it as he turned into the fairground.

"It could happen," he said.

Jim was in Columbus for a nostalgic visit on the occasion of his twentieth high school reunion. He had been born and raised in Columbus, the third of five children in a working-class family. His father, at various times, worked in a factory, painted houses, ran a small grocery store. The kids worked, too. Jim caddied, worked in a pizza parlor, and traveled with a carnival. Starting in his early teens, he got jobs at the state fair, selling brightly colored junk to other kids, picking up balls at the cat throw, eventually running his own carny games. One year he had the misfortune to run a booth next to Ronnie and Donnie, the Siamese twins. The endless tape-loop announcement beckoning people to see them—"They're joined at the waist! They're alive!"—nearly drove him crazy. Another year, he claimed, he'd messed around with the daughter of a king of the Gypsies, who worked the fair too, and had to hide from her bodyguards.

Twenty years later, wandering the fairground with Dave, Jim stopped for a hot sausage called a Bahama Mama and watched the suckers throwing baseballs at wooden milk bottles. He stopped for spare ribs and strolled through the sheep exhibit building. He had a peach cobbler and a glass of Dave's iced tea.

When he stopped for an ear at the Ohio Roast Corn stand, he noticed a man with a grizzled beard who was supervising the busy operation. "I know you," Jim said. "I used to work for you."

The man looked up with no trace of recognition. "Could be," he said. "I've been here eighteen years."

"You've been here longer than that," Jim said. "I worked for you longer ago than that."

"I guess you're right," the man said. "I guess I have been here longer than eighteen years."

"Yeah," said Jim. "I used to work here."

One of the counter girls looked up, pausing in her endless routine of handing out corn and taking in money. "What made you give it up?" she asked.


Jim was always enterprising.

A friend from high school recalls that Jim once proposed that they pool their resources and buy a car, despite certain limitations: "He couldn't drive. I couldn't drive. The car didn't run. He said it would be a good investment."

After he learned to drive, Jim devised another plan, one he was reminded of as he drove around his old neighborhood on the day of his reunion:

"I was driving down the freeway one night. I had an old Nash Rambler, and I'm driving along, and I saw some guy weaving real bad, weaving all over the road. I thought, 'Shit, this guy's drunk. And he's not going fast enough to hurt me. I think I'll let him hit me, and I'll get the insurance money, get some cash out of the deal.' I followed him, and the next thing I knew the sucker had hit two or three bridges, railroad overpasses, smacked them and just kind of glanced off of them, and the next thing I know he's making a U-turn over a median and going back the other way on the freeway, so I got a U-turn and go back. So then I put my brights on him, and I figured I'd confuse him a little bit, since he was obviously real drunk. I hit the brights on him a few times, and then I pulled up alongside of him and just waited. Finally he drifts over, and as soon as he hit me I locked him up so he'd put some skid marks down in case the police wanted to see that. Then I turned my wheel into him and we come to a grinding halt. Immediately I jumped out of the car and told him that he'd hit me and that I wanted money for my car. He said, 'We're gonna call the cops. Call the cops.' I said, 'Nah. You're real drunk. You don't want to call the cops. That's a real bad mistake.' He said, 'Nah. Call the cops. Fuck you. I ain't paying nothing. I knew what you were trying to do.' I said, 'Hey, pal, a couple hundred bucks cash right now, and I'm out of here.' He was driving a big Lincoln and we were in a pretty rich part of town. He said, 'I ain't doing that.'

"About that time a truck driver stopped across the road and he comes running over and says, 'I saw the whole thing, son. I called the police for you.' I said, 'Great. I just wanted this guy to give me a couple hundred bucks and I'm out of here.' The truck driver said, 'Nah. That's a bad idea. You get the police here and have this whole thing investigated.' Well, the cops show up and they talk to the guy. I say, 'I got to tell you, I've been behind this guy for quite a while, and when I tried to pass him is when he hit me. I wouldn't let him drive home. It's a real bad idea to let this guy drive home. I don't want to say he's drunk or anything, but he has some kind of a problem.' He tells the cops he's on medication, and he's a doctor, and this, that, and the other, and that's why he's weaving. The cop does the insurance deal and tells me to take off.

He says, 'You just call the insurance company tomorrow.' So I leave.

"Next day I call the insurance company and said, 'I want to see about getting my car checked out. This guy hit me last night. Dr. Brown or whatever his name was hit me.' And the guy said, 'Oh, you must be Mr. Williams.' I said no. He said, 'You're Mr. Jones.' I said no. He said, 'You must be Mr. Smith.' I said, 'No, I'm Mr. Teal.' He said, 'We don't have any Teal down here. He didn't hit any Teal last night.' Pause. 'Oh, you were the *first* one.' I said, 'What do you mean I was the first one?' He said, 'Oh, after he hit you, the cops let him drive home and he crushed five parked cars on the way home.' So then the deal was my car only had a dent in it. I figured, 'Shit, they're not going to give me no money for just having a dent.' I was working for Kentucky Fried Chicken at the time, so we took the car and went down through the driveway of the Kentucky Fried Chicken store at Cleveland and Duxbury, and I cut the wheel real hard and tried to slide into a light pole to smash the back end of the car up. And I did it. Then I go into the body shop and told the guy, 'I need to get an estimate on the car. I think it might have some real damage to it.' And the guy says, 'What kind of car is it?' And I said, 'Nash Rambler.' He said okay, and he pulls out a sheet and he writes, '1961 Nash Rambler. Totaled.' I said, 'What do you mean "totaled"? You didn't even look at the car.' He said, 'Pal, if it's a Nash Rambler, if you scratched it it's totaled as far as I'm concerned.'

"So I smashed my car up for no reason. The insurance company gave me four or five hundred bucks, and I was still driving it. Then I parked it in front of my house one morning, and my mom came upstairs and woke me up and said, 'I think you got a problem. You better go outside and look at your car.' I go downstairs and look out and there's this little MG sports car buried in the engine of my car with a girl dangling behind the wheel and people all gathered around. She was a neighbor that lived down the street and had dropped a cigarette in her lap and smashed the car again. This time the insurance company came out and gave me another check for a couple, three hundred bucks and towed the car away for good. And then about two months later she killed herself at the same intersection. She dropped another cigarette in her lap and ran a stop sign and a guy hit her head on and killed her, which goes to show that smoking can be deadly."

Driving through his old neighborhood, looking around, Jim passed the yellow brick elementary school he'd walked to every day, and the Northeast Church of Christ, where he went every Sunday until he was about thirteen and quit going to church, and the site of the whites-only swimming pool where, barely understanding race, not understanding racism, he swam every summer until the owner, ordered to admit blacks, bulldozed the place instead.

The neighborhood now was mostly black. Jim stopped the car in front of his old house, a large, well-tended place with sixty-foot pines in the front yard that Jim's family had planted when he was a kid. Jim approved of the way the current residents were keeping things up.

He drove again, past a park where he'd played, past the Valleydale Ballroom where he saw Frankie Valli and the Four Seasons twice, past a restaurant where he'd worked as a teenager and one day, careless with a knife, sliced off his fingertips:

"My boss threw me the keys to his car, and I drove down to the emergency room in his big Lincoln convertible, like President Johnson used to have. And I've got the top down, and I've got the towel wrapped around my hand, blood pouring everywhere.

"I go in the emergency room and I say, 'Sew the tips of my fingers back on. I don't think I completely severed them.' So they do it, and the nurse says—she knows I'm working at Casino Pizza—'Why didn't you bring us a pizza?' I said, 'Well, at the time I wasn't really thinking about bringing you a pizza. I was more thinking about bleeding to death.' And she says, 'Well, next time you're back, bring us a pizza.' And I said, 'I hope not to *be* back.'

"About two weeks later, I've healed up considerably and, being a young stupid kid, I have forgotten that knives hurt, and I'm playing with the bread, and I chop the tips of my fingers off again, and I chop them off this time a little better than the time before. So I yell over to Bill Casino, 'I'll need the keys to the car and a large pepperoni.' "

Jim stopped his rented car again in front of the house of his high school girlfriend. It was small and shabby; there were toys scattered in the yard. Jim's high school girlfriend had been beautiful and smart. Somebody had told Jim she was back living in this house again, after all the years. Jim thought about it. He decided not to knock on the door.

After high school, Jim had considered marrying this girl. But he knew that wives demanded a lot of their husbands' time and attention. His married friends were always being nagged to spend more time at home. Jim wanted to be successful, and he had picked a career that he knew would require all of his time and energy. A wife would hold him back.


Jim started working for Kentucky Fried Chicken part time during his senior year in high school. His brother Dave was the assistant manager of a Kentucky Fried Chicken store where Jim used to hang out. Sometimes he borrowed his brother's car while Dave was working. Dave finally told him he couldn't have the car any more unless he worked a couple of hours a day for free, breading chicken. This kept Dave's labor cost down and made him look good in his reports to the company.

Jim eventually started getting paid a dollar an hour for his labor. He preferred breading chicken to frying because he'd seen people get burned at the fryer, but once he was on the payroll Dave made him fry too. When he finished high school, Jim had no desire to sit in classrooms any more, and Dave proposed that he come to work for Kentucky Fried Chicken. Jim hesitated; he didn't see much of a future in part-time breading and frying. But Dave said, "You'll be full time. You'll be management." Jim thought it over. Dave, who hadn't gone to college, was doing pretty well. He was making over ten thousand dollars a year. He lived in a nice apartment and had a nice car. It looked like a pretty good deal.

Jim started full time at fifty-five dollars a week. This was actually a cut from his part-time pay, since he immediately found himself working sixty-five to seventy hours. The work was not glamorous. He spent a lot of time breading chicken in a Kentucky

Fried Chicken store that had been converted from a gas station. The kitchen was so small Jim had to push the breading table up to the bathroom door and stand in the bathroom while he breaded.

There was some excitement once at another store. A bunch of black kids who hung out at a nearby McDonald's had more or less declared war on Kentucky Fried Chicken. They threw rocks at the store and beat up one of Jim's co-workers. So Jim and his colleagues took action:

"I got a bunch of chicken pots, and I got the shortening smoking at about 450 degrees, which is right below the flash point. And I come walking out of the back door with a couple of kids. We had hot pots of shortening, like in the old medieval days. And we walked around to the front of the store, and we snuck up on them, and we said, 'You boys want to have a little talk now?' They all had rocks in their hands, and we're standing there with the hot shortening, which could nail them. And they retreated back to McDonald's and kept throwing the rocks. Next night we hid up on the roof, and we had two or three shotguns that we had smuggled into the store. We were going to shoot them if they came over. This was all against the rules of Kentucky Fried Chicken, of course."

Fortunately, a supervisor came by and imposed an armistice.

Even in routine times, Jim enjoyed the camaraderie of Kentucky Fried Chicken. The staffs and managers of several stores hung out together. They were all young and enthusiastic and excited about the potential of their careers. They worked together six days a week. After work they drank and chased women and played poker together. On their days off they came in and hung around the stores. Working for Kentucky Fried Chicken in Columbus, Ohio, in the late 1960s was like being in a fraternity. It was an all-encompassing way of life.

Within six months, Jim was promoted to assistant manager. Within a year, he was running his own store. He was making almost $12,000. Life was good. When he wasn't working, he was still hanging around with his Kentucky Fried Chicken pals, including a guy named Dave Thomas. Thomas was an older guy—in his thirties. He was the boss and part owner of all the Kentucky Fried Chicken stores in Columbus. He lived in a nice

house where he had built a chicken-shaped swimming pool.
Sometimes Jim and his Kentucky Fried Chicken friends came
over and swam in the pool, and Dave Thomas fried chicken for
them.

Both Jim and his brother continued to rise in the organization. By the time Jim was twenty, he was supervisor of nine
Kentucky Fried Chicken stores in Virginia Beach, Virginia. He
was making $14,000 a year and had a company car and was
living on the beach. Then he got a call one day from Columbus.
Dave Thomas had left Kentucky Fried Chicken and was planning on starting a new hamburger restaurant, and Jim was
invited to work for it. Jim was skeptical. The last thing America
needed in 1969 was another place to buy hamburgers. But Dave
Thomas had been good to Jim, and Jim decided to stick with
him. He moved back to Columbus to work for the hamburger
restaurant, which didn't even exist yet. It was going to be named
after Thomas's daughter Melinda. Her nickname was Wendy.


Frances, radiantly pregnant, accompanied Jim to Columbus
for his reunion. After six weeks of marriage, things were still
going well. Their luxury honeymoon cruise to Alaska on the
$1200-a-day *Sea Goddess* had been a great success. They
made friends, and drank champagne and ate Beluga caviar in
their private Jacuzzi every night, and Jim had been voted gros-
sest passenger. Jim's only complaint was that it was hot in
Anchorage, and their hotel, the best in town, had not been air-
conditioned; he vowed he would never return to Alaska in the
summer.

During their visit to Ohio, Jim and Frances met each other's
mothers for the first time, and the marriage weathered that as
well. They called on Jim's mother (who was divorced from Jim's
father) at her small house, where she spent much of her time
making art. On the porch was a plastic goose she had found in
the trash; she had painted it pink and put a turban on its head.
Inside the house there hung a series of eerie masks she had
made and a piece of black fabric from which a plaster face and
hands emerged like a ghost rising out of its grave. She was

working on a new piece that incorporated a dress and bonnet that had belonged to her great-grandmother.

Jim's mother embraced Frances and gave her some baby pictures of Jim, which Frances found endearing.

Jim met Frances's mother the next day on the world's largest trapshooting range, next to the Dayton airport. Frances's mother and her second husband had traveled there from Connecticut so he could compete in the North American Clay Target championship. Frances's mother embraced Frances when she arrived and then kissed a friend of Jim's who had come along for the ride and welcomed him to the family. Frances pointed out her actual husband, and her mother greeted him, too. Frances's stepfather, an amiable man called Jiggs, gave Jim some solid advice about trapshooting: "Keep the wood [your head] on the wood [the gun stock]."

Frances talked to her mother for an hour, then she and Jim drove back to Columbus. Jim never called his father, who didn't even know that his son was married.


On their second day in Columbus, Jim and Frances stopped for lunch at a Wendy's. Jim tried the new chicken nuggets for the first time and concluded that they were "fucking horrible." Wendy's had introduced them in response to the enormous success of McDonald's chicken nuggets. A big mistake, Jim said. "Why be a me-tooer? Wendy's at one time was the leader in the industry."

Jim also took exception to the level of cleanliness of the restaurant. "If I was the manager here, they'd get rid of those flies," he told Frances. "Go in the bathroom and look at how filthy it is. When I was in charge of a store, you would never see that. And when Dave Thomas was directly involved you would never see that. Now Dave Thomas is off on his ninety-foot yacht. And of course you have four thousand stores now. There's no way you can keep up with what it used to be. . . ."

In the official history of the Wendy's corporation, there is a photograph of Jim at the site of this very Wendy's. The year is 1970. Jim is slim and clean-shaven and wearing a hideous brown suit. He is standing next to Wendy Thomas, Dave's daughter, who is lifting a shovel filled with dirt, breaking the ground for this restaurant, which was the second in the Wendy's chain.

At the time, at the age of twenty-one, Jim was general manager of the company. When he had quit Kentucky Fried Chicken to work for Dave Thomas the year before, the world's first Wendy's was still under construction in a former automobile showroom in downtown Columbus. Jim helped to paint the place himself. When it opened, he recruited the staff and co-managed the restaurant, working behind the counter in a white chef's hat and black bow tie. He soon moved up to general manager of the corporation, which was administered from a small office over the store. Dave Thomas dropped by from time to time to see how things were going.

Thomas, then thirty-seven, had been in the restaurant business for twenty-five years. When he was twelve, he had lied about his age to get a job as a soda jerk. (Even then, a Wendy's press release claims, he dreamed of "operating a really good hamburger stand.") He quit school at fifteen to be a busboy at the Hobby House restaurant in Fort Wayne, Indiana. After a stint in the Army, where he managed an enlisted men's club, he returned to the Hobby House in a managerial position. In 1955, he met Harlan Sanders, an honorary Kentucky Colonel who was driving around the Midwest trying to convince restaurant owners to adopt his secret recipe for fried chicken and pay him a royalty of five cents a bird. Sanders walked into the Hobby House one day and told Thomas about his recipe. Thomas liked it, but he hated the Colonel's logo. ("His symbol at the time was a couple of little chicks hatching out of an egg," Thomas told an interviewer from the Harvard Business School years later. "Awful! Chickens are hateful creatures!") Hobby House was soon selling Kentucky Fried Chicken, with a redesigned logo.

In 1962, Thomas moved to Columbus to take over four failing Kentucky Fried Chicken stores. He turned them around and built six new ones. In 1968, the Kentucky Fried Chicken company, which had grown considerably since the days when the Colonel sold his recipe door-to-door, bought out the Columbus operation, netting Thomas $1.7 million. He worked as a Kentucky Fried Chicken executive for a while after that and then worked briefly for Arthur Treacher's Fish 'n' Chips. Then he decided it was time to realize his alleged childhood dream of owning a really good hamburger stand.

This was a time when conventional wisdom held that America had just about as many hamburger stands as the market could bear. And skepticism about Wendy's was not diminished when Thomas announced that his burgers would cost fifty-five cents. "Dave, that's stupid," Jim told him. "No one is going to buy a fifty-five-cent hamburger." McDonald's cost eighteen.

But Thomas planned to grill a better burger. He would use fresh beef, not frozen. The patties would weigh one quarter of a pound (McDonald's weighed one tenth of a pound), and they would be square, so people could see the burgers sticking out from under the buns. Every Wendy's hamburger would be cooked fresh to order. If the grill person happened to cook too many, instead of being preserved under heat lamps the extra patties would be dumped into the chili.

Thomas had some interesting business concepts as well. He realized that the labor cost of preparing a 55-cent hamburger was the same as that of an 18-cent hamburger, so his labor cost as a percentage of sales would be lower than McDonald's. He saw the advantages of a limited menu (Wendy's opened up serving hamburgers, chili, shakes, fries, beverages, period). High school kids working part time could be easily trained to make a few things well, and it was simpler to keep fresh-cooked burgers coming off the grill in the right numbers if you knew that everybody who walked in the door was probably going to order a hamburger. Starting with the second Wendy's, Thomas put drive-through windows in his stores. Drive-through customers didn't take up seats or parking spaces, but they still paid cash for their food.

Wendy's grew slowly at first (after two years, it had three stores), but it grew, and Jim's job grew with it. When Wendy's moved into the Dayton market, Jim was made area director there, supervising construction, hiring staffs, lining up suppliers. He became area director in Columbus and Toledo, and then he became a regional director, supervising Dayton, Columbus, Toledo, and Cincinnati. He enjoyed his work, especially getting out in the field, working with the crews in the stores, and he enjoyed his success. In his mid-twenties, he was making $35,000 a year and getting stock options. When he moved to Toledo, he bought a house with an indoor swimming pool. When he was eighteen, he had promised himself that his first house would have an indoor pool.

But as Wendy's mushroomed, Jim grew discontented. By 1976, Wendy's had five hundred stores and a swelling bureaucracy. Jim loved getting into a troubled store and working with the staff to turn it around. But he wasn't good at dealing with bureaucracies. He didn't get along with his boss, the vice president of operations, who, Jim complained, "couldn't work a french fryer." He hated the company rule that he had to wear a dopey blue-striped Wendy's uniform on the job. And, seeing the profits his stores were making for the company, he began to feel shortchanged both in his salary (which had been frozen at $35,000) and in the number of stock options he received.

Still, the stock options kept on coming.

Jim's high school reunion was held in a Columbus motel ballroom. Jim thought the place was a dump. He and Frances arrived in a chauffeured limousine. A band played hits from the 1960s, and people danced. The lights were kept very bright for the benefit of a crew making a souvenir videotape.

Jim regaled several male classmates with tales of his days as proprietor of a male stripper bar. The customers were all women, and they were whipped into a sexual frenzy by the dancers, who were all gay. As one of the few heterosexual males on the premises, Jim enjoyed certain fringe benefits. . . .

Later, Jim ran into a woman who had been a childhood playmate and, briefly, an adult girlfriend. "How did you come up smelling like a rose?" she asked.

Another woman shared her wonder: "Jim has succeeded more than we ever thought he would."

After seven years with Wendy's, shortly after being named regional director for Tampa, Jacksonville, Atlanta, and Louisville, Jim and the company parted ways. In a farewell meeting with senior executives, he announced that he was exercising every stock option to which he was entitled and that he would like to become a Wendy's franchisee. That was fine with Wendy's. Eureka, California, was available. So were a couple of towns in Iowa and the entire state of Vermont. But those places didn't appeal to Jim. Finally, Austin was mentioned. There was a single Wendy's store down there, and it had failed twice. Jim flew to Austin and checked the town out. It looked good to him.

Back in Columbus, Jim packed up his things. On Christmas Day, 1976, he visited with friends and family. Then he climbed into his Corvette and headed south. He owned Wendy's stock worth more than a million dollars. He owned his own business. And he was going to become a Texan.

# "A Promising Tropical Breed"

CLAMBERING OFF their chartered DC-6 at Miami International Airport, the cattle looked airsick. They walked uncertainly down a ramp from the plane, which had just carried them on a five-hour flight from the island of St. Croix, to a truck that was waiting to haul them to Texas.

The ramp was as wide as three cattle, but it was beyond the cattle to realize that. They moved down in packs that kept getting wedged tight. The jams broke up and the cattle surged forward until they wedged again. A man followed behind, hosing off cowshit, which the cattle dropped on the ramp and on each other.

One of the animals, a calf born a few days before departure from St. Croix, wasn't moving at all. The trip had been too much for it. A man carried it off the plane and laid it in a pen where it wouldn't be stepped on. "Get a little milk in him," counseled the waiting truck driver, Curtis Villines of Fayetteville, Arkansas. "He'll be all right." A few minutes later, he examined the limp calf again. "Better call a doctor," he said. "I don't think he's going to make it nohow." He took another look. "He's dead."

"Not yet," said Frits T. Lawaetz, a sturdy fair-haired man who had accompanied the animals on the plane and spoke with a curious sing-song accent.

"Call the doctor," said Villines. "I hate to put him on the truck with him already dead."

Lawaetz bent down to examine the calf and reconsidered his opinion. "He is dead," he said.

"He's not *plumb* dead," Villines protested. But he was wrong. The calf was totally dead, which actually came as a relief to Villines. He preferred to have it die at the airport than on his truck. "It really makes 'em feel bad," he said, "when you bring 'em a dead one."

The animals that survived—twenty-seven heifers, three cows, and two calves—walked onto Villines's eighteen-wheeler, where he packed them close in pens inside the trailer, so if he made a quick stop he wouldn't have a cow come flying through the cab. He had already laid down a nice layer of hay for them, to cushion their feet from the shocks of the road and serve double duty as a refreshment.

The cattle were tired and hardly shifted at all as Villines raced up U.S. 27 through the center of Florida, watching for police cars and talking on his CB. Passing another big rig headed in the opposite direction, Villines hailed him: "Lookin' good, southbound, as far as Haines City," meaning he hadn't seen any cops on that stretch. "How's it lookin' up north?" Near a small town in the middle of the state, a woman's voice came over the radio. She was a hooker working the truck-driving trade. Villines chatted with her briefly but kept on moving.

He was pleased to be carrying this load of purebred Senepol cattle. For one thing, he knew they hadn't eaten since leaving St. Croix, so they'd left most of their shit in the plane and his trailer wouldn't get too messy. For another, purebred cattle and their owners were a pleasure to deal with. The cattle were likely to be in good health, and their owners were likely to write good checks. Villines's boss made a point of courting ranchers developing new breeds. A ground-floor connection with such people could be good for business if a breed caught on.

Just before dawn, Villines rolled over the Georgia state line. He got on the CB and called into the darkness: "I wonder where Rome, Georgia, is. Does anybody know?"

A voice came back: "Yep. North of Atlanta."

So Villines drove north. He pulled into a truck stop near Cordele and checked his load. Through slats in the trailer, he could see one heifer lying on its side. "It's probably just airsick and carsick and has sore feet," he said. Then he napped for a couple of hours himself before continuing toward Rome, where some of the cattle were to be dropped off at Berry College for study by the agriculture department.

An enthusiastic reception committee—professors, ag students, and a photographer from the school paper—was gathered at Berry to witness the arrival of the Senepol, a breed they had never seen before. As soon as Villines pulled up to the college pens, a dozen people ran to the trailer and peered inside. "Is that cow daid?" a woman called out. The airsick heifer was still on its side. "Don't step on its haid!" the woman shouted to the other cattle.

Villines was embarrassed. He should have stopped outside the college gates and made sure all the animals were standing. It didn't look good to have one down.

The cattle that were staying at Berry got unloaded, and the ones that were traveling on (including the prone heifer, which rallied itself) got off the truck, too, for a rest. Villines took his second short nap of the trip. Then, with seventeen Senepols aboard, he set off on a nonstop eighteen-hour drive, heading west, toward Hopes Creek Ranch.

The two-day journey of the Senepol from the Caribbean to Texas was only the latest step in the century-long voyages of the red-haired breed. The female ancestors of the cattle on Villines's truck were N'Dama cattle from West Africa, a hardy breed with a natural immunity to troublesome insects and diseases and a long-developed tolerance to tropical heat. In 1860, a herd of N'Dama were imported from Senegal to St. Croix, then a Danish possession, by a rancher who thought they might do well there. The N'Dama, called "Senegalese" on the island, did just fine, and the offspring of the original herd were rapidly acquired by other Cruzan farmers.

In 1918, a Cruzan estate owner named Bromley Nelthropp decided to make a good thing better. He sailed to Trinidad and bought a Red Poll bull named Captain Kidd. The Red Poll is a beefy English breed, larger than the N'Dama, that was originally developed for milk production. The British had sent the bull to the

Caribbean to upgrade the local cattle, but Captain Kidd was a flop on Trinidad. He, and most of his progeny, were polled (hornless), and West Indian farmers preferred horned cattle, because it was easy to yoke them by their horns to pull wagons and plows.

So Captain Kidd was sold to Nelthropp, who took him home to St. Croix, renamed him Douglas, and set him to work impregnating N'Dama cows. Douglas had the time of his life in the service of Nelthropp's project—creating a new kind of cattle that would combine the best traits of the Red Poll and the N'Dama. For thirty years, Nelthropp supervised the breeding of Douglas and his descendants, carefully selecting some animals to carry on the line while their rejected siblings were sent, childless, to slaughter. For his breeding stock, Nelthropp selected animals with the Red Poll characteristics of hornlessness (because horned animals sometimes injured their handlers or one another), red color (because Nelthropp liked red), and general heftiness, and the N'Dama characteristics of heat tolerance and fertility. He selected as well for good meat and milk production, and he insisted on animals that had "gentle, pet-like" dispositions.

Eventually, the cattle born in Nelthropp's herd were displaying those traits consistently. He had created a new breed. It was sometimes called the Nelthropp breed but finally took its name from a contraction of "Senegalese" and "Red Poll"—Senepol.

Nelthropp died in 1950, but not before selling most of his herd to Ward M. Canaday, who was chairman of the Willys-Overland Corporation of Toledo, Ohio, manufacturer of the Jeep, and also the largest private landowner on St. Croix. Canaday installed the Senepol on his Annaly estate in the northwest corner of the island and left the herd under the supervision of his general manager, Frits E. Lawaetz.

Lawaetz's parents were Danish and had arrived on St. Croix when it was Danish, too. (The United States bought St. Croix, St. Thomas, and St. John from Denmark in 1917, creating the U.S. Virgin Islands.) Lawaetz (pronounced La-*vetz*) was born in 1907. As a teenager, he spent several years in Denmark, working on farms. Back in the Caribbean, he worked in a sugar factory on St. Croix, as a cowboy in Puerto Rico, as a foreman in a rum distillery, and as the manager of an estate producing sugar cane and cattle.

He went to work for Canaday in 1940, at a time when there were only eighteen cattle on the Annaly estate, all of which died soon after when arsenic-laced water from a tank used to dip cattle for ticks accidentally drained into a pond where the cattle drank.

Lawaetz was a poker-playing buddy of Bromley Nelthropp and, when the Nelthropp herd became available, Lawaetz encouraged Canaday to buy it. He was convinced it was the breed St. Croix needed—rugged enough to climb the steep hills on the Annaly estate, survive the island's periodic dry spells, gain weight on rough grass during the hottest months, and, through it all, produce a steady crop of healthy calves. With the breed in his care, Lawaetz worked hard to build it up. He began keeping detailed performance records on every animal, and he sold bulls to other Cruzan farmers, spreading the breed all over the island. On the side, he pursued a career in politics, serving for twenty years in the Virgin Islands Senate, where he was known as "the Bull from Annaly."

In 1964, Lawaetz was joined in the cattle business by his son Hans, who had earned a B.S. at Cornell and then served five years as a captain in the Air Force. In 1974, they were joined by Lawaetz's youngest son, Frits T. The three Lawaetzes bought the Senepol herd from Canaday and, after he died, leased the Annaly estate from its new owners. Operating as Annaly Farms, the Lawaetzes sold beef to island butcher shops, supermarkets, and individual retail customers, and they made a living.

But the island meat business was changing. Small butcher shops were being replaced by supermarkets. Supermarkets, for convenience, were beginning to import their beef in precut frozen trailer loads. The future of the beef business for island producers looked grim. The Lawaetzes consulted with other Senepol breeders (apart from Annaly Farms, there were two major herds and several minor ones on the island), and, together, they began to think about marketing their Senepols in a totally different way—not to eat but to breed.

This would be a great deal if it worked. The same animal that sold for $500 to be turned into steak and hamburger might be sold for $2500 for breeding purposes if ranchers could be convinced the Senepol had valuable genetic characteristics (and a $2500 cow wouldn't cost any more to raise and prepare for its place in society than a $500 cow). The Senepol breed already enjoyed some renown in the Caribbean. For years, bulls had occasionally been sold to farmers on other islands. A 1956 postage stamp of the British Virgin Islands pictured a Senepol bull. But the Caribbean cattle market was a piddling one. The Senepol breeders cast their gaze at the southern United States, a territory where a warm-weather breed like the Senepol would likely do well, and also a territory that happened to be the richest cattle market in the world.

The notion of marketing a new breed to American ranchers was not a novel one. There are no native American cattle breeds; every cow in America traces its family tree to another continent. Columbus imported the first cattle to the New World (and landed them in the Caribbean). Since then, dozens of breeds have been imported by ranchers aiming to improve their stock—and promoters hoping to make a buck. English Shorthorn cattle arrived on the East Coast in the eighteenth century. Henry Clay imported the first Herefords in 1817. The Angus arrived in the mid-nineteenth century, as did the first Brahman cattle. The 1960s and '70s saw a boom in the importation and promotion of "exotic" breeds—mainly large European varieties—as American cattlemen went through an infatuation with size. The Simmental, a Swiss breed that had been largely ignored during earlier introductions, arrived once again in the United States in 1967 and soon achieved great popularity. The Chianina, an Italian breed promoted as "the world's largest cattle," arrived in 1971. Others followed.

Many cattlemen grew disillusioned with the exotics, however. Their size did not always translate into economic efficiency, and giant bulls cross-bred with normal-sized cows sometimes produced calves that were literally too big for the cows to bear. These disappointments led to a generalized backlash against new breeds. Ranchers who felt they'd been burned once didn't even want to hear about yet another new breed that was going to solve all their problems, especially one from a tiny island they'd never heard of.

In this atmosphere, the St. Croix breeders launched their marketing effort in 1976 by organizing the Virgin Islands Senepol Association of St. Croix. And they had some immediate success. An executive of the American Simmental Association who had given the Senepol breeders some advice on how to organize their group told a Kentucky Simmental breeder that the Senepol looked impressive, and the Kentuckian flew down to the island and bought some. Meanwhile, a semen collector dispatched from the mainland to bring back samples from Senepol bulls for the insemination of research animals in Florida mentioned the Senepol to a Mennonite Georgia beefalo breeder, and *he* flew down and bought some, too. The first Senepols ever to set foot on the American mainland flew off from St. Croix, twenty-two strong, in 1977.

Over the next several years, the breed spread slowly. The original importers sold some of their animals, the islanders made a few more sales, and a couple of dozen small herds of Senepols were developed, mostly in the southeastern states. By 1985, there were about 500 Senepol cattle on the mainland (and some 2700 on St. Croix). No one had gotten rich selling Senepols, but the breed had established a toehold in the United States.

As the eighth annual meeting of the Senepol Association approached, the island breeders were looking forward to making some sales there. They'd heard that the largest mainland Senepol operation, a partnership of ranchers in Tennessee and Virginia, was thinking of buying more animals for its herd. And Hans Lawaetz had got word that "a gentleman from Texas A&M" was coming to the meeting and "was maybe interested in buying some cattle."

When, as a graduate student at Texas A&M, Pete Binion had been assigned to a research project on the Senepol (after his father-in-law's casual business proposal had cut short his Brangus study), the first thing he did was to go to the library. Pete had never heard of Senepol cattle. In this, he was like the vast majority of American ranchers. The Senepol had garnered a little publicity in its day, but not much. A 1955 article in *The Cattleman*, a major industry magazine, had described it as "a promising tropical breed." A 1963 *Cattleman* article reported that Senepols "are gentle and are good rustlers on grass." A 1981 article in *Beef* commended the breed's "favorable beef production and efficiency, tolerance to high temperatures, foraging ability, gentle disposition and good looks." Despite these reviews, the word had not spread. If you said "Senepol" to an American rancher, he thought you were mispronouncing "Simmental."

Pete read everything he could find about the Senepol, and he was impressed. In fact, the breed sounded too good to be true. If the Senepol was all it was cracked up to be, then why wasn't it being raised all over America?

Pete was still wondering about that when he finished his research project. He compared the offspring of Hereford cows bred to Senepol bulls (via frozen semen imported from St. Croix) to the offspring of Herefords bred to Angus, a breed renowned for its high-quality beef. The Hereford-Senepol crosses stacked up well against the better-known animals.

Pete was talking about his project at Texas A&M one day when he ran into a graduate student who said he had a friend in Tennessee who actually owned some of these Senepols. The friend was John Niceley, who, with his brother Frank, had recently entered into a partnership called American Senepol Limited with a local veterinarian and a former coal-mine operator in Virginia. Pete called the Niceleys and then flew up and visited them. With backing from Dr. McCall, his new partner, Pete paid the Niceleys $5000 for a Senepol bull (the Niceleys' partnership retained a one-quarter ownership share in its semen), and he borrowed three Senepol cows, with the understanding that he would breed them and split their offspring with the Niceleys. He also bought one hundred units of frozen Senepol semen.

The animals arrived at Hopes Creek Ranch in 1984. They were the first Senepols ever to set foot in Texas, which is not only the biggest cattle state in the country but also, at least in its southern portion, a state that requires a heat-tolerant animal (that is, an animal that will spend hot days grazing and gaining weight instead of collapsing with exhaustion under a tree). Texas was potentially an enormous market for the Senepol. But it would not be an easy one to crack.

Several cattle breeds had already left their marks on the state. First and most celebrated was the Longhorn, the legendary creature of the great cattle drives of the years following the Civil War. The Longhorn evolved naturally on the Texas range at a time when there were no fences and cattle were left to live or die without human intervention. The strongest survived. They were a mix of the cattle the Spanish had brought to North America three centuries before and English and Northern European breeds brought to Texas by Anglo-American settlers. The Longhorn was an ugly, wild beast, but it was fertile and resilient. "They could walk the roughest ground," wrote Texas chronicler J. Frank Dobie,

> cross the widest deserts, climb the highest mountains, swim the widest rivers, fight off the fiercest bands of wolves, endure hunger, cold, thirst and punishment as few beasts of the earth have ever shown themselves capable of enduring. On the prairies they could run like antelopes; in the thickets of thorn and tangle they could break their way with the agility of panthers. They could rustle in drouth or snow, smell out pasturage leagues away, live—without talking about the matter—like true captains of their own souls and bodies.

They could not, however, gain weight fast enough to satisfy the economics of the cattle business after 1880. Grassland had become too valuable to allow cattle years of grazing. Railroads had eliminated the need for a breed that could walk a thousand miles to market. And the invention of barbed wire in the 1870s had made it possible to fence off the range, which in turn made it possible to control which cows were bred by which bulls. Ranchers began to import bulls of the English beef breeds to add bulk to their stock. The Shorthorn came first, followed by the Angus. And then came the Hereford, which prospered so well on the range that it rapidly displaced the Longhorn almost completely. By the turn of the century, the Longhorn was a curiosity.

Around that time, on the hot ranges of South Texas, there appeared a strange-looking animal with a large hump over its shoulders and enormous droopy ears. The Brahman (or Zebu) was a native of India. It thrived in hot climates and had spread to tropical areas all over the world. Texas Gulf Coast cattlemen tried crossing Brahmans with their Longhorns, and they were pleased with the results. Soon ranchers throughout the South and West were crossing Brahmans with a variety of European breeds, to get the Brahman's hardiness and heat tolerance and the Europeans' superior beef. New breeds resulted, including the Santa Gertrudis (developed on the King Ranch from Brahman and Shorthorn), the Barzona (developed in Arizona from Santa Gertrudis, Angus, Hereford, and Africander), and the Beefmaster (a blend of Brahman, Hereford, and Shorthorn). There also arose the Brangus (Brahman plus Angus), the Braford (Brahman plus Hereford), the Brahmousin (Brahman plus Limousin), the Charbray (Brahman plus Charolais), the Braler (Brahman plus Saler), and the Simbrah (Brahman plus Simmental).

When Pete went into the Senepol business, Brahman-cross cattle were the staples of hot-weather ranching in the United States. But Pete thought the Senepol offered advantages over the Brahman. Brahmans tend to produce tough meat, and they have occasional reproductive problems; the Brahman also has a reputation for being an ornery beast, hard to handle and even dangerous in some situations. The Senepol appeared to offer the same heat tolerance as the Brahman while it lacked the Brahman's drawbacks; its meat was fine, its fertility was excellent, and it had always been prized for its "gentle, pet-like" disposition.

As of January 1985, however, the Texas Brahman establishment had little to fear from Pete Binion. He owned exactly one Senepol. And he still had some doubts about the Senepol himself. He needed to see where the animal came from and what the foundation herds of the breed looked like. He wanted to see if the animals were well cared for and if they were being selected and bred to maximize their genetic potential. Flying down to St. Croix for the eighth annual meeting of the Senepol Association, he was afraid he might find a bunch of amateurish, would-be Caribbean cowboys sitting around wearing ten-gallon hats and drinking Lone Star beer, with their cow herds staked out in their front yards.

Hans Lawaetz met Pete at the St. Croix airport, where he deplaned into a crowd of golf club-toting tourists and local Rastafarians. For the next four days, he toured the island with a dozen other mainland ranchers, inspecting herds of Senepols grazing in pastures that overlooked white sand ocean beaches and on hillsides surrounded by tropical rain forests hung with vines. Pete was impressed by the animals and by the management skills of the St. Croix breeders. He was put off only by the landscape; it reminded him of Vietnam. He barricaded the door to his room with chairs every night and still had trouble sleeping. At a cocktail party one evening at a renovated old mill where Ward Canaday had once entertained Harry Truman, Pete talked for a while with several other guests on the rooftop patio. He couldn't believe it when they descended to the bar. Why would they abandon such a good lookout, especially at night?

Despite these flashbacks, Pete pursued his Senepol business with diligence. He inspected nearly every animal on the island, those that were shown on the tours and those that were not. Hans Lawaetz noticed him jotting down notes all the time and couldn't imagine what all he was finding to take notes *about*. When the other visiting ranchers took an afternoon sail on a chartered catamaran to view a spectacular underwater reef, Pete stayed ashore and looked at more cows.

At the end of the week, the Cruzan breeders got great news. American Senepol Limited was buying eighty head. And Pete told Hans Lawaetz that he was buying eight heifers, at $2500 apiece. Lawaetz was excited by the big sale, but he was also pleased to have a new customer, for whom he predicted great things. "Pete's going to a completely new location," Hans said. "Texas is a big state. He'll be a big man with these cattle in Texas."

Twenty months later, Curtis Villines pulled his eighteen-wheeler into the dirt road that leads to Hopes Creek Ranch. He braked the truck to a halt, climbed down from the cab, and walked back to the trailer to examine his cargo—the third load of Senepols Pete had imported from Annaly Farms. Villines did not want to repeat the mistake he'd made at Berry College, and, sure enough, that same heifer was down again.

Villines thought that maybe the animal was feeling homesick now, or maybe that was the way these Senepol cattle took their rest—lying on their sides with their heads down, like horses. But Villines didn't care. He wasn't going to pull onto another customer's property with an animal down.

He stuck an electric prod through a slat in the trailer and gave the heifer a shock. It jerked, but it didn't get up. Villines shocked it again. The heifer bellowed. Villines shocked it some more. It moaned, and it rocked on its side, but it didn't stand up.

Villines gave up the prod. He climbed into the trailer, kneeled down, grabbed the animal's head, and tried to twist the heifer to its feet—a reverse wrestling move. The heifer resisted. Just a few hundred miles back down the road, after a shower at a truck stop, Villines had put on a clean shirt, but he paid it no mind as he grappled with the heifer in the muck-covered hay. He was stained with shit when he finally got the animal to its feet. He got back in the cab, fired up the engine, and rolled down the road to Hopes Creek Ranch, with all the cattle in the back looking fine.

It was 1:00 p.m. on a cloudy Sunday afternoon when the truck pulled in next to the big open-sided shed where Pete stored his hay. Pete drove up a few minutes later in his Blazer; he'd rushed back the eight miles from College Station, where he'd been attending a meeting of the youth soccer league of which he was president. His two ranch hands—Wendell, his half brother, and Bryan, his brother-in-law—were already guiding the cattle from the truck into a pen. Pete's three little children— three-year-old Mollie, six-year-old Pauline, and seven-year-old Wade—were watching the excitement from atop a pile of hay bales. They were wearing socks but no shoes.

Pete climbed into the pen to look the cattle over. Number 4904 (all the cattle were branded) had a clear fluid draining from its rectum. That didn't worry Pete, but 5008 had a bloody discharge, which could mean trouble. All of the cattle were thin; they'd lost a hundred pounds each from the rigors of the trip. "They need hay in front of them *all* the time," Pete instructed Bryan. "Nonstop?" asked Bryan. "Nonstop," said Pete. Overall, he was pleased with the animals' condition.

In a pasture across the road, and in another beyond the one-story ranch house, other Senepols grazed. Pete had about eighty on the ranch now, sixty-five from St. Croix and the rest born in Texas. Some of the animals belonged to him, some to him and Dr. McCall, some to the Universal I limited partnership, and some to Annaly Farms, which had sent them on consignment in an effort to develop its own market in Texas. Pete would get a commission if he sold them. So far, he hadn't sold any animals, but he had just sold six Senepol embryos for $1500 apiece to a man named Louper. Pete wasn't worried about selling cattle at the moment. He'd built up his herd to be ready for the Universal II limited partnership. And now it was big enough.

With the new animals set to chomping on hay, Pete retreated to the patio behind the house for a snack of tortilla chips, cheese, and peppers. Dinner was beef shish kebab. Pete looked out at a pasture as he ate. "I really like to see Senepol, Senepol, and Senepol," he said. "Pretty soon there'll be Senepol all over the place."

After dinner, he sat down in the living room with Wade, who was having a little trouble in school, and a set of flash cards.

"Nine minus seven," said Pete.

Wade, seated in a worn naugahyde chair that was too big for him, looked around. "Three," he said.

"*Nine* minus *seven*," said Pete.

"One," said Wade.

"*NINE* minus *SEVEN*," said Pete.

"Two," said Wade.

"Eight minus four," said Pete.

The next morning was cool, with a light mist hanging in the woods beyond the pastures. Becky, Pete's wife, was outside early, planting flowers. Pauline and Mollie alternated between helping her and climbing halfway up a TV antenna that rose fifty feet high by the side of the house. (Despite the antenna, the Binions got only one channel, and that one badly.) A few yards from Becky's garden, Wendell and Bryan were digging a ditch to expose the pipe that drained the kitchen sink.

Pete was at work in the office he'd set up in a small room in the hay barn. He shared the cramped space with Keith Newbill, his ranch manager, and Lisa Christiansen, an efficient young woman he'd hired as his secretary. Lisa was typing a letter on the Apple II while Pete and Keith discussed arrangements for the upcoming "Senepol Stampede," the ranch's second annual open house. "Are we going to have tables this year?" Keith asked.

"I don't like tables," Pete said. "I like the hay bales."

Keith was leaning back in his chair. He was wearing his hat and had spurs on his boots. A handwritten list headed "Things To Do—Sept" was taped to the wall above his desk. It included:

worm all cattle
corner posts and gate on hill
get 100 embryo pregnancies
finish back fence

"If we can get it catered for four bucks a head," Keith said, "we'll do it."

"We'll take a hard look at it," Pete agreed.

Four bucks a head was a pretty good deal, but Pete was worried about all the money he was spending. Until—unless—the limited partnership shares in Universal II were sold to investors, Hopes Creek Ranch would be running in the red. A year before, Pete had borrowed $55,000 from a bank in Bryan for operating expenses. He was making his payments—to the bank, to his father-in-law Billie Pratt (from whom he rented Hopes Creek Ranch for $500 a month), and to everybody else—but he tried to be cautious. There had been some delays in the paperwork for Universal II. It still wasn't even officially on the market.

One new prospect had recently presented itself. A group of investors had been referred to Lundelius by a Houston accounting firm. Lundelius was trying to interest them in Universal II or, failing that, a cattle-feeding program. Pete called Lundelius often to see how the talks were progressing. He knew he called him more often than Lundelius appreciated being called. But Pete, frustrated at not being able to do anything himself for himself, wanted to know what was happening. He needed to know.

Keith headed off into town. Pete told him to get a ten-pound bag of ant poison. Then he picked up the phone and dialed Lundelius.

"Howdy . . . ," Pete said. "Doin' good. Any late-breaking developments? . . . Good. . . . Sounds encouraging. . . . If he'd like to get into a cattle-feeding program, we'd like a shot at putting it together."

After a few minutes, Pete hung up. "I hate talking to him," he reported. "He always sounds so positive. It gets me fired up. . . . "

He shuffled through some papers on his desk.

"The only good thing," he reflected, "is there's been no bad news. No bad news is what has me feeling good."

# "Penguin Lust"

J IM WAS THINKING about having another baby.

Frances, his bride of three months, was still pregnant with Jim's first child, but a unique opportunity had arisen. A friend of Jim's who owned a ranch on the Rio Grande employed a part-time maid from an impoverished Mexican village across the river. The woman, a widow, had suddenly died, leaving four children. Three were going to be adopted by a woman in El Paso. That left an infant daughter. "I can't stand the thought that ten or eleven years from now that little girl will be a prostitute in Juarez," Jim's friend had told him. Jim said he would take the baby.

This transaction had taken place in an Austin restaurant where Jim had run into his friend. The next afternoon, sitting in his office, Jim still thought it was a great idea. Frances had wanted to have a daughter, and the baby she was carrying was a boy. This Mexican baby had blond hair and blue eyes (Jim's friend said it had Spanish blood). Jim had always believed in adoption. And he was going to have one little rug rat running around; how much more trouble could another one be?

It was a slow day in the office anyway. Jim's partner, Gary, was out of town. The clerical and warehouse staffs were taking orders and shipping T-shirts. There wasn't much for Jim to do. His main accomplishment of the day so far was starting a diet; he did that at 11:00 a.m. by swallowing some diet pills. Like the baby, the pills were Mexican. People in Texas were flocking across the border to buy them; Jim knew several who'd lost thirty pounds on the pills in a month. "Everybody understands that they're just fucking speed," he said, "but there's supposed to be something in there to slow you down, too."

Jim wanted to lose at least twenty pounds—he was up to 233. Photos mounted on the wall behind his desk, taken during his fast-food days (Jim with Dave Thomas, Jim with "Wendy" Thomas, Jim with Colonel Sanders) showed a much slimmer Jim than the Jim who now sat in his green leather desk chair looking over some proposed new T-shirt designs ("There is no joy in Mudville/Mighty Casey flunked his urinalysis"). Jim and Gary were doing well in the T-shirt business, but they wanted to do better. They wanted to grow, and that meant adding new designs; they were always looking for new designs. Jim considered the prospects on his desk for a while. "In this business," he reflected, "you never know what somebody is going to want to put on their chest."

He would not make any decisions today. Instead, he turned his attention back to the office TV, which had been on much of the afternoon. He had watched "Jeopardy!" as usual (and been peeved that a phone call had distracted him from learning the answer to the Final Jeopardy question: "Contrary to U.S. government predictions, this state had the smallest population in 1985"). Now he was watching a baseball game, which was suddenly obscured by a burst of fuzz on the screen.

Jim was annoyed again. "How the fuck can you run a business," he demanded, "when your cable keeps going out?"

Somehow, Jim had managed.

During a decade in Austin, he had run through half a dozen businesses, starting as a hamburger mogul, ending as a budding T-shirt magnate. If he had not been as successful as he had once dreamed, he still felt he was doing pretty well for a kid from Linden-McKinley High School.

When he'd packed up his belongings and driven from Columbus to Austin in 1976, he entered a small and lively city that exemplified all that was appealing about the Sunbelt. It was surrounded by rivers, lakes, and parks, and the sun shone on them three hundred days a year. There was an exciting live music scene on a youthful nightlife strip where an outgoing newcomer could easily make friends. The city's economy was anchored by its status as state capital and the presence of the University of Texas, and a boom was in the works. High-technology companies were moving to Austin. The population was swelling with newcomers from out of town and out of state. High-rise offices and hotels were replacing the old stone buildings downtown. Everything was growing; everything was changing.

It looked to Jim like a ripe market for a quality burger.

The single Wendy's store that Jim took over had nearly gone bust twice, but Jim was confident he could turn it around. It had a good location—on "the drag" next to the University of Texas—and it seemed to Jim that its problems could be blamed on its previous absentee owners. Jim was anything but absentee. As soon as he got to town, he started cutting tomatoes and slicing onions and frying hamburgers and trying to figure out why people weren't coming into the store.

He applied some classic remedies—distributing discount coupons and making sure the store was clean and well staffed (by working there himself ten to twelve hours a day)—and business picked up. So Jim decided to expand. He had purchased (for $80,000) not only the single store but also the right to build more stores, and he did. He had already used his Wendy's stock as collateral for a loan to buy and operate the first store. Now he borrowed more to build a second store, and then a third. Within three years, he had six Wendy's. The Austin newspaper ran an article about him with the headline: "A Millionaire Before 30; Burger Magnate Took a Gamble That Paid Off." Jim was "a true workingman's hero," the article reported, and it quoted his business philosophy: "The secret is solving problems quickly and never quit hustling."

By this time, Jim was $700,000 in debt, which would have been fine if business was good. But it wasn't. This was mystifying to Jim. He was doing everything right, everything his years of experience in the business had taught him; he had clean stores, good crews, decent locations, and people simply were not walking through the doors. Meanwhile, the economy was going haywire.

Interest rates topped 20 percent; real estate prices were skyrocketing; the price of hamburger went from 65 cents a pound to $1.47 in one eight-week period.

On top of all that, or because of it, Jim was getting tired. He was tired of dealing with the Wendy's organization, tired of managing sixteen-year-old employees, tired of frying hamburgers, and simply worn out from more than ten years of twelve-hour days and seven-day weeks. Not even the grand opening of a new store could excite him any more.

And Jim was getting scared. The value of his Wendy's stock had plummeted from more than $1 million to $300,000. He owed more than twice what he owned. He risked losing everything.

So he sold out. The hamburger business still looked like a good bet for the long haul, at least to a friend of Jim's named Charlie Ogle. Ogle bought Jim's whole operation for $50,000 down and another $400,000 to be paid over a period of years. Most important, he assumed all of Jim's debt. So Jim got his Wendy's stock back free and clear. He still had his base, something to work with, something to play with.

He started out playing. He'd always wanted to bum around on a boat, so he went down to Florida to crew on a yacht Ogle owned. When that turned out to be less fun than Jim expected, he flew back to Austin. For the next couple of years, he concentrated on living the good life of a bachelor in the bars and hot tubs of the town.

He dabbled in a few businesses. Ogle was involved in something called the Electric Cowboy Music Festival in Tennessee. Jim invested $5000 and never saw it again. Ogle was also importing kerosene heaters from Japan. They looked like a good product to Jim, so he became a distributor and lost $20,000.

He opened a hot tub rental parlor, which did great until people began to worry about sexually transmitted diseases. He had a friend with a plant nursery who needed a $40,000 loan to put it over the top. Jim helped him out. Two years later, Jim got his $40,000 back, with no interest. It was his best deal of that era, which left him, when all was said and done, with one valuable lesson ("Don't go into something you don't know anything about"), a tangle of litigation over the hot tub business's debts, and one physical souvenir:

his hot tub company's logo—a man in a tub—was etched on a crown in the back of Jim's mouth.

Then things picked up.

Several years before, Jim had become aware of the phenomenon of male stripper bars while he was working for Wendy's in Toledo, Ohio. He lived with a girlfriend there who had come from the West Indies and married a bartender to get a green card. When she and Jim split up, her husband, with whom Jim had become friendly, moved into Jim's house as his roommate. This was the house with the indoor swimming pool. The bartender worked in a club that occasionally presented male strippers. Men were barred from the place on those nights, but the bartender took Jim inside, and Jim was impressed: "I saw hundreds of women going crazy. They just loved seeing these goofballs running around in their little bikini pants and jock straps."

Jim kept it in the back of his mind.

A couple of years after he got out of the hamburger business, his lawyer introduced him to two experienced male stripper bar managers who were looking for money to open their own club in Phoenix. Jim put up $50,000 and guaranteed some loans in exchange for 53 percent of the business. The two operating partners got 17 percent apiece (lawyers got the rest). Jim's partners moved to Phoenix and started setting things up. Jim visited from time to time.

What he saw there was not encouraging. His partners had taken over an old restaurant way out of town. It was the worst location for a nightclub Jim had ever seen. It was in the middle of the desert.

His partners made a television commercial featuring the dancers wearing white tuxedos, top hats, and canes. They performed a little one-step while an announcer said, "Cheeks. A ladies' club," and gave the address.

No television station would air it.

Jim's partners told him not to worry. Jim foresaw doom.

But his partners were right. By 3:00 p.m. on the afternoon of the day the club was to open, there were one hundred women camped out in lawn chairs in the parking lot in 102-degree heat. By early evening, there was a traffic jam in the desert. The Phoenix television stations came out to cover the scene, one with a helicopter. Jim was amazed that the same stations that wouldn't show the dancers in their tuxedos in the commercial showed "their bare butts in G-strings" on the news. Cheeks was a big success.

Jim continued to visit regularly, working with his partners and the dancers. Most of the latter were gay, but Jim thought "that didn't make them bad people; they were good friends." One day, however, he made a sarcastic comment to one of them, and the dancer burst into tears and sought comfort from another dancer. Jim was amused at the sight. "They were both adult grown men. They had only G-strings on, with their cowboy boots, and they might have had cowboy hats. The one was sitting in the lap of the other one, and they were both crying their eyes out, and one didn't even know why they were crying. He just knew there was a crisis, and he was patting the other fella on the back and saying, 'It's okay, it's okay. Jim's a meany.' "

The business continued to thrive, but Jim started to wonder about things when he flew out to Phoenix and one of his partners picked him up at the airport in a year-old Ferrari. This struck Jim funny, "because five months earlier the guy couldn't put a down payment on a fifteen-year-old car." Back at his partner's new condo, Jim saw a second Ferrari in the driveway. "So I decided his seventeen percent was probably worth a lot more than my fifty-three percent." Jim sold out for an $80,000 profit and walked away happy.

Then he went into the telephone business.

A friend of his brought him some literature about an incredible new computerized phone being sold by a company in Florida. The phone would time and track the cost of long-distance calls as they were made and print out a report; it could assign an account number to each call so that lawyers, for example, could maintain a record for billing their clients. It could do a few other gee-whiz things as well, and Jim was impressed. This was the new business opportunity he was looking for. He called his old friend and fellow Wendy's alumnus Gary Shuster, who was working for a fast-food chain in Chicago, and invited him to come to Austin and be his partner. He promised to pay Gary's moving expenses and match his salary; he knew that Gary, who was tall and bearded with intense dark eyes, was an aggressive go-getter who would put a lot of energy into any new business venture. Gary moved to Austin. Jim flew to Florida and wrote a check for $60,000 for exclusive rights to distribute the telephone in the 512 area code.

Jim and Gary set up a company called Austintatious and started selling phones. It soon became clear, however, that the phones worked only erratically. Also, they were overpriced (the top-of-the-line unit retailed for $2500). Also, they were rapidly being made obsolete by new microcomputer technology. Also, there turned out to be two other "exclusive" distributors in the 512 area. But the biggest problem with the phones, from Jim's point of view, was that they would occasionally explode. He had one in his house and, when it burst into flames one day, he called the business quits. He sued the manufacturer in federal court in Miami and won a judgment for $150,000, which just about covered his investment and legal fees. The company went bankrupt the next day. Jim's lawyer offered to try to collect anyway, for another $25,000 fee. Jim declined to press on. He told the lawyer, "I've had about as much fun for my hundred and fifty thousand dollars as I can stand."

Jim flew back to Austin, where Gary had now settled (he was living with Jim), and considered his options. He and Gary were still young, they were bright, they had business experience, and Jim still had some money. They needed something to do.

They were playing backgammon in a bar one night when the manager, who knew Jim was some kind of businessman, came over and asked if they would talk to a guy about armadillo cartoons. The guy's name was Joe Waldon, and Jim remembered him from when he'd been a doorman at the bar. Even then, Joe had been drawing cartoons. Now he'd assembled a collection featuring the armadillo, which is the unofficial national animal of Texas. Texiana was hot at the moment—people all over the country, deeply impressed by *Urban Cowboy,* were walking around wearing cowboy boots—and Jim and Gary thought an armadillo cartoon book had promise. They told Waldon to meet them the next morning for breakfast at 9:00 a.m.

Their reasoning here was that artists are inherently flaky and irresponsible and probably tend to be late sleepers as well. If Waldon showed up at 9:00 a.m., that would be a good indication he was reliable.

He showed, and Joe Waldon Enterprises was created, with Jim, Gary, and Waldon equal partners. Jim put up the money, Waldon created the art, and Gary operated the business. They published five thousand copies of *Too Much Tongue: Facts and Humor Featuring the Texas State Varmint* and spent every weekend selling them from card tables at flea markets, craft fairs, and chili cookoffs.

Soon they branched out into armadillo T-shirts. A couple of years before, Waldon had designed a T-shirt featuring a boy holding up an armadillo by its tail and asking, "Can I keep him Ma?" Waldon had a few shirts printed up, gave them to friends, and then left town for a while. When he returned, he discovered that the printer had liked the shirts so much that he had kept on printing them—and started selling them. Jim and Gary thought this T-shirt business was worth looking into. (For one thing, Jim reasoned, T-shirts wouldn't present the technological complications of computerized telephones. "A T-shirt's not too technical. You put it on.") Gary paid a call on the printer, told him that Joe Waldon Enterprises owned the rights to the shirt he'd been selling, and threatened to sue for $50,000. The printer made a counteroffer: he'd hand over one thousand dollars and do a thousand dollars worth of printing for free. Jim thought this was a hell of deal—they weren't even in the T-shirt business yet and already they were two thousand dollars ahead of the game.

So Joe Waldon Enterprises started producing the T-shirt known as "Can I keep him Ma?" Waldon designed another shirt with the legend "Ski Texas" that pictured a man who looked like a water skier standing in the desert; he was holding a rope attached to a pickup truck and two armadillos were strapped to his feet. With these and two more new designs, also with armadillos, the partners hit the road again, selling shirts at craft shows, chili cookoffs, and fun runs. They started buying small ads in regional magazines and signed up a few commission salesmen, including one in New York. They were building a small business.

Jim decided that maybe it was time to expand beyond armadillos. When Waldon hesitated, Jim had another idea. He'd always been a big fan of comic strips, and one of the funniest he'd ever read, called "The Academia Waltz," had run in the University of Texas student newspaper while Jim was operating the Wendy's at the edge of the campus. Jim had noticed that the student cartoonist, whose name was Berke Breathed, had, since graduating, launched a nationally syndicated strip called "Bloom County." The strip appeared in only a handful of papers, but Jim thought it was as funny as "The Academia Waltz." Now that he was in the T-shirt business, he thought it might be worthwhile to call Breathed and talk about doing shirts for him.

Jim had Gary make the call. This was the pattern in their partnership: Jim considered himself the "idea man," Gary was the "detail man." (A friend of theirs put it this way: "Jim has the nose for it [finding a new business]. Then he gets bored with it, and Gary gets in and whips it to death.")

So Gary called, but Breathed's reaction was negative. He said he doubted there was a market for "Bloom County" T-shirts, and he was, in any case, offended by the rampant commercialization of comic strips. He had, in fact, recently introduced a character called Bill the Cat as a parody of Garfield, the popular and much-merchandised comic-strip cat. Garfield (who by 1987 was identified with four thousand licensed products, from underwear to chopsticks) was cuddly and sassy. Bill the Cat was an eyesore. He sat perpetually in a cloud of fleas, drooling and retching. Later, Bill the Cat's role in the strip would expand—he had a torrid affair with Jeane Kirkpatrick, he was exposed as a Communist spy, he confessed to cocaine addiction on the David Letterman show—but in his initial appearance Breathed's target was merchandising. "Never ones to pass up a hot trend and a chance for some major bucks, we're introducing a new character," a narrator in the strip announced. While Bill gagged and barfed in the background, the narrator urged readers to run out and buy Bill the Cat shirts, tote bags, mugs, toys, wallpaper, lunch pails, toilet-seat covers, and flammable children's pajamas.

Breathed told Gary he didn't want to do T-shirts.

Jim told Gary to call Breathed back once a month.

Eventually, Breathed called Gary. He was offering a few hand-drawn T-shirts as prizes for a contest in the strip, he said. In case he got inquiries about buying "Bloom County" shirts, would Jim and Gary be interested in handling them? Gary said sure. He and Jim flew to Washington to meet with an executive of the Washington *Post* Writers Group, Breathed's syndicate, and they got the rights to produce a "Bloom County" T-shirt. It pictured Opus, a sweet-natured penguin Everyman who was the emotional center of the strip; he was holding a top hat and looking dim. Beneath him, for no obvious reason, appeared the legend "Penguin Lust."

Joe Waldon Enterprises started marketing "Penguin Lust" and, soon after, a second "Bloom County" design. Simultaneously, Jim and Gary were attempting to get Joe Waldon his own syndicated strip (without armadillos). As soon as they appeared to be making some progress, however, Waldon abruptly quit the partnership, announcing that henceforth he would be a stand-up comedian. Jim and Gary changed the name of the company to Lin-Tex Marketing and threw their efforts into selling "Bloom County."

And here, as with Wendy's, Jim proved to have picked a winner. "Bloom County"—a strange and witty strip that combined whimsy, childhood emotion, and social and political satire (in 1987 it would win the Pulitzer Prize for editorial cartooning)—became an enormous success. Within four years it was running in a thousand newspapers. "Bloom County" anthologies were major best sellers. And Jim and Gary had the T-shirts.

Spearheaded by Gary's relentless energy, they extended their marketing across the country. They added more "Bloom County" designs, and they obtained the rights to other strips (an effort that assumed special urgency when Breathed was injured in a crash of his ultralight plane and it was briefly feared that he would never draw again). In the early days, they acquired the T-shirt rights to "The Rock Channel," which soon folded, and "Pavlov," which never did much. Within a couple of years they were signing more popular strips—"Shoe," "Mother Goose & Grimm," "The Neighborhood."

They dabbled in specialty T-shirts as well. While Waldon was still with the company, they produced a "McReagan" shirt with Ronald Reagan as Ronald McDonald. Attorneys for McDonald's immediately dispatched a flurry of correspondence demanding that Lin-Tex surrender the shirts or face a lawsuit for trademark infringement. Waldon wrote back that he had not intended to harm McDonald's, "even though the burgers are horrible." Gary told the lawyers that twenty shirts had been produced, thirteen had been sold, and that he would gladly turn over the remainder except for two he wanted as souvenirs and one that was to be buried in "our company time capsule."

A risqué "Sexual Trivia" line sold even worse than "McReagan." (Lin-Tex ultimately tried to give the shirts away as premiums at a retail outlet; the only customer to take any, an old woman who couldn't read English, brought them back the next day shouting "Filth! Filth!") During the Falkland Islands war, Jim wanted to put out a shirt with the legend, " 'Don't Falk With Me, Argentina'—Margaret Thatcher." Gary attempted to stall until Jim changed his mind but only succeeded in delaying the appearance of the shirt until after the war was over.

Despite these setbacks, and a period during which Breathed's father was also selling "Bloom County" shirts (Jim and Gary eventually bought him out), the business grew steadily. In its first year, Joe Waldon Enterprises had gross sales of $20,000. Five years later, Lin-Tex Marketing had sales of $1.5 million.

And it was growing still. The day Jim sat in his office complaining about the cable TV, his company had just concluded a $314,000 month. Including weekends and holidays, it was selling 1600 T-shirts every day.

"Watch out for cops," said Jim. "There's a speed limit on this lake." Standing by the wheel of his 22-foot Hammond Chal-

lenger with a 260-horsepower motor, Jim was taking a late afternoon spin with a visitor on Lake Austin. He was wearing a
"Shoe" T-shirt on which a character in a bar was saying, "I'll
have what the gentleman on the floor is having." A George Strait
song was playing on the boat's built-in stereo as Jim pushed the
craft up to fifty.

He raced up the narrow serpentine lake, which had been
created forty-six years before by a dam built with federal funds
obtained by Lyndon Johnson when he was an ambitious young
congressman from the Austin district. Jim appreciated it. He
cruised by the dock of a dentist he knew, who was enjoying
cocktails on his patio and invited Jim in for a drink. Jim declined
but suggested a round of golf the next day.

At the approach of sunset, Jim accelerated toward home.
The sky was blue and pink; the steep wooded hills that ran down
to the lake were in shadow. Jim turned on the boat's lights.
There had been a lot of bad collisions on the lake at night.

At his private dock, Jim hoisted the boat out of the water in
a sling and covered it. He drove up the hill to his house, where
three Mexican-Americans wearing "Bloom County" T-shirts
were hacking at high grass around his satellite dish. Inside, he
was greeted by Ashley the Pomeranian and Frances, all blond
and pregnant, who was excited about the Mexican baby. "Isn't
it great?" she said. "I want a girl but I don't want to have another
baby for five years. I want to get back in shape."

The house hadn't changed much since Jim's bachelor days.
The crap table still stood opposite the front door, with a painting
of Willie Nelson on the wall behind it. There had been minor
adjustments. Frances had banished a video game from the living
room to the garage, and she'd had the sofa and barstools re-
covered ("There were too many memories on them," she explained). A magazine rack now held copies of both *Good
Housekeeping* ("8 Dreamy Kitchens") and *Cheri* ("Golden God-
desses and Big Boobs").

Over the pool table there still hung twenty paintings by Rich-
ard Wawro, a legally blind Scottish autistic savant whose work
Jim admired. Other walls were now decorated with paintings by
A. D. Greer, an elderly Western landscape artist for whom

Frances had worked before her marriage. Greer specialized in mountains and waterfalls, Jim explained. "In one painting the waterfall is on the left; in the next he'll move it over to the center; in the one after that he'll put it on the right."

"Some of his paintings have sold for one hundred and fifty thousand dollars," Frances said. "This is fifteen thousand." She pointed to a woodsy scene hanging in the living room, then to a small painting of trees by a pond. "That took him ten minutes to do. That's two thousand dollars for ten minutes work."

An amateur painter herself, Frances had received many of the paintings in lieu of pay. "He didn't like to pay cash," she said. "It didn't matter to me. They're going to go up."

Frances laid the dinner—frogs legs and peas—on the dining-room table, and she turned to the visitor, who was Jewish, and said, "I've got something I want to ask you about." She produced a copy of a pamphlet entitled "The Conspiracy to Destroy All Existing Governments and Religions." It described an ancient plot to "enslave the human race" and "impose the Luciferian ideology upon the Goyim (human cattle) by means of Satanic despotism," a plot supported by the House of Rothschild, the Rockefeller and Ford Foundations, and the "Synagogue of Satan," a term that did "not, repeat not, mean the Jews" but rather "those who call themselves Jews, but are not, and do lie."

"A.D. gave it to me," Frances said. "He's very interested in the Jewish religion. It's very interesting talking to him. You learn so much."

Is that so, said the guest.

"It's an interesting little book," said Frances, in perfect innocence.

"Sit down and eat," said Jim, "if you're not too busy conspiring to destroy all governments and religions."

The next day Jim had a lunch date with a man named Leonard Smith who had called him after reading an article about Lin-Tex in the Austin paper. Smith said he had contacts with Taiwanese manufacturers and maybe they could do something for Lin-Tex. At the moment, Jim was in fact looking for a supplier for a new line—he wanted to introduce Lacoste-style polo shirts with little embroidered Opuses and Bill the Cats instead of alligators—so he made the appointment.

They met at an Austin restaurant where the only main course on the menu was pan-fried steak. Smith and a colleague were wearing long-sleeved shirts and ties. Jim wore shorts and a golf shirt; he ordered a double salad.

Smith said he was in partnership with some Taiwanese in Houston whose relatives back home might be able to manufacture Jim's shirts. In the meantime, he said, "They have a good source for shoes. Would you like to do 'Bloom County' shoes?"

"I think we'll stick to shirts for now," Jim said.

"How about phones?" asked Smith. "They're bringing in these cheap phones."

Jim shook his head. "Not just now."

Well, said Smith, he and his people might be interested in becoming Lin-Tex's sales reps for Florida and California.

Jim allowed that he was not at the moment well represented in Florida, and he was open to offers. "We're interested in anything that sells shirts and doesn't cost us money. We grossed three hundred thousand dollars last month and made eighteen percent. We want to get that up to a million dollars a month and make twenty percent, and we don't care what anybody else makes."

Smith said he'd be in touch, but Lin-Tex never did any business with him. And the baby deal fell through, too. The lady in El Paso took all four.

# "Cows, Income Taxes, and Bull(s)"

**P**ETE WAS TORMENTED by hope. The Universal II limited partnership shares still hadn't been put on the market, but Lundelius, the investment banker, remained sublimely confident
that they would sell. Assuming they did—an assumption Pete hesitated to make for fear of being disappointed—Universal II would
raise $1.8 million. A quarter of a million dollars of that would
promptly find its way into the coffers of Hopes Creek Ranch.

Pete knew exactly what he was going to do with the money.
He was going to hire a man to take over the ranch's hay operation.
The man he had in mind was a qualified bulldozer operator. Pete
was going to have him dig fifteen "tanks" (ponds) at points where
soil was eroding along the banks of Hopes Creek, which twisted
through the ranch. Pete was going to stock the tanks with catfish,
a popular food in Texas. He was going to harvest the fish and
process them in a catfish and beef-processing plant he was going
to build on the ranch. The way Pete saw it, "vertical integration"
was the key to success in agriculture. His meat plant would process
excess Senepols produced by the Universal II breeding program.
The meat would be lean and hormone-free, and Pete was going
to market it under the brand name "Texsen." He would sell it to
food stores and directly to consumers in his own hamburger restaurant in College Station. "A survey of other hamburger places
in town showed that to be a profitable venture," he said. "It would
be done by bringing in somebody who knew the restaurant busi-

ness, who would work on a profit-sharing basis plus a base salary. We're talking about a young, clean-cut, twenty-five to thirty-year-old with experience."

But before Pete had a bulldozer operator, or catfish ponds, or a meat plant, or a hamburger restaurant, the partnership shares in Universal II had to be sold. Pete called Lundelius at least once a day to see how things were going. Lundelius blamed part of the delay in getting to market on Pete's insistence on drafting the legal documents himself (having rejected the $30,000 lawyer Lundelius had suggested). Pete had composed a one-page escrow agreement that was totally inadequate, Lundelius complained. A member of Lundelius's staff had to rewrite the thing.

Nevertheless, the offering plan was moving forward, and Lundelius considered that there was still plenty of time to sell it. Autumn was the season when people with money began to feel the chill of approaching tax deadlines and their thoughts turned to tax shelters. Universal II would be there when they needed it.

There were many varieties of tax shelters from which people with money could choose, of course. There were real estate shelters, oil and gas shelters, equipment-leasing shelters, and motion picture production shelters. All of these were cleverly structured investment arrangements designed to give investors big upfront paper losses that they could deduct from their incomes for tax savings. In Texas, tax shelters involving the breeding or feeding of cattle were particular favorites. A good portion of agricultural ventures in the state, in fact, owed their existence to the tax benefits doctors and lawyers in Houston and Dallas derived from them. (Also, people in Texas just liked to own cows.) The role of tax shelters was so strong in the cattle business that Pete, unsophisticated in finance, had made a point of looking into them early in his career. "The United States can import beef cheaper than it can grow it," he concluded. "The entire cattle industry exists only because of tax advantages. Beef has nothing to do with it." He wrote up a little memo summarizing his findings with the title "Cows, Income Taxes, and Bull(s)." The title expressed his skepticism. This was a hell of a way to run the industry he loved. But Pete was up for the game. If this was how business in America worked, this was how he would play.

The purpose of the Universal II limited partnership, according to the offering plan Pete drafted, was to establish a herd of pure-blood Senepol cattle in Texas. The plan told the story of the breed's origin on St. Croix and praised the breed's heat tolerance and general economic efficiency. Senepol cows, the plan said, possessed "excellent maternal ability and fertility"; Senepol bulls exhibited "excellent libido"; Senepol calves were "growthy and alert." "Given enough exposure and time," the plan concluded, "the management of MB Universal Programs believes that Senepols will be a viable and popular alternative to other breeds of cattle, particularly in the South and Southwest."

Universal II was going to begin by buying a base herd of Senepols from Annaly Farms on St. Croix, the plan said. It was also going to buy a herd of "commercial" (mixed-blood) cows to serve as surrogate mothers to Senepol embryos. Via intensive use of embryo transfers, the partnership would build up the herd for seven years. Along the way, it would generate income by selling off surplus and second-rate animals as well as Senepol embryos and semen. After seven years, the entire herd would be sold and the partnership liquidated. "With very few Senepol cattle presently in the United States and given the cost of importation, the price demanded for quality [Senepol] cattle should and will remain high," the plan predicted.

The entire project, the plan said, would benefit the American consumer (because Senepols produce "the lean beef that modern consumers prefer") and the American rancher (because Senepols offer "many advantages . . . not readily available on the present market").

It was also going to give its investors a great tax break.

Each investor (or "limited partner") was being asked to contribute $20,000 ($6000 in the first year, $7000 in the second, and $7000 in the third) and to assume $16,000 in debt on behalf of the partnership. By drawing on the borrowed money, the partnership would in its first year (the end of which was only a few months away) spend far more cash than the investors had personally contributed. While each investor would be making an immediate payment of only $6000, the partnership would be spending $11,976 per investor to get the herd started. Since the partnership would have no business income in the first year, it would show a loss of $11,976 per investor. Each investor would be entitled to show that loss on his personal tax return and deduct it from his other taxable income. Assuming he was in a 50 percent tax bracket, that would cut his tax bill by $5988. He would also be able to claim as his own $403 of the investment tax credit the partnership would receive for its purchase of animals. So the investor would save $6391 on his tax bill, for a net *gain* of $391 after taking into account his $6000 investment.

There would be similar, though lesser, tax benefits in succeeding years. After three years, the investor's net out-of-pocket cost would reach its peak at $3412. Assuming all went well, after seven years he would have a net profit of nearly $20,000.

There was one dark cloud hanging over this happy picture. As Pete and Lundelius were preparing Universal II for the market, the United States Congress was lurching toward passage of the tax reform bill put in motion by President Ronald Reagan, who was then serving in his second term and remained popular beyond all reason. The bill before Congress would put new limits on the benefits of tax shelters and, by lowering tax rates, reduce the value of any benefits that remained. Even under the proposed legislation, however, Universal II looked okay. In the first year, instead of gaining $391 from his $6000 expenditure, an investor would have a net cost of $12. After three years, he would be $7177 in the hole instead of $3412, and his ultimate net gain would be $13,525 instead of $20,000.

These numbers were still respectable, especially considering that the rewards of all other tax shelters would be reduced as well. And Universal II would still benefit from its reliance on embryo transfers, which happened to be not only a great agricultural technology but also a great tax gimmick. The IRS required that many limited partnership expenses be allotted over a period of years, which diminished their tax-reduction effect. But the cost of an embryo transfer could still be deducted in full the moment the technician inserted the fertilized egg into a cow. A large proportion of Universal II's first-year expenditures (and thus a large portion of its first-year tax benefits) was allocated for embryo transfers.

Lundelius saw this giving the program a competitive advantage over other tax shelters on the market.

"Pete's writeoff is driven in the first year by one activity," Lundelius said, "and that's embryo transfers. . . . He's got over one hundred transfers scheduled for this program, and he's got to perform those by the end of the year. He will be very busy."

Lundelius, sitting in his plush office in his tailored suit, foresaw an odd kind of New Year's Eve party on the ranch, frantically stuffing embryos into cows as the clock approached midnight: "We may be up there, all of us. I'll volunteer to hold the cow's head, I guess. That's about as close to it as I want to be."

But that was still in the future. For the moment, nothing was happening.

In the lull, Pete was following a few other leads. An Australian rancher had inquired about buying some frozen embryos. A patient of Pete's partner, Dr. McCall, told McCall he exported food products and had contacts in Latin America. Pete had met with the man and was tentatively planning a Senepol sales trip to El Salvador.

Pete sometimes talked about these deals as if they were practically concluded. He was daring to hope. He was even talking about the successor to Universal II—Universal III. It was going to raise $5 million.

# **M**AGIC Show

**I**N A BUBBLE-DOMED ANNEX to the Los Angeles Convention Center, the owners and staff of Lin-Tex Marketing were applying the final touches to their display. It was early evening. In the morning a major trade show called MAGIC, for the Men's Apparel Guild in California, would commence. Menswear manufacturers from all over the world had come to Los Angeles and set up elaborate exhibits; thousands of buyers from stores big and small would stroll the long aisles of the hall to peruse the offerings of Stanley Blacker, Oscar de la Renta, Evan-Picone, Bill Blass, and Levi Strauss. Thousand-dollar suits and fine silk ties were on display; so were jeans and socks and underwear. And this year, for the first time ever, there were Bill the Cat T-shirts.

Jim and Gary were arranging their goods in booth B106 under the arched ceiling of the inflated annex. "Bloom County" designs, which still accounted for the bulk of Lin-Tex sales, were mounted next to designs from newer Lin-Tex properties. There were T-shirts with characters from "Mother Goose & Grimm" (Grimm, the dog, burping contentedly over what appeared to be the remains of Mickey Mouse) and "Hagar the Horrible" (Hagar adrift on a raft surrounded by sharks, declaring, "I need a volunteer to go for beer"). There were several designs from a single-panel strip called "The Neighborhood," including a popular shirt picturing a dump-side stand advertising "Fred's Fill Dirt and Croissants."

Gary, in pink corduroy shorts, was running a hand steamer

over another "Neighborhood" design (two fishermen in a boat nervously watching four bears approach in a boat of their own). As he got the last wrinkle out, he declared, "It would have been great if my mom had had one of these." He was referring to the steamer, not the shirt. When Gary was a child in Columbus, his mother had taken in ironing to help make ends meet. She was an aspiring singer who performed with local big bands under the name Jeannie L'Amour (her real name was Jeannie Louise Moore) and told people she was French. Gary grew up thinking *he* was part French.

In fact, he was part German, part Pennsylvania Dutch, and part Chippewa Indian. He did, however, inherit a fine tenor voice from his mother. One of his first ventures with Jim had been a musical one. In junior high school, Gary had been lead singer and bongo player in a band called the Afterbeats; Jim, who couldn't sing a note, was the manager.

Jim and Gary also caddied together at a country club in suburban Columbus. They worked together at the Ohio State Fair. And, eventually, they worked together at Wendy's. Gary joined Wendy's as assistant manager of its first and only store when Jim was general manager of the company. One day the store manager ran off with a counter girl, and Jim promoted Gary to the job. Like Jim, Gary flourished in the organization; he reached the position of area director for Cincinnati. Also like Jim, he eventually quarreled with corporate officials. Unlike Jim, he lost his temper and left the company before his stock options vested.

A few months before the MAGIC show, Jim and Gary had sent a copy of an Austin newspaper article about the success of Lin-Tex to the former Wendy's executive who had driven them both from the company. They attached a note: "Thanks." (The former executive wrote back: "You're welcome.")

The article appeared at a time when Lin-Tex Marketing was attempting a major transition. In the company's early years, it had sold T-shirts primarily through co-op advertising in newspapers. Lin-Tex provided newspapers with camera-ready ads which the papers ran for free (preferably opposite the comics page); when orders came in, Lin-Tex filled them and sent the papers a 15 percent commission.

That was a good business (Lin-Tex paid $3 to have the shirts produced and collected full retail—$11.95—when it sold them), but the mail-order market was inherently limited. Six months before the MAGIC show, Jim and Gary had decided that their future lay in being T-shirt wholesalers, and they started selling shirts to retailers. Between March and September they acquired six hundred accounts.

And now they were attempting something bigger still. Most of their accounts so far were small T-shirt and gift shops. Coming to the MAGIC show was the first shot in a campaign to break into mainstream clothing stores and even department stores. Gary thought the time was right. In the past, department stores had looked down their noses at T-shirts. But the recent popularity of surfing styles from a company called Ocean Pacific had opened some department store doors. Coca-Cola clothing, which included T-shirts, was a hit in department stores. And Spuds MacKenzie was on the horizon.

In reaching for bigger markets, Lin-Tex was taking a risk. Big stores took ninety days to pay their suppliers, and, because of its rapid growth, Lin-Tex already had a problem with cash flow. To sell to big stores, you had to have a full line. "You can't go to a department store with four 'Bloom County' shirts," Jim said, "even if those shirts sold one million dollars last year." So Lin-Tex had pushed to sign up more strips and had pushed the cartoonists to deliver promised designs. Lin-Tex built up its inventory and incurred new marketing costs, including hiring sales people and, far from least, renting space at the MAGIC show, designing a booth, and staffing it. Lin-Tex was paying for all this with money it didn't quite have.

But Jim and Gary seemed relaxed as workmen hammered the last bits of the booth into place. It was a striking display, constructed of mock black brick, with shirts highlighted in showcase windows surrounded by moving marquee lights.

Jim and Gary looked it over approvingly. Then they went out to dinner to celebrate Gary's birthday and the opening of the show. They took a dozen guests—the booth's designer, two carpenters, some Lin-Tex staffers, and the models who had posed in T-shirts for a new Lin-Tex brochure. The tab came to $1400. Gary had been ordering $120 bottles of Roederer champagne, thinking he was ordering $65 bottles. But he took this news in stride. He reached for the check.

"Do you take the gold card?" he asked.

The waiter said yes.

Gary produced a cardboard gold card that was good for a 50 percent discount at any Wendy's in Austin.

The bill was settled by other means, and, in the morning, the MAGIC show began:

### DAY ONE

Jim and Gary show up at the booth in tuxedos. "So that people can ask us why," Gary explains, "and we can say, 'Because we're selling T-shirts.' "

The Lin-Tex exhibit is pristine, fully stocked, untouched, as Jim and Gary loll around, waiting for customers. Jim walks across the aisle to check out the booth of another, larger T-shirt company called Changes, which features designs with Buckwheat and other characters from the 1930s comedy shorts variously packaged as "The Little Rascals" and "Our Gang." Changes also has Beaver Cleaver, Ralph Kramden, Ed Norton, Maxwell Smart, Sergeant Bilko, and the zany gang from the prisoner-of-war camp in "Hogan's Heroes."

Rock music is in the air, emanating from the Surf Fetish booth down the aisle. Riding the surfwear wave, Surf Fetish has brought in some musclehead male models to dance in front of its booth wearing T-shirts with stylized drawings of palm trees and the company slogan: "No Nerds Not Anywhere."

Lin-Tex has a model, too. Her name is Havoc Oliver and she is encased in an Opus penguin costume. It's hot in there, but Havoc has spirit. She dances along to the Surf Fetish music. Children visiting the show with their parents stop to have a few words with Opus, as does a middle-aged salesman from the next aisle who keeps pressing for a date. Havoc isn't interested.

Business is slow. Everybody in the Lin-Tex booth perks up when a young woman buyer from Millers Outpost stops by.

Millers Outpost is a clothing chain ubiquitous in America's shopping malls. The buyer sits at a table with Jim and Gary and pores over a sample book of Lin-Tex products. She pauses at a "Mother Goose & Grimm" design of Snow White being flashed by a dwarf. Snow White is saying, "And you must be Sleazy."

"I wore that shirt into a bar the first night after it came in," Jim volunteers, "and I must have had fifteen women offer to buy it off my back."

If the woman from Millers Outpost is impressed, she doesn't show it.

She finishes paging through the book and walks off down the aisle.

"She said she's going to walk the show," Gary reports. "The trouble is she doesn't know anything about comic strips."

"She has no earthly idea what a comic strip is," Jim complains.

"She never reads them," Gary says. "I said, 'Do yourself a favor. Call R. Dakin and ask how Opus does compared to Garfield.' " (R. Dakin & Company, a leading manufacturer of plush toys, produces both Opus and Garfield dolls.)

"If she wanted to," Jim says, "she could write a hundred-thousand-dollar opening order."

He shakes his head and walks across the aisle to the Changes booth, where he has made friends with the company's owners. "How big is your Millers business?" he asks.

"Close to a million dollars a year," one of the owners says.

Jim sighs.

The Changes owner says his most popular shirts are the Buckwheat designs, a result of Eddie Murphy doing Buckwheat routines on "Saturday Night Live." Changes has shirts with Buckwheat surfing and Buckwheat playing electric guitar. It also has Buckwheat as Rambo ("Buckbo"). "Some white retailers worry about stocking Buckwheat [who is a funny-looking black child]," the owner says, "but it does great in black areas. We put it in a Harlem street fair, and it blew out of there. It does well in Detroit."

There are some Buckwheat problems, however. The rights to Buckwheat are being fought over by the owners of "The Little

Rascals" and the owners of "Our Gang." And the son of the child actor who played Buckwheat is trying to get into the act as well. "He says he ought to get something," says the Changes owner. "He's selling his own T-shirts. There's a lawsuit. Legally, he can use his father's picture but not the name Buckwheat."

So what name can he use?

"George Thomas."

## DAY TWO

Lin-Tex makes its first sale of the show—thirty polo shirts with little embroidered Opuses and Bill the Cats. The streak continues when the owner of a store in Anchorage stops by and buys fifty-nine T-shirts. One design she declines to buy pictures Grimm running comically. The front of the dog is on the front of the shirt; the back is on the back. "It's too cute for us," she explains. "You have to understand that our biggest seller is 'Nazi Punks Fuck Off.' We sell seven-hundred-dollar leather coats, too."

What on earth is she talking about?

No one has the slightest idea.

Lin-Tex still hasn't recouped the cost of the opening-night dinner.

But now a stocky crewcut blond man with his left arm in a cast has stopped to admire some "Shoe" shirts. The "Shoe" comic strip, drawn by editorial cartoonist Jeff MacNelly, concerns some birds who publish a newspaper. One of the birds has a nephew, a skinny little bird named Skyler, who, every summer, thinking he is heading to summer camp, gets packed off instead to Marine Corps boot camp. Several shirts mark these occasions, including one that is headed "We're Looking for a Few Good Men" over a picture of scrawny Skyler, in fatigues, who adds, "But we've been known to stretch the rules."

The crewcut blond identifies himself as Major Schoppe from the base exchange at Parris Island, the Marine Corps training camp. He says he likes the "Shoe" Marine shirts, although he has a problem with the "We're Looking for a Few Good Men" design. "Our command is very image-conscious," he says. "We couldn't take that one by itself." He is enthusiastic, however, about an embroidered design of Skyler with the legend "Counselor, Camp Lejeune." "If you could do something like that for us, we'd be very interested."

Jim practically snaps to attention. "I just had lunch a few weeks ago with Jeff MacNelly, a three-time Pulitzer Prize-winner," he tells Schoppe. "He said the main thing he wants to do now is get involved with the military. He loves the Marines. You tell us what you want. He'll draw it for you, and he'll come down and help you sell it. Just get him a ride on a jet or something."

Major Schoppe nods and says he'll be back.

Jim turns to his fellow Lin-Texans and announces, "Just made the show, folks."

"He's only one base," somebody points out.

"If we get in one base," Jim says, "we'll get in all of them."


DAY THREE


There is something profoundly wearying about sitting day after day in a booth at a trade show. Most buyers walk by without stopping. Most who stop don't buy, but only after asking a lot of stupid questions. The Surf Fetish muscleheads are still dancing in the aisle, but Havoc Oliver, who is a freelance designer as well as a model, has shed her penguin head and is showing people a portfolio of videocassette covers she has designed. A Canadian manufacturer says he'd like to come over to her place and see the rest of her portfolio. She tells him to forget it.

The Lin-Tex crew is listless. When a buyer does stop and inquires about shirts, Jim says, "There's our national sales manager," and pushes him over to Gary.

Major Schoppe returns, and Jim and Gary arrange to meet him in two weeks in Chicago, where Jeff MacNelly lives. Schoppe is excited about meeting MacNelly and possibly getting MacNelly to visit Parris Island, but he is dubious about arranging a jet ride for the celebrated cartoonist. "If it's Joe Shmuck," he explains, "we can sometimes do it, if the commander isn't a hardass. But someone like that . . . if there's a problem . . . if we kill him. . . . "

A woman from United Media Licensing shows up to discuss some of its properties. Would Lin-Tex like to do "Nancy" T-shirts? "Frank and Ernest" T-shirts? "Born Loser" T-shirts? "Alley Oop"?

Jim seriously doubts that there are many hard-core "Nancy" fans just dying to own "Nancy" memorabilia, but he thinks "Nancy" might be "a fashion shirt," one that sells because the image is interesting irrespective of its content.

Jim and Gary sit and talk with the woman. Nothing is resolved. Everything is possible.

## DAY FOUR

Jim is outraged. An article in the L.A. paper reports that Wendy's has spent a million dollars conducting taste tests and has determined, among other things, that the best order to stack condiments on a burger is, from bottom to top: mayonnaise, ketchup, pickle, onion, tomato, lettuce. This is the way Wendy's has been doing it all along. "They spent a million fucking dollars to find out what we knew by gut instinct in 1969!" Jim rants. "You know what this study cost *me*? Three hundred and twelve dollars and fifty cents. I have 31,250 shares of Wendy's stock. *You* figure it out."

Meanwhile, back at the booth, Gary makes a $1380 sale, for a final show total of $2500.

"But we got the Marines," Jim says, "and UCLA could be a hundred-thousand-dollar account." A buyer from the UCLA bookstore has stopped by and said he'd buy "Bloom County" shirts if he could put the letters "UCLA" on them. In the past, Berke Breathed has forbidden any changes in his designs. "We might just go ahead and do it while Berke's in Antarctica," Jim says. *Life* magazine is sending Breathed there to write about Opus the penguin's search for his mother.

The show winds down. The buyers are all gone by early afternoon. The exhibitors begin to pack up.

Jim puts an embroidered Bill the Cat diaper on his head, just for fun, and goes across the aisle to trade some "Bloom County" books for "Buckbo."

# Texas Sports (Aggie Football)

**O**N THE LIVING-ROOM WALL in the house at Hopes Creek Ranch, Becky Binion had hung one of her prized possessions, a copy of "The Aggie War Hymn" autographed by J. V. "Pinky" Wilson, the man who wrote the lyrics:

> Hullabaloo! Caneck! Caneck!
> Hullabaloo! Caneck! Caneck!
> Good-bye to Texas University,
> So long to the Orange and White.
> Good luck to dear ole Texas Aggies,
> They are the boys that show the real old fight.
> "The eyes of Texas are upon you. . . ."
> That is the song they sing so well,
> So good-bye to Texas University,
> We're going to beat you all to . . . Chiggarroogarrem!
> Chiggarroogarrem!
> Rough! Tough! Real stuff!
> Texas A&M!

Generally, war hymns are reserved to nations and military forces, not universities, but Texas A&M (home of the "Aggies") is no ordinary university; it has the flavor of a nation and the history of an army. Until the 1960s, the school was all male and all military. Students belonged to the Corps of Cadets, which functioned (and functions still) as an ROTC unit for the Army, Navy, and Air Force. When the United States entered World War I, the entire senior class resigned to join the Army. ("Pinky" Wilson wrote "The Aggie War Hymn" while standing watch on the Rhine.) During World War II, more American officers came from Texas A&M than from any other school, including the military academies. The center of campus life is the Memorial Student Center, a building dedicated to Aggies who died in the world wars; as signs of respect, students are forbidden to walk on the surrounding lawn or to wear hats inside (a significant proscription in cowboy-hat country). A corridor honors Aggies who have won the Congressional Medal of Honor.

Texas A&M is coed now, and membership in the Corps (also now coed) is optional, but it is still the largest ROTC unit in the United States. Its two thousand members live in Corps housing under military discipline, and their uniforms and rituals are prominent on campus. Freshman cadets in duck-billed caps are required to "whip out"—greet upperclassmen wherever they encounter them. A freshman meeting *two* upperclassmen will blurt, "Howdy howdy," one "howdy" for each. Campus restrooms are filled after every class with cadets straightening the razor-sharp ironing creases on their shirts; being caught with a crooked crease can subject one to disciplinary action.

Even non-military aspects of campus life are suffused with tradition and lore. The world's largest bonfire is set ablaze each year on the eve of the football game with arch rival University of Texas (the "Texas University" of "The Aggie War Hymn"). The campus mascot is a dog named Reveille. Her predecessors have all been buried, with full military honors, at the entrance to the football field, "so they can see the scoreboard." Every year on April 21, the anniversary of the Battle of San Jacinto (when Texas rebels won independence from Mexico in 1836), Aggies gather wherever they are, all over the world, for "Muster," a ceremony that reaffirms their loyalty to A&M and their fellow Aggies and honors Aggies who have died in the previous year. A roll call is read, and living Aggies call out "Here!" for their departed comrades.

"Aggies" include not only current students at A&M and

alumni of A&M but also anyone who ever attended A&M, even for a day. There is no A&M "alumni" association, only a 125,000-member Association of Former Students. "Once an Aggie," they say, "always an Aggie."

Considering these feelings of Aggie kinship and the Aggie backscratching that eases the paths of many Aggies through life, it is baffling that one Aggie pastime is the telling of Aggie jokes, which revolve around an image of the Aggie as a dumb and unsanitary hick. Bookstores around campus sell eight volumes of a series called *101 Aggie Jokes*. Volume One, now in its thirteenth printing, introduces the Aggie who got cufflinks for his birthday so decided to have his wrists pierced, the Aggie who wanted a formal wedding so he painted the shotgun white, the Aggie elevator operator who lost his job because he couldn't learn the route, and the cannibal who went to a jungle restaurant and inquired why baked Aggie was the most expensive thing on the menu. "Aggies aren't scarce," he protested. "No," replied the waiter, "but did you ever try to clean one?"

Hopes Creek Ranch (located just eight miles from the A&M campus) was imbued with Aggie spirit. Pete was an Aggie and wore his class ring with pride. Becky's dad, Billie, was an Aggie; he had even played on the football team. Becky had attended A&M for a couple of semesters before flunking out, so she was an Aggie, too. Bryan wasn't an Aggie, but he had been named for the town of Bryan, which adjoins College Station. Becky and Bryan's older brother, the pride of the Pratt family, was a student at A&M when he was killed in a car crash and thus became the subject of another Aggie tradition—Silver Taps. On the first Tuesday of the following month, the flag in front of the Academic Building was lowered to half-mast. At 10:15 p.m., chimes began to play in the bell tower and the campus lights were dimmed. A squad from the Ross Volunteers, an elite unit of the Corps of Cadets, slowly marched to a central lawn where the student body had gathered and fired a twenty-one-gun salute. Then buglers from the Fightin' Texas Aggie Band played Taps.

Pete and Becky met because of the Aggie connection. When

Pete moved to Burnet in the late 1970s to manage a ranch there, he naturally became acquainted with local lawyer and fellow Aggie Billie Pratt. Billie's daughter Becky, a tall, spirited woman who had been a high school basketball star, became acquainted with Pete in turn, and she liked him. She remarked to one of her girlfriends at the time, "Someday I'd like to marry a guy like Pete, or a preacher." A lot of the guys she met seemed "weak." She figured a preacher would be strong-minded, and Pete seemed to be not only strong-minded but as if he knew how to have a good time to boot.

These speculations were strictly hypothetical, however; Pete was married at the time. The marriage was a troubled one, but there it was. Becky knew Pete only as a fellow who did some real estate business and talked Aggie talk with her father, for whom she worked as a secretary. Then one night, on the eve of the Burnet cattle show, Pete and Becky turned up at the same party. Pete was looking for his wife, but he never found her:

"Becky and I danced. We really didn't know each other at all. Never had really talked to each other hardly at all. Somehow Becky and I danced two, three, four dances. There was another party at a doctor's house. Becky said, 'Why don't you go with us over there?' So we go to this party, and there's all these people there, and I'm feeling good. They're all out at the pool swimming, a bunch of Aggies. Lots of Aggies. An all-Aggie family. Aggie doctor after Aggie sons. Well, I picked Becky up—she was in her high heels and her dress—and threw her into the Jacuzzi on top of all these guys. 'Cause they were all talking big-time, and I'm feeling ready to raise some hell. So the next thing I know—the cattle show was starting at eight o'clock—I wake up. I've been in bed with Becky all night long, at her house. The sun comes through the window, hit me in the eye. The show was fixin' to start, and I'm giving the opening ceremonies, and my clothes are soaking wet on the floor beside the bed. I leave. Becky's asleep."

She awoke soon after, her own memory a haze:

"I wondered, 'Did I dream it? Did I spend the night with a married man?' "

Two days later, Billie invited Pete to come with him to a

football banquet to watch an A&M coach show some Aggie game films. Pete said sure. His wife came with him. Becky came with Billie. Over dinner, the two women got to talking. Pete's wife asked Becky if she'd seen Pete the night of the party; had she noticed if he'd been dancing with any of the girls?

Pete and Becky hadn't talked since that night, and they still didn't talk until a couple of weeks later when Pete called Billie's office to discuss a real estate deal. Becky answered the phone. Pete said he supposed they ought to have lunch sometime. Becky said, "Today?"

Six months later, they were married.

And it was a happy and fruitful marriage. Wade, Pauline, and Mollie were born in the next five years. Pete wanted to have kids close together so they'd have each other to play with if the family lived in the country; his own siblings had been crucially important to him during his isolated childhood. But Pete vowed also that his kids would be no more isolated than they had to be. His own lack of social contact as a child, he believed, had caused him to be tongue-tied and feel inferior well into adulthood in the presence of anyone who "either wore a tie, worked at a bank, or was an engineer, or anything." This wasn't going to happen to his kids if he could help it, so he and Becky were constantly driving them to play on soccer teams, train and compete in a swimming league, to ballet lessons, art classes—everything the university town of College Station had to offer three bright and active children.

Family was the heart of Pete's life—he took care to schedule Senepol business meetings so they did not conflict with his duties as coach of Wade's soccer team—but it sometimes threatened to overwhelm him, for he lived at the center of an extended family. When the Binions had moved onto Hopes Creek Ranch (which they rented from Becky's dad), they brought Becky's brother Bryan with them. Bryan was tall and well built and a tirelessly strong worker. His reasoning powers were limited (the only arithmetic he was good at was keeping score at dominoes, a game his grandfather had taught him), and he was careless with heavy machinery, but he could drive tractors and trucks (Pete let him drive the older ones) and do any kind of chore. He bowled in College Station one night a week, went to church with Becky and the kids on Sundays (Pete stayed home), and dreamed of having a wife or girlfriend:

"One day I'll have my chance of meeting a girl. One day, I don't know when it's goin' to be, maybe when I be forty. One day, one day my dream will come true."

After a year on Hopes Creek Ranch, the family had expanded again to take in Wendell Binion, Pete's half brother and the only child of his mother's second marriage, which had ended with the disappearance of Wendell's father. (Pete was at one time going to change his last name to Rand, his own father's name, but he retained Binion to give Wendell a sense of family.) Wendell was tall and good-natured but alarmingly thin and plagued by large facial cysts. He had adjusted slowly to becoming a cowboy—for one thing, he didn't like the way cows smelled—but he, like Bryan, was a good worker. *His* dream was to own a house with three walls of hard-covered books and the other wall a picture window.

For the moment, he stayed with his girlfriend Aleta in a cinder-block annex to the cinder-block house. (Bryan lived in the annex, too; Wendell and Aleta were serenaded to sleep every night by Bryan singing along to his Walkman in the next room.) Aleta, who had been named by her father for a character in the "Prince Valiant" comic strip, arrived on the ranch with Wendell and her Pekinese, named Pudge, who settled in as the least likely ranch dog in Brazos County. Petite and placid, Aleta spent her days vacuuming and revacuuming the shag living-room rug, which was endlessly muddied by kids and cowboys, and making peanut butter sandwiches and spaghetti for the children.

The final resident of the ranch was Keith, the manager, an A&M graduate in his mid-twenties who had a trim mustache and looked more like a junior executive than a cowman. He lived in a mouse-infested cottage down a long dirt drive behind the main house.

The whole scene was a bit much for Pete sometimes. Aleta and Bryan tended to engage him in more conversation than he cared to partake of. He never knew who might be in the living room. His retreat was the bedroom he shared with Becky. It was a dark, chaotic landscape of papers and clothes, but it was a place to get away, to think about his plans, and to worry in peace.

On a fresh October night with a full moon rising, Hopes Creek Ranch was ablaze with activity. Bryan was sitting on the back patio with a towel wrapped around him as Becky cut his hair. Becky's mom Beverly was in the kitchen trying to cook while Pete's brother-in-law Rodney—whom everybody called Brother—was installing a new stove. Aleta was vacuuming. Wendell and Keith were out at the main cattle pen trying to straighten a gate, which a Senepol bull had bent in a vigorous effort to get at some cows. Wendell and Keith had the gate off its hinges and lying on the ground, and Keith was driving his pickup over it, but they still couldn't get it bent back in shape. So they propped it on a mound of dirt and Keith jumped up and down on it. That did the trick.

This ranch beautification program was inspired by the imminent approach of the second annual Senepol Stampede, scheduled for the following afternoon, when Hopes Creek Ranch would be thrown open to visitors. Ranchers who were interested in Senepols—or might conceivably become interested in Senepols—had been invited, and the local television station had promised to send a reporter and camera crew. So all the pen gates had been freshly painted maroon. The hay field had been cut so it looked neat. Bales had been arranged on the lawn next to the house to spell out "HCR." And pounds and pounds of ant poison had been spread. South American fire ants were a troublesome pest on the ranch (and in most of East Texas); nobody wanted a visiting rancher to have his contemplation of handsome Senepols interrupted by a few hundred nasty biting ants crawling up his leg.

Over dinner, Pete was exuberant, plotting strategies for the next day. When the TV crew arrived, he said, "We're going to have cowboys blasting by on horseback—GIDDYAH!—and Bryan'll run up and say, 'We just had five embryo calves!' " Pete turned to Brother, who lived in Houston with Pete's sister

Gretchen and had come up for the weekend to help out, and commanded, "You got to drive up and get out in a suede suit and say, 'I need a hundred Senepol!' "

The prospect of the open house was exciting to everyone; it was fun to show off the ranch. And that wasn't the only big event on the next day's agenda. Wade had a morning soccer game, which Pete would be coaching. And the Aggie football team would be playing old rival Baylor; the Senepol Stampede had been scheduled to take advantage of the presence of tens of thousands of old Aggies in town for the game. Pete had four goals for tomorrow, he announced: "Let's win the soccer game, get through the TV interview, beat Baylor, and make sure the meat's cooked right. Any of those could depress me."

The meat—Senepol beef—was already marinating in several coolers in the kitchen. "That was number thirty-eight," Keith said, pointing to the meat in one cooler when he came in for a glass of iced tea. "She raised her head and ran from me one too many times."

"I thought it was number thirty-six," said Wendell.

"Nah," said Keith. "*She's* in the freezer."

Out in the living room, Brother and Pete were taking down the front door to the house, which was cracked. They laid out the replacement and started banging on hinges. Insects poured in through the empty door frame, causing some discomfort to Becky, who was walking around barefoot and kept stepping on them. When Brother and Pete finally got the new door up, they discovered it didn't fit. It would have to be planed.

But that would wait for the morning. A few minutes before midnight, Pete and Becky took off in the Blazer for the Aggie football field. It was time for midnight yell practice.


Aggies don't "cheer" at football games. They "yell." The yells, carefully rehearsed and precisely delivered, are directed by male "yell leaders" who signal which yell to do when by a complex series of hand motions, which all Aggies learn as freshmen.

Aggies don't sit at football games. All current students stand, all game long. This symbolizes their readiness to be "the twelfth man," to rush down onto the field and join the team if necessary. The "twelfth man" tradition derives from a game in 1922 when the Aggie coach, after his team had suffered several injuries, summoned a former player named E. King Gill from the stands and asked him to suit up. Gill was not used in the game, but he became an Aggie legend. His statue stands at the entrance to the field.

Aggies don't just show up at home football games at kickoff time. They come first at the previous midnight.

And so, in the eerie half-light of dimmed bulbs and the moon, Pete and Becky and twenty-five thousand students filed silently into the field and stood in the stands in a half-ring that stretched from one end of the fifty-yard line to the other. The playing surface below was empty until, all of a sudden, the all-male Aggie band (all members of the Corps of Cadets but now in civilian clothes) burst pell-mell running onto the turf, accompanied by their dates. In the end zone, an artillery squad fired a howitzer. As its roar echoed through the murky bleachers, more members of the Corps lined up around the edge of the field as if guarding it. Behind them, band members vied against one another in spontaneous pushup competitions.

The yell leaders, crew-cut and trim in white T-shirts and denim overalls, appeared at the foot of the stands and gestured with their hands. Students who could see the signals repeated them for the benefit of students farther back. Each signal prompted a yell. No words were spoken, except for the words of the yells:

> Yeaaaaa, gig 'em, Aggies!
>
> Farmers, fight! Farmers, fight!
> Fight! Fight!
> Farmers, farmers fight!

A student sitting behind Pete tapped him on the shoulder and reminded him to remove his Senepol cap.

He and Becky, like everyone else, did not merely yell the yells. They *humped* them, with their hands on their knees and their bodies bent forward. (When A&M was an all-male school, humping included squeezing one's left testicle, so one could share the pain being experienced by the Aggie team.) During some of the yells everyone stood up on the benches at particular passages and then climbed down again. Everyone knew when to do this without direction.

The band played "The Spirit of Aggieland" and "The Aggie War Hymn" and everybody sang. During a moment of silence, tradition required that Aggies kiss their dates or hold aloft a flame if they were dateless. Pete embraced Becky.

At the edge of the field, members of the Corps were wrestling with rebellious "civilian" students who had attempted to run onto the playing surface, which by tradition is off-limits to all but the band and the football team. A similar incident two weeks before had ended with students who ran on the field being beaten by Corps members. "Those are the 'two percenters,' " Becky said of the students who ran on the field, "the two percent of Aggie students who don't have the spirit."

The wrestling soon stopped, with no apparent injuries. The band was still playing and, during breaks, doing pushups. There were more yells, and there were speeches on the subject of Aggie pride. One speaker was David Eller, chairman of the A&M Board of Regents and president of the Granada Corporation, a big agricultural company (and marketer of limited partnerships) that Pete considered to be a competitor to his fledgling Senepol business. When Eller was introduced, twenty-five thousand students applauded. Pete put his hands together in the praying position, wagged them, and hissed the Aggie "horse laugh," a traditional yell of contempt.

At 1:30 a.m., the crowd filed out, moved and energized. Pete looked around for a moment before leaving the field. "Everything I have I owe to this university," he pronounced.

He and Becky were quiet on the ride home until Pete noticed that signs pointing the way to the Senepol Stampede had not yet been posted. They were Becky's responsibility. Pete said he had not been satisfied with last year's signs; they weren't sufficiently clear and prominent. He wanted this year's signs done right. "You want to do it?" he asked Becky. "Or you want to quit? If you don't want to do it, I'll assign it to somebody else."

Becky, exhausted, sighed. "I feel like quitting," she said, "but that's not the ranch spirit."

In the morning, Becky put up the signs, and they were good ones. Wade's team came from behind to win the soccer game, 2–1. And, before a crowd of nearly seventy-five thousand people, Texas A&M beat Baylor, 31–30.

Everything was going fine.

# Texas Sports (Topless Golf)

O N THE CHARTERED BUS heading to the Sugar's golf tournament, the golfers were drinking heavily. Beer, screwdrivers, and Bloody Marys—all included, in unlimited quantities, in the tournament entry fee—were being passed up and down the aisle by Sugar's hostesses. It was almost 9:00 a.m.

"Attention, golfers," one of the hostesses announced on the public address system. "To determine handicaps, would everyone please take out their penises so we can measure them."

Everyone ignored her. A pot-bellied man in a yellow shirt was standing in the back of the bus with a pair of panties on his head. Jim and Gary, skipping work for the day, were sipping drinks and watching the highway roll by in bright sunshine. It was still pleasantly cool outside; the heat was coming.

A slim young woman with short dark hair took the seat in front of Jim and struck up a conversation. She said her name was Déjà and that she'd been a hostess at the previous Sugar's tournament, where she'd had a frightening accident: "Angel drove our cart over a ten-foot cliff. I was holding a Bloody Mary and looked down and thought I was bleeding all over."

She wasn't, but her leg was pinned under the cart. "I had to dance in tennis shoes for six weeks."

Déjà did her dancing at Sugar's, a big Austin topless club with a history of innovation. Its owner, Rod Kypke, claimed to have introduced "couch dancing" to the state of Texas. In the mid-

1970s, while working at a Houston club called The Booby Rock, he had flown with the owner to Tampa, Florida, to check out a place called Odyssey 2001, which had pioneered this new ecdysiastic art. Couch dancing consisted of a conventional topless dance except that the customer sat on a couch and the dance was conducted about three inches from his face. It looked like just the thing for Houston.

Couch dancing was a hit at The Booby Rock and, when Kypke and a partner took over another Houston club and renamed it Sugar's, they instructed the dancers there to try it. "And these girls wouldn't couch-dance," Kypke recalled later. "They said, 'We're not gonna do anything nasty like that.' And I said, 'Fine.' So I called down to The Booby Rock and I said, 'I need four girls over here.' They sent four girls over, and they went in there and couch-danced, and they made about one hundred and fifty dollars in tips in about thirty minutes. And I never had another girl say she wasn't going to couch-dance."

Kypke's next big new idea was a golf tournament, which he tried at Sugar's in Houston and considered a success ("it generates a lot of goodwill"). When he opened the Sugar's in Austin, he brought along both the couch dancing (since evolved into table dancing) and the golf.

Kypke saw Sugar's as an upscale establishment: "We built the club for American Express Card-carrying businessmen as opposed to blue-collar workers or whatever." And the golf tournament fit that concept. "Someone's got to be able to afford seventy-five dollars and take a full day off. Our players are boards of directors of companies, managers, general managers, advertising executives, lobbyists."

And Jim and Gary, who had played several times. They displayed an enormous triple-tiered Sugar's tournament trophy on a shelf in their office, and Gary liked to tell the story of the tournament hostess with no pubic hair. In exchange for a tip, this young woman had pulled down her shorts and exposed hairless genitals. "Oh!" Gary cried. "Chemotherapy!"

The woman was puzzled. "No," she said, "I had a birthday party."

Now Gary was puzzled.

She explained that at a high point in the festivities, she had lathered up, handed out razors to her guests, and invited everybody to have a go.

The bus pulled into the Pine Forest Golf Club in Bastrop, Texas, thirty miles from Austin, and the golfers and hostesses tumbled out into the glaring sun. "There's Kimberly," said a dancer as she stepped down from the bus. "I knew that bitch would show up."

Kypke, who'd arrived in his own car, was pleased to see that the turnout was good. He never had any trouble getting golfers; there were ninety on hand, in brightly colored shirts and slacks, and he had a waiting list. But his dancers were reluctant to get up early in the morning, and he didn't encourage just any dancer to come. "They have to pass the daylight test," he explained. "We have red lights in the club. *Everybody* looks beautiful. We don't have red lights on the golf course."

While the twenty dancers who had shown up prepared for their hostess duties—"They're out there as more or less goodwill ambassadors," Kypke said—the golfers toted their clubs across the parking lot to their designated golf carts. Waiting for each golfer was a little gift package containing tees, ball markers, an Old Grand-Dad key chain, a hot drink recipe book, a golf shoe cleat cleaner, a certificate of participation in the tournament (suitable for framing), and a pocket-sized bottle of cheap vodka.

Jim and Gary located the third member of their foursome—their friend Patrick Nugent, Austin businessman and former son-in-law of Lyndon Johnson (he was divorced from Johnson's daughter Luci). Nugent carried in his golf bag the late President's woods; they were Ben Hogan models, engraved "LBJ." Nugent was wearing a long-sleeved rugby shirt that he never took off, even in the heat of the day, and he puffed on a pipe. Throughout the tournament he was a model of probity, possibly because of the presence of the fourth member of the foursome, a writer from New York. Nugent abstained from drinking—"Drinking beer in the sun gives me a headache," he explained—and he kept his eyes on the ball.

The golfers mounted their carts and fanned out over the green and hilly course to the eighteen tees for a shotgun start. The tournament was "best ball." Each foursome comprised a single team and combined their best shots for a single score. Since each group had four tries at every shot, the scores tended to be low.

There were some countervailing influences, however. All day long, golf carts piloted by dancers in short shorts and loosely fastened tops ferried sandwiches and beer to the players. Encouraged by tips, the hostesses periodically consented to perform. Many a golfer's concentration was interrupted, midway through a backswing or putt, by the cry of another golfer from an adjoining fairway: "Show us your tits!"

Jim introduced himself to the hostesses as George Smithers. After twenty minutes of play, he complained, "This is the second hole, and we ain't seen no pussy." Gary lined up for a short chip shot and shanked the ball. As it skittered off at an angle, he shook his head, perplexed. "I usually play *better* when I'm drunk," he said. On the green, all the members of the foursome missed a five-foot putt for a par. They gave themselves a par anyway. "Everybody cheats," Gary explained. "This ain't the U.S. Open."

On the sixth hole, a short dogleg left, Jim and Gary encountered a cart filled with dancers at the edge of the fairway. Gary called out, "Five dollars for the first tits of the day." The other cart's driver, a young woman who looked like she'd cheated on the daylight test, pulled back one strap of her halter top to expose her left breast. She put the strap back, then pulled back the other strap. She looked bored by the effort. Gary handed her five dollars. She put it in her pocket and drove away.

Jim and Gary approached the next green to find another foursome still putting. A buxom brunette with dark makeup underlining her eyes was doing a split in the center of the green. Her shirt was off; a name tag that said "Shelley" was stuck on the bare skin above her left breast. She pulled one leg up behind her head acrobatically, then rolled over spreadeagled behind the hole as the group on the green continued to putt. "No fair!" Gary shouted. Her spread legs could have channeled the ball into the cup.

Waiting to drive on the next tee, Jim and Gary chatted with a couple of dancers who had just pulled up to deliver beer. ". . . But I'm a good kisser," Gary was telling them, "and I've got a cute way of getting on and off."

Nugent was impatient. "Come on," he said. "You're up."

The writer from New York, whose turn it was to hit, ignored him. He was mesmerized by the beauty of one of the women. Her name was Ivory, and she remarked that today was her twenty-first birthday. She wore a hot pink blouse with matching pink sunglasses and was tall, with long brown hair, a guileless smile, jutting breasts, and a slender waist. She leaned over to say something to the New Yorker. As she moved closer, he opened to receive her words. "You're standing on a fire-ant nest," she said.

He looked down to find the fierce biting insects crawling over one of his shoes. He started to brush them off with his hands. "No," Gary shouted. "Stamp your feet." If you brush off fire ants with your hands, you get fire ants on your hands, as the visitor from New York learned about five seconds too late.

Déjà, Jim's friend from the bus, appeared on a beer cart a couple of holes later. She smiled at him. "What are you up to?"

Jim, who was struggling with his golf game but didn't care, replied, "About six three, two hundred and thirty pounds."

"That would crush me," Déjà said. "I only weigh ninety-five."

"Want to try?" asked Jim. Before she answered, he pointed to her cutoff denim shorts, which had been trimmed with lace. "I never saw lace on cutoffs before."

"My mom said, 'I'm tired of seeing your cheeks hanging out,' " Déjà explained.

Jim pointed to a light scar on her thigh. "What's that? From the cart accident?"

"That's where I was child-abused," Déjà said.

---

The beautiful Ivory appeared again on the back nine. She was driving by with another dancer when Gary hailed their cart to a stop. They listened patiently while he explained to Ivory why she should take off her clothes.

"This is the fifth Sugar's tournament we've been in," Gary reasoned. "We have a big trophy in our office from one year that we won. *He* came all the way from New York for this. *He* came from Harlingen. And we haven't seen anything yet."

Ivory was not moved.

Gary kept selling. "I'll do it with you," he said. "I'll give you ten dollars to do what I do."

"What's that?" Ivory asked cautiously.

"Take off your shirt and shorts."

"But I'm not wearing any underpants," she protested.

"Neither am I," Gary said.

Ivory conferred with her colleague, then announced, "I'll do it if you give her ten dollars to do it, too."

Nugent, looking annoyed, walked away and teed off.

Gary and the two women lined up facing the remaining members of the foursome. Gary started to wiggle his arms like a hula dancer and gyrate his hips. The women stood watching him.

Gary took off his shirt and threw it to the ground. Ivory and her friend pulled up their blouses. Ivory's large breasts sprung out erect.

Gary, still dancing, spun around and bent over, pulling down his pants and underpants in a single motion, mooning his partners. Ivory and her friend turned and bent, too. They dropped their shorts, offering a quick rear glimpse of their lower parts before pulling up their shorts and turning around.

Jim protested. "You had your backs to us!" He sounded aggrieved.

"That's the way we *always* drop our pants," Ivory answered. "We're *titty* dancers."

---

Gary was distracted by a hostess wearing a shirt with a design of comic-strip panels. "Did you buy that because you thought it was a cute fashion or because you're a comic fanatic?" he asked, conducting some impromptu market research. The hostess didn't know how to answer. Gary put a hand over her eyes. "Don't look," he instructed. "Name the comics on this shirt."

"I don't know," she said.

Gary nodded, digesting this information.

On the seventeenth tee, several foursomes were backed up waiting to shoot. Jim was talking to Shelley, who was standing with her shirt open. She had some mud on her thigh which, she told Jim, she'd acquired during an unpleasant experience with another golfer in the rough. Jim nodded sympathetically. Shelley spoke into his ear.

"Three hundred dollars?" Jim exclaimed. "What are you selling? Krugerrands?"

Another dancer, feeling frisky, peeled off her shirt and did some back flips. The waiting golfers applauded. "You're a limber little minx," one remarked. A second dancer, encouraged by the attention, did the same thing.

By the time it was the turn of Jim and Gary's group to drive, Shelley was lying on her back at the rear of the tee. A drunk golfer from another foursome was lying on top of her, sucking her breasts.

Jim borrowed Lyndon Johnson's driver from Nugent and drilled a long one down the middle of the fairway.

With a moderate amount of cheating, Jim and Gary's foursome finished at six under par. The winners came in at a credulity-straining seventeen under. Gary was a little disappointed. "Last year," he said, "we came in third, *and* we had a blow job on the second hole."

# The Senepol Stampede

**A** COUPLE OF HOURS BEFORE the guests were due to arrive at the Senepol Stampede, Keith, Wendell, and Bryan were washing the cows. Pete had selected a few of his best-looking animals to display in temporary pens on the lawn next to the house. The pens were freshly painted. The lawn had been decorated with red mums set in old cowboy boots. Becky had hung her autographed copy of "The Aggie War Hymn" on a tree. Now the cows were having their baths.

Bryan went into the house and returned with a bottle of Sunlight dishwashing liquid from the kitchen while Wendell fetched a hose from a shed. The three cowhands shooed the cattle, one at a time, into a narrow chute and stuck a bar in behind them so they couldn't back up. While the animals bucked and bellowed in protest, Keith sprayed them with the hose; Wendell applied the dishwashing soap; Keith hosed it off; then Bryan set upon the wet Senepols with a brush.

The entire procedure offended Keith. "I hate all this foo-foo crap," he complained. "This isn't what a cow is for."

But the Senepols' rich red coats did look pretty when the men were done with them. (The men, on the other hand, looked awful; they were spotted with mud kicked up by the squirming cattle.)

Pete, meanwhile, was talking to the press. A young woman reporter and a camera/soundman had arrived from KBTX-TV, Channel 3, in College Station and its sister city of Bryan, and set up near the cattle chute. Pete, in a clean white shirt and new-looking jeans and the Senepol cap he always wore as part of his promotion effort, stood stiffly in front of the camera and recited the virtues of the Senepol: "They're very heat-tolerant and appear to be disease-resistant. Their ancestors came from central Africa, and they were one of the few animals that exhibited natural immunity to the testy [sic] fly."

Behind him, a cow going under the hose bawled loudly and clattered against the chute, but Pete pressed on, explaining the role he expected the Senepol to play in the Texas cattle industry. He wasn't looking for the average rancher to start raising purebred Senepol, he said. Rather, he hoped cattlemen would use the Senepol as they used other breeds—to improve the quality of their mixed-blood "commercial" cattle by adding some Senepols to the genetic stew.

"What are your hopes for this breed of cattle?" the reporter asked.

"In my dreams," Pete said, "I see myself driving across Texas and looking out at different pastures and seeing a lot of F1s [hybrid cattle] and commercial cows with Senepol blood in them. . . . My long-term goal is to see them spread out across the Southwest and into Mexico and South America."

The interview wrapped up, and Pete surveyed the scene. The cattle were shiny; the lawn was neat. The hay bales laid out to spell "HCR" were ready to serve as tables and chairs. A girl singer Pete had hired, backed by a guitarist, was rehearsing "The Streets of Laredo" over and over again. Wendell and Keith had hauled out two large display boards with photos of Senepols and large-lettered slogans: MATERNAL ABILITY, CATTLE THAT WORK, DOCILITY. A keg of beer was in place, and so was a rented machine that converted ice, tequila, and syrup into frozen Margaritas. Now all Pete needed was guests.

Here was the final step in his formula for success with the Senepol. He had found the breed and brought it to Texas. His herd was established and looking good. His effort to secure long-term financing was under way (Universal II was finally on the market). Now he only had to convince other ranchers that the

Senepol was a breed they needed. To this end, he had mounted a display at the Houston Livestock Show earlier in the year and been rewarded with a nice article in the *Houston Chronicle* that ran with a photo of him and Dr. McCall and reported: "A Deer Park physician and a Bryan rancher have joined economic forces to bring the Houston Livestock Show and Rodeo what is likely the latest breed of cattle, the Senepol." Becky, who functioned as the Hopes Creek Ranch publicist, had sent out copies of that article and won a follow-up write-up in the *Brazos County Farm Bureau News*. The Senepol Stampede was another important means of getting the word out. The television interview was the latest triumph for the media blitz.

The guests started to arrive after the A&M football game. They drank the beer and the Margaritas, ate barbecued Senepol, and eyed the live Senepols in their pens. Some guessed the weight of a cow-calf pair to compete for a door prize (ten pounds of Senepol beef), but, as buyers, their mood was cautious.

"You have families who've been raising cattle for a hundred years," an A&M grad student explained. "They think they know how to do it [i.e., without Senepols]. You can't brush aside history."

A rancher named Jim Bob who was strolling around with his girlfriend Mandy (and who aroused Pete's suspicions about his credentials as a cattleman because his belt buckle, his hat, and his talk were all a little too big) refused to commit himself even to doubt. "I just thought I'd come out and have a look" is all he would say.

Circulating among the crowd of about one hundred were Dr. McCall, Pete's partner, and Charles Lundelius, the investment banker, who looked wildly out of place in a brightly striped Ralph Lauren rugby shirt. Lundelius had yet to sell any of the shares in the Universal II limited partnership, but he was still confident the offering would succeed. He could have brought some potential investors to the party but had elected not to. "There's not a whole lot of need for me in my marketing effort to drag someone over to actually see the cows," he said. "The pictures are very nice and they're wholly sufficient. I think Pete might not understand that and might even be a little offended. He points to an animal and says, 'Isn't that pretty?' And I say, 'Well, I guess so.' "

Dr. McCall was in a contemplative mood. A fifty-one-year-old friend of his and a twenty-nine-year-old patient had both recently died of sudden heart attacks, and Dr. McCall seemed to be questioning the pressures to which he subjected himself in his high-volume medical practice. He'd recently told Pete that he wanted to help out with the Senepol embryo transfers. He spoke fondly of the cattle business, although he did note, "My wife has pointed out to me that if I took the money I put into the cattle business and just put it aside, I, uh, wouldn't have to work as hard."

Now McCall was buttonholed by a young German resident of Guatemala who was a graduate student at A&M. The German said he was very interested in getting some Senepols to Guatemala. He noted that the United States government (in an effort to reduce dairy production and thus the amount of surplus dairy products it had to buy) was currently paying dairy farmers to slaughter or export their herds. Perhaps some dairy cows were being shipped to Guatemala, the German said. If so, Senepol embryos could be implanted in their wombs before the trip. This would make transportation costs, for the Senepols, very reasonable.

"Okay," said McCall when the German was finished. "We'd like to see the cattle get there any feasible way."

The American ranchers at the Stampede were more restrained in their interest in any arrangement that involved exchanging their money for Pete's Senepols. Being ranchers, they were congenitally conservative. They had been subjected to so much hoopla about new breeds that they were skeptical about another one. And, no matter how eager to experiment they might otherwise have been, they were constrained by the fact that the American cattle business was only just beginning to emerge from a major slump. Over the previous decade, annual per capita beef consumption had fallen from 94 pounds to 79 pounds. Cattle prices had tumbled 30 percent in six years. Consumers had been wooed away from beef by the innovative marketing of a dynamic chicken industry and scared away by stories that eating red meat was bad for their health. This latter notion seemed to sting cattle producers more than anything

else, even more than the drop in their incomes, and it was vig-
orously disputed by the Senepol Stampede's featured speaker, a
gray-haired A&M lecturer in animal science named Frank Litterst.

"We have to do something about getting people's appetite back
wanting to eat beef," he said. "I can't see why they don't. I've been
eating beef ever since I was a little kid, and I'm not a spring
chicken. I took a physical recently in Houston, and my cholesterol
count is lower than the Chinamen's are over in China, where all
they eat is rice with no cholesterol, and I've been eating steak, so
that's a bunch of baloney."

As Litterst addressed the crowd, the sky was darkening over
the hay meadow behind him, and the crickets began their nightly
clamor. Mollie Binion and another little girl were chasing each
other over the hay bales on the lawn, leaping from the "C" to the
"R" and back again.

"Whatever happens, you need to eat all the beef you can,"
Litterst urged. "The National Cattlemen's Association just came
out with a release, right here it is, black and white, that you got
to eat beef because it supplies amino acids that affect your sex life.
. . . If you quit eating beef, you're going to just be lagging behind."

He concluded with an endorsement of the Senepol—"I think
Senepol cattle are going to be a damned good breed because they're
good brood cows"—and a warning to Senepol breeders to avoid
the quick-buck mentality that had tainted some of the purveyors
of other new breeds:

"Don't breed trash. Don't breed junk. Castrate the bottom forty
percent if you can. That's the way it ought to be, and that's the
way it used to be. . . . Go slow. Don't be in a big hurry. If you
hurry, if you're just looking for the dollar, I guarantee you you're
gonna fall like the Roman Empire. I've seen them all my life. Every
breed has its day. It rises and falls. And if you don't build it on
solid rock, by golly, it's gonna fall. You have a good time. You have
cocktail parties. But, if you don't do it right, after the laughter are
gonna come the tears."

There was enthusiastic applause for Litterst, and then the
crowd drifted away until only a few friends and relatives of the
Binions remained, huddled around the Margarita machine. Pete
set up a TV on the lawn, now illuminated by candles in brown

paper bags, just before the eleven o'clock news, and everybody gathered round. The report on the Senepol did not appear during the first half, which concluded with an announcement that the weather would be next.

"Weather?" Keith demanded impatiently of the screen. "The weather's great!"

The weatherman corroborated this, and the anchorwoman said, "Thanks, Bob. We'll be right back."

"With *what*?" Pete demanded.

As if in reply, a beautiful still shot of a Senepol bull appeared on the screen with the caption: "Coming Up." Everybody cheered. "That's about the best picture of a bull I've ever seen," Pete declared. "If I was just watching TV and saw that picture, I'd stop." Everyone else on the lawn agreed that they would, too. When Pete went to bed a couple of hours later, he was still pumped up by the TV report. It alone, he thought, had been enough to make the party worthwhile.

At nine-thirty the next morning, Pete's brother-in-law, Brother, was fiddling with the Margarita machine. "How do you fire this thing up?" he called out. He got it going and poured himself a drink.

Other residents and weekend guests at Hopes Creek Ranch, waking slowly from the excitement and Margaritas of the night before, one by one rolled out of bed into the vicinity of the machine, where Brother ladled out the drinks.

After contemplating the morning over a couple of Margaritas, Pete decided he wanted to go fishing, so he, Billie Pratt, Brother, Bryan, and the kids all piled into a pickup truck and drove two hundred yards to the ranch's largest tank, a fishing and swimming hole that Pete had stocked with bass. The men balanced their Margaritas on their laps during the drive, which took about forty-five seconds.

Everybody climbed out of the truck and walked over to a rowboat beached upside down at the edge of the water. The plan was to take the boat to the raft in the middle of the tank and then sit on the raft and fish. But the boat turned out to be resting directly on top of a fire-ant nest.

Universal dismay among the fishermen.

Brother set his Margarita carefully on the ground and snuck up on the boat. With help from Bryan, he flipped it over. There were about a million ants on it.

Pete sent Bryan back to the house to get some gasoline to pour on the ants. Brother walked over to Keith's cottage to get insecticide spray. Before using either of the fluids, the men decided to get the ants off the boat by dunking it in the tank. While the children—Wade, Pauline, and Mollie—wandered about unconcerned, Brother and Bryan wrestled the boat under the water. Mollie picked up a fire ant and admired it as it crawled over her hand, while Brother and Bryan leapt about swatting fire ants off their bodies and wincing as they were stung. They managed to rinse most of the ants off the boat and doused the rest with gasoline and insecticide; Mollie, oblivious and seemingly immune, continued to play with some of the survivors.

Finally the boat was ready to go. Pete looked for fishing rods and discovered there weren't enough to go around. Wade had been given a new one just the day before, but he'd left it in the Blazer, and Becky had driven the Blazer to church. Some rubber worms Pete wanted were in the Blazer, too.

"We'll have to share poles," Pete decreed. "Now, where did I put my drink?" He found it on the roof of the pickup.

He looked up to see Billie, Bryan, Wade, Pauline, and Mollie sitting in the ant-free boat, about to cast off.

"Mollie," Pete called. "You got to get out of there." He explained to the others: "If the boat goes down, she'll sink."

Mollie started to climb out of the boat, then hesitated.

"Come on, Mollie," Pete called again.

"She can't," Brother called back. "She's got the bait." He was kneeling by Mollie, untangling a lure that was hooked on the pink sweatsuit she'd been wearing since the previous day.

It took him a while to separate Mollie from the lines.

The boat sailed off and left Pete ashore.

He never did get to go fishing.

# II. GETTING IN DEEP

# "Do You Like Bank Jokes?"

A FEW DAYS AFTER the Sugar's golf tournament, Jim went out to get a $100,000 loan.

Christmas was coming, and Lin-Tex expected it to be a merry one. The company's sales in November and December of the previous year had been just over $300,000; this year Jim and Gary expected year-end sales to reach one million dollars. But they couldn't sell T-shirts unless they had T-shirts to sell. And they didn't have enough.

Lin-Tex sold its shirts for roughly double what it paid for them, so, to sell a million dollars' worth, it needed a half-million-dollar inventory. In fact, its inventory stood at about $350,000. That was enough to have a nice Christmas, but not a great one. Lin-Tex's supplier could deliver more shirts in November, but it would want to be paid for those shirts in November; even if Lin-Tex sold the shirts promptly, it would not be paid by *its* customers until December or January.

This would pose no problem if Lin-Tex had a wad of cash on hand. But it did not. Sales had been increasing steadily, but so had expenses. The switch from the mail-order business to the wholesale business had entailed substantial marketing costs; participating in the MAGIC show alone had cost $40,000. General overhead was running about $50,000 a month; that included Lin-Tex's rent in an unglamorous office/industrial park on a highway in an Austin suburb, salaries for a dozen full-time employees, and Jim and Gary's business trips (generally first class).

Every dollar that came into the Lin-Tex office went right back out again as soon as or, more likely, *before* it arrived. Gary, the company's chief operating officer, had made an art form of playing the "float" in the Lin-Tex checking account. He carefully estimated when each account receivable was likely to be paid. A few days before he expected a payment to arrive, he would dispatch a check of like amount to Lin-Tex's T-shirt supplier or some other creditor, calculating that the money to cover it would show up by the time the check cleared. Occasionally, Gary miscalculated and checks bounced. But the resulting embarrassment, and the ongoing tension of the floating art, mattered less than being able to run the company as if it were as much as $100,000 richer than it actually was on any given day.

There was nothing unusual about any of this. Playing the float is a time-honored practice of American business. And the cash-flow crunch that inspired Gary's performance is a classic problem of growing companies. As their sales increase, they need more product, but they can't afford to buy more product until they sell it, and they can't sell it unless they have it. The more successful a business is, the greater the strain—and frustration.

Lin-Tex had tried to deal with the problem by requiring its customers to pay for their shirts COD, but that was an ungainly solution, and it prevented Lin-Tex from pursuing sales to big stores and chains, which would insist on terms of sixty to ninety days. The operating profits that Lin-Tex produced had already been plowed back into the company's not insubstantial inventory, but there wasn't enough money coming in fast enough to take advantage of the growth that seemed to beckon from just around the corner.

Lin-Tex needed a loan.

As Jim drove off from his office to get one on a bright October afternoon, it did not seem to him that he should have much trouble. In his early years in Austin, he had easily borrowed $700,000 to build and operate his Wendy's stores. Granted, those loans had been secured by his Wendy's stock, but, after leaving the hamburger business, he had obtained one $65,000 loan solely on his signature.

Jim had done that banking during Austin's boom years, when the city was blossoming as a high-tech capital and real estate mania swept the town. Property values were racing up, businesses were expanding, and bankers were cheering the show on with lending policies that might politely be described as enthusiastic. Lin-Tex was born in that era, and it obtained a $200,000 line of credit from the United Bank of Texas to finance its initial growth. A couple of years later, United Bank hit hard times and it cut off new credit to Lin-Tex, but Jim and Gary simply moved their business to Lamar Savings, the largest Austin-based savings and loan. Lamar was an aggressive and promotion-minded lender; it had recently formally applied to open a branch on the moon. Lamar lent Lin-Tex half a million dollars, which Jim and Gary used to pay off their debt to United, to buy Berke Breathed's father out of the "Bloom County" T-shirt business, and to operate the company and expand.

Now, when Lin-Tex needed more money, everything had changed. The collapse of the price of oil had staggered the Texas economy. In Austin, bankruptcies were up, and retail sales were down—even passenger traffic at the city airport was down—and the Austin real estate market, a classic bubble, had exploded. The city was littered with empty office buildings and half-finished condo developments. Builders couldn't make their mortgage payments, and banks and savings and loan associations found themselves repossessing hundreds of millions of dollars' worth of properties they didn't know what to do with. Their balance sheets turned red, and their lending policies turned cautious.

It was a bad time to be looking for a loan.

Jim and Gary had already knocked on the doors of half a dozen banks and been turned down everywhere. But today Jim had an appointment with the president of a small bank who had sought out Lin-Tex, not the other way around. He seemed eager to make a loan.

Jim only had to make a couple of stops to pick up some things the banker had asked for.

Jim stopped first at the downtown tower of the United Bank of Texas. United, which once had been Lin-Tex's bank and still was Jim's personal bank, was an institution with many troubles, some of them rooted in the construction of the opulent mahogany and marble-adorned edifice into which Jim now strolled. United's chairman, an X-ray-technician-turned-real-estate-developer-and-financier named Ruben Johnson, had transformed United from a small neighborhood bank into Austin's fifth largest. After a decade of astounding growth, however, the bank had begun to lose money in 1984, when other Austin banks still flourished, and had come under close scrutiny by federal examiners, who criticized its lending practices. Soon after, several tenants in the United Bank Tower, which was owned not by the bank but by a partnership headed by Johnson, had been outraged to learn that Johnson had received secret kickbacks from the contractors who did interior work on their offices. A lawsuit against Johnson was now about to go to trial. (Ultimately, the jury would order Johnson to pay the plaintiffs $1.2 million, a sum it calculated by totaling damages and then tacking on a 15 percent surcharge—the same percentage the contractors' bills had been padded to provide Johnson's kickbacks.)

"Good news!" Jim said as he strode into the office of a United vice president, Bush Bowden, who sat in a deep leather chair beneath an Audubon print. "Wendy's stock is at fourteen."

Bowden punched some numbers into a calculator—14 times 25,000. "That's three hundred and fifty thousand," he said. "That helps."

Jim had an outstanding loan of $313,000 from United Bank (most of which had gone to build his house). The loan was secured by 25,000 shares of Wendy's stock, the bulk of his holdings. The price of the stock moved up and down; it had been 20 within recent memory, then had fallen to 11. Jim was pleased to see it at 14. At that price, the value of his stock exceeded the amount of his loan by a sufficient margin, he hoped, for the bank to release one other item it was holding as collateral—the title to his Mercedes. He needed that to make up part of the collateral for the loan he expected to get for Lin-Tex. Lin-Tex had no hard assets of its own to put up—its inventory and receivables were already pledged against its big loan from Lamar Savings—so Jim was going to put up some assets of his own.

"How will you get a hundred thousand dollars on a twenty-thousand-dollar car?" Bowden asked.

"It's that plus some other securities," Jim said. "When can I get the title?"

"Thursday," said Bowden. "It's not approved yet."

"Have you heard anything about Cattlemen's Bank?" Jim asked. "They called me the other day."

"They're a bank that hasn't been in business long enough to make too many bad loans," Bowden said.

Jim nodded. It might be another place to turn.

"How are *you* doing?" Bowden asked.

"Great," said Jim. "We should have tons of cash after Christmas."

Bowden congratulated him. "It's good to hear some good news."

Jim's next stop was the downtown office of Merrill Lynch. As he entered the open area of brokers' desks, he glanced up at the electronic ticker and winced. Wendy's had dropped to 13½.

Keeping an eye on the ticker, Jim conferred with his broker. Jim had a Merrill Lynch margin account consisting of some Wendy's stock, assorted other securities, and some debt. Its net value was $90,000, and Jim needed a statement to that effect to take to the banker who was considering the Lin-Tex loan. There was some question, however, as to whether a margin account could serve as collateral for a bank loan, since some of the assets in the account already collateralized Jim's debt to Merrill Lynch. The broker suggested that Jim could simplify things by selling his Wendy's stock and taking the cash. Jim shook his head. He liked to own Wendy's stock. He always owned Wendy's stock. He had an unreasonable sentimental attachment to Wendy's stock. He would rather borrow against it than sell it.

Jim left the office with a letter attesting to the value of his account and feeling a little better; Wendy's was back up to 13⅝.

The offices of Greater Texas Bank, Jim's final stop, were in a low-rise building on a suburban highway. Compared to United Bank, the place was spartan. On the other hand, it was solvent.

Jim was ushered into the office of the president, Tim Lear, the man who'd said he wanted to give Lin-Tex a loan. Jim handed him the letter he'd brought from Merrill Lynch.

Lear looked it over, then placed it aside. "You cannot assign a margin account," he said. "I called another broker and asked him. . . . I don't know what else to do. Were you able to get the car title?"

"I'll get it Thursday," Jim said, and he shifted ground. "I don't know if you like bank jokes. I'm giving these to all our bankers." He handed Lear some bank-related gags from the "Frank and Ernest" comic strip, the T-shirt rights to which Lin-Tex had recently acquired. In one panel, the comic's hobo-like characters were sitting in a banker's office and telling him, "We'd like a 'let the good times roll' loan."

Lear, a neat, balding man with wire-rimmed glasses, seemed to think this was very funny. He laughed out loud.

Jim handed Lear two new "Bloom County" T-shirt designs featuring Opus the penguin wearing a hat adorned with fruit. He showed Lear a clip from *Gift Reporter* magazine that described an Opus doll as a "best bet" gift item. He gave Lear several articles about Berke Breathed, the acclaimed "Bloom County" cartoonist.

"Berke Breathed was on the Today show this morning," Jim said. "He's the hottest thing in America. We own exclusive rights to him. That's worth a bunch of money. I know that's all ambiguous. But two hundred thousand dollars in orders in our office aren't ambiguous."

Lear was listening.

"We've got to make a deal here or forget it," Jim said. "We don't have time to start going through committees at some other bank. I've got two hundred and fifty thousand dollars in prebooked business for November."

"If I were a hundred-million-dollar bank," Lear said, "we wouldn't be talking. You'd have the money. But I'm a twelve-million-dollar bank. I have to ask, 'What's our incentive?' Ordinarily, it's that by giving you a loan I guarantee that you'll continue banking with us. But the likelihood of your banking with us long term is not there. We can't provide the services you're going to need. We're too small."

This sounded almost encouraging. Jim suggested that maybe

Lear could put something together with other banks in the holding company that controlled Greater Texas.

Now Lear shifted his ground. "This is an asset-based loan, and the assets aren't there."

"But they are there," Jim protested. He picked up the clippings about Berke Breathed. "If you can't take those articles and see that's an asset. . . ."

"Oh, I see that is an asset," Lear said. "But who's the authority? Who can tell us what the value of that asset is?"

"Jim Davis, 'Garfield,' " said Jim. "Charles Shulz, 'Peanuts.' "

Lear smiled sympathetically. "I know you need the money to make money. I know what you're going through, and I've already committed to lending you money. I want to lend you some money. But I've got to have some assets."

Jim picked up the Merrill Lynch letter. "I can't imagine I can't write a document saying I won't trade the account without your approval and get the broker to acknowledge that he won't act on calls from me without your approval."

"Let me call my attorney and see if we can work something out," Lear said. "Meanwhile, if I can lend you some money on your car. . . ."

"That's only thirty thousand. That won't do much good."

"Right."

Jim was halfway out the door. "It's going to break my little heart if on December Fourth I've got to say, 'We're shut down for the year.' "

"When are you going to slow down and let profits finance expansion?"

"Never," Jim declared. "It's just gonna get better. The day our profits catch up with us is the day we go out of business."


The next day, Jim was still in business. He still needed a loan. And he was still fuming about his conversation with Lear, who, Jim was convinced, could have made the loan with *no* collateral if he'd wanted to.

Jim's mood was not improved by the early morning discovery of a nest of baby rats in his washing machine.

He retreated to his office, where he sat in his big green leather desk chair wearing khaki pants and a pink golf shirt and took a long chain of phone calls.

They didn't improve his mood either.

The first call came from a T-shirt manufacturer that Jim and Gary had regarded as their ace in the hole. A few weeks before, a salesman from the company had called offering them 25,000 shirts on sixty-day terms. That was enough to save their Christmas. But now the company had changed its tune. It wanted a letter of credit from a bank guaranteeing payment for the shirts.

"We've pretty much extended our lines of credit here," Jim explained to the caller. "If I could get a letter of credit to give *you,* I could just go with our regular supplier."

That was the end of that.

A friend of Jim's called with another idea. He knew of a company in Houston that sold computers. He thought it and Lin-Tex were good candidates to merge and then issue stock to raise money. Jim listened to this patiently. "How much money do they have lying around?" he finally asked. "We need a deal tomorrow. I don't mean meeting to *talk* about it tomorrow. I've got all these orders. I'm maxed out on my lines of credit. And I'm running out of time."

Jim knew this deal would never happen.

Then he got a call he liked. It was someone from Dun & Bradstreet, the credit-rating firm, with a request for information. The caller remarked that Lin-Tex had a very high credit rating. Jim was proud and pleased to hear it, even though it wasn't doing him a bit of good.

The next call was from a colleague of Leonard Smith, the man Jim had talked to about polo shirts from Taiwan. Jim and Gary were still planning on introducing polo shirts with little embroidered Opuses and Bill the Cats, but they had not been able to finance the purchase of the shirts beyond an initial test batch. Smith and his colleague had said they had connections with some Taiwanese in Houston who had relatives back home who owned a shirt factory. They had also mentioned easy terms. Now they were asking for $100,000 upfront for a container of shirts. "It seems like every time we talk, the deal changes," Jim said. "If we could put up the money, I guess we could go to Taiwan ourselves and buy the container. . . . If you get the shirts, we guarantee that we'll use them over a six-month period. Otherwise, I don't think we're really interested."

Then Jim got a call from Jim Akins, his banker at Lamar Savings. Logically, it was to Lamar, which had already lent Lin-Tex half a million dollars, that Lin-Tex should have been turning for another loan. But Lamar was at the head of the list of Austin financial institutions in deep trouble. It was about to end the year with a $90 million loss. Its net worth was negative $27 million. Akins had told Jim he would like to lend Lin-Tex more money, but there was no money to lend. His own job was in jeopardy. Lamar had also postponed its plans for a branch office on the moon.

"I met with Greater Texas yesterday," Jim told Akins. "They said if we put up five hundred thousand dollars cash, they could loan us fifty thousand dollars at ten points over prime. . . . He called *us* and said they wanted to be our banker. Then yesterday he says, 'What's the incentive for us? You're too big for us.' I just sit there and say, 'God, why do I have to listen to this crap?' I'm listening to bankers all day long when I need a hundred grand to buy shirts for next week. . . . You're in a town where nobody pays their bills, where the real estate developers say to the banks, 'Nah, you can take the land back.' And here's a company that pays its bills, and they won't lend us money to make money. I don't understand it at all."

Akins offered an explanation: "You're not trying to borrow money on overpriced real estate. Why would they lend you anything?"

Jim asked Akins to call Lear and put in a word for Lin-Tex. Akins said he would.

Then Jim called an Austin Mercedes dealer to arrange leasing two new company cars—one for him and one for Gary. They were going to have a nice Christmas, no matter what.

# "How Much Are We Charging for a Pregnant Recipient?"

**N**O SALES HAD BEEN RUNG up at the Senepol Stampede, but Pete was not discouraged. For one thing, Universal II was finally on the market. Lundelius was still confident that investors would snap up the limited partnership shares despite the passage a few weeks earlier of the new tax law, which limited the benefits of tax shelters. In fact, Lundelius told Pete, the new law would actually *help* sell Universal II. Beginning with the new year, the law cut the top federal tax rate from 50 percent to 28 percent. This provided strong incentive to defer income from this year to future years, and one function of tax shelters like Universal II was to do just that. Moreover, the paper losses generated by tax shelters would no longer be deductible from real income—unless the tax shelters were purchased before the President signed the tax bill, which was expected to occur any day now. "I think those investors who procrastinated are now going to go out and furiously look for tax writeoffs," Lundelius predicted.

Some of them were going to find Pete's prospectus for Universal II, which Lundelius's firm had distributed to small brokerage houses in Texas and elsewhere. Directing the marketing effort was Trudy Cass, a twenty-seven-year-old Lundelius associate who had never handled an offering by herself before. In between fielding daily phone calls from Pete asking how things were going, Trudy spent her time making sales calls to brokers and financial advisers, including the adviser to the rock group ZZ Top. She was encouraged by the fact that the Granada Corporation, a major Texas packager of cattle limited partnerships, had already sold out its program for the year, opening the field to Pete.

Trudy told Pete every time he called, day after day, to be patient, his program would sell. Pete was encouraged, but he hedged his bet. He decided to market individual Senepol investment deals himself via an ad in the *Wall Street Journal*. The *Wall Street Journal*, however, wouldn't accept an ad from just anyone. It sent Pete a batch of forms asking for references and particulars about his organization.

A couple of days after the Senepol Stampede, Pete sat in his little office beneath his championship plaque from the Brazos County Hay Fair and a framed article about the Senepol from the *Schulenburg Sticker* and worked on filling out the forms.

At the next desk, the phone was ringing with promising news.

Keith picked up a call from a Guatemalan friend of the German Guatemalan who had been at the Stampede. The Guatemalan said he wanted to try out the Senepol in his country. He wanted to know if somebody could fly down with a frozen embryo in his luggage, or if perhaps an embryo could be implanted in the womb of a dairy cow and shipped.

Keith covered the telephone mouthpiece with his hand and turned to Pete. "How much are we charging for a pregnant recipient?" he asked.

"Fifteen to eighteen hundred dollars," Pete said. "What are they after, basically?"

"They want a live animal to see how it does. They don't have much money right now, but they could buy a lot more next year."

"If they want a live animal," Pete said, "we'll get them one. Tell them we'll work with them."

Keith objected, "But then if they decide to be fly-by-nights. . . ."

"We're out one animal," said Pete. It was a risk he was willing to take. He'd always thought, considering the depressed state of the American cattle industry, that some of his best prospects for Senepol sales lay abroad.

Keith assured the Guatemalan that they would be pleased to work something out, and then the phone rang again. It was a man from Granada Sire Services, a subsidiary of the Granada Corporation, who said he had a buyer for Senepol semen in Paraguay. Could he come out to the ranch and, for a fee, collect some from one of Pete's bulls? Keith and Pete discussed whether they could trust to have someone from Granada, a potential competitor, looking around at their operation. Pete decided that if Granada wanted to go into the Senepol business, it didn't need to spy on Hopes Creek Ranch; it could just go to St. Croix and buy a herd.

He told Keith to tell the semen collector to come on out.

# "Up Against the Wall, Yew Maggots!"

JIM AND GARY FLEW to South Carolina to sell T-shirts to the Marines.

Major Gerald Schoppe, the officer who had approached them at the MAGIC show, had come through with an $11,000 opening order for "Shoe" T-shirts featuring Skyler, the little bird who joined the Marines by mistake. The T-shirts were going on sale in the base exchange at Parris Island on the occasion of the 211th anniversary of the founding of the United States Marine Corps; the "Shoe" cartoonist, Jeff MacNelly, was flying in to make a personal appearance. Jim and Gary, delighted with Schoppe's order—they saw it as the opening wedge in a campaign to sell Lin-Tex T-shirts on military bases everywhere—were coming too.

Lin-Tex's Christmas cash crisis had still not been resolved. No loans had been forthcoming from Greater Texas or any other Austin bank; Jim and Gary were now looking elsewhere. In recent weeks, several people had called to talk about putting money into the company—in exchange for part ownership of the company. One such group had been referred by a bank that turned Lin-Tex down for a loan, leaving Jim fuming: "The guy who owns the bank wants to buy part of our company, but it wasn't good enough to lend money to." Gary was starting to worry about "creepy guys who want to steal your business."

There was, nevertheless, still plenty of cash coming in to cover Lin-Tex's operating expenses, including the usual first-class travel arrangements for Jim and Gary. The day before they were due at Parris Island, they checked into the Hyatt Regency on the posh resort island of Hilton Head, forty miles away, and played a round of golf. They could have stayed instead at a modest motel in Beaufort, six miles from the base, but they didn't see the point. Why cut corners to save a few hundred dollars on a business trip? Travel expenses were tax-deductible. And if they weren't working so they could enjoy themselves in nice hotels, limousines, and the first-class cabins of airliners—places they could only dream about when they were kids frying hamburgers in Columbus—then what the hell *were* they working for?

They had, in any case, just made a move that would reduce their travel costs from now on. To buy air tickets for this trip, Gary had called a small travel agency near the Lin-Tex office. The woman who answered the phone said she was sorry but the agency had just gone out of business. Gary asked if the owner was there. The woman put him on, and Gary bought the travel agency.

He bought it with Jim (for the assumption of $10,000 of debt and an additional sum to be paid out of future profits). This made Jim and Gary travel agents. They would henceforth be entitled to travel in luxury at travel agents' discounts.


The Marine Corps Recruit Depot at Parris Island is renowned for transforming American teenagers into Marines. Sometimes this is harshly done; in the past the base was occasionally shaken by scandals resulting from the fatal abuse of recruits. Reforms have long since been introduced—drill instructors (DIs) may no longer strike, or even touch, recruits (except to demonstrate a correct position) nor may they address them as "maggots"—but Marine Corps basic training, which basically involves disassembling personalities and then putting them back together again, is still not a gentle process. As Jim and Gary drove onto the base, passing picnic tables and live oak trees hung with moss, they were curious about what they would see.

Jim had never been in the armed forces. As a high school graduate facing the draft, he had attempted to join the Marine Reserve but made the mistake, when asked why he wanted to join, of answering honestly: "To avoid going to Vietnam." This was not an acceptable answer.

Rejected by the reserve, Jim was resigned to being drafted when he was saved by Kentucky Fried Chicken. It was, specifically, a well-connected chicken purveyor turned Kentucky Fried Chicken executive who lent Jim a hand. Jim had dropped off his upward career path at the chicken company to await the Army's call when he happened to mention his situation to the executive. "Why in hell are you going to get drafted?" the executive asked. "Do you want to go in the Army?"

"Fuck, no," said Jim.

"Well," said the executive, "why didn't you tell me you were going to get drafted?"

"I didn't know I *should* tell you," said Jim.

"Fuck, yeah," said the executive. "I can get you out of that deal. What draft board are you in?"

A few weeks later, at his pre-induction physical, Jim told the doctors he had bad knees, an authentic but minor condition he never expected would keep him out of the Army. But it won him a 4-F. Jim never learned exactly what the chicken executive had done for him, but he knew he had done something.

Gary, on the other hand, had spent three years in the military, including a few days in Vietnam and singing appearances at several state fairs.

He joined the Navy immediately after graduating from high school and was dispatched to Chicago for basic training. During the initial processing period, an officer asked the new recruits if any of them wanted to join the Navy Bluejacket Choir. Gary had heard that being in a special unit like the choir made basic training a more pleasant experience, so he raised his hand, and so did about three thousand other recruits who had heard the same thing.

One by one, the volunteers were called onto a stage to pick up sheet music and sing a few notes. The song Gary picked up happened to be "The Naval Hymn (God of Our Fathers)," which he had sung many times in church and the Youth for Christ choir. He sailed through the audition and got into the Navy choir, which did turn out to be a good deal. His first duty of the day was choir practice at 8:00 a.m.; everybody else got up at five-thirty and started doing pushups and marching around. The choir appeared at the California, Illinois, and Wisconsin state fairs while Gary was a member and once almost appeared on the Ed Sullivan show.

Meanwhile, Gary was training as a radarman. After nine months of school, he was assigned to a destroyer that was briefly posted off the coast of Vietnam. Gary was sent ashore once to meet up with a platoon of Marines, scout the location of some enemy fuel tanks, and use the Marines' radio to send target coordinates back to his ship's artillery. A small boat ferried Gary in to a beach, where he was dropped off alone with instructions to march half a mile inland to meet the Marines. Navigating by compass, he walked half a mile and found no one there. He explored the area and still found no one. He tried to return to the beach where he'd landed, but he couldn't find that either.

He didn't know where to go, so he returned to what he thought was the rendezvous point, dug a hole, and hid. He heard gunfire once and thought about walking toward it, but then he thought, "What if it ain't *our* gunfire?" He stayed where he was. After two days, some Marines happened by. Gary, starving, covered with insect bites, not entirely coherent, rose out of his hole to greet them. They almost shot him, and then they burst out laughing. Gary spent two days in the hospital on an aircraft carrier recovering from his mission.

Gary saw action once more during his naval career—in Italy. He was driving his captain to Mediterranean fleet headquarters in Naples and carrying a load of ship's mail to the fleet post office when he came around a corner into the middle of an angry street demonstration. Surrounded by protestors, who started rocking the car, Gary unholstered his service pistol and fired once into the air through his half-open window. The gun kicked up, hit the window frame, and bounced down into the window, shattering it. The crowd had scattered. Gary made a U-turn and drove off. He dropped the captain at headquarters, and he got the mail through.

The night before the arrival of the Lin-Tex team at Parris Island, Major Schoppe was so nervous he had trouble sleeping.

He was worried that no one on the base would show up for Jeff MacNelly's personal appearance.

To mark the Marine Corps' anniversary, there would be a traditional morning celebration on the base parade field. A band would play, and Marines would march by in the uniforms of every era in which the Marines had seen action, from the American Revolution to the invasion of Grenada. Then the oldest Marine on the base (a fifty-two-year-old colonel) and the youngest (a seventeen-year-old recruit) would step forward to take ceremonial bites from a Marine Corps birthday cake that the commanding general would slice with his saber.

The ceremony would end at 11:00 a.m., and all permanent base personnel had the rest of the day off. The next day (Veteran's Day) was a holiday, too. Major Schoppe was afraid that everyone would take off on vacation and no one would hang around to see MacNelly. (The recruits in basic training would still be on the base, but they were given only one hour of free time a day, and they had to spend it in their barracks.)

Major Schoppe, who had been an artillery officer before he transferred into retailing, had done everything he could to keep people around. He'd had flyers distributed promoting a one-day sale, and he had chosen that day to open the exchange's Christmas Toyland. He considered MacNelly (who produced not only "Shoe" T-shirts but also a Pulitzer Prize-winning editorial cartoon) a major VIP, and he wanted to make a good impression.

Major Schoppe drove to the Savannah airport himself to pick up MacNelly and drove him back to the Bachelor Officers' Quarters, where MacNelly was to spend the night. Jim and Gary were waiting there along with the warrant officer to whom Schoppe had delegated the task of provisioning MacNelly's suite. Schoppe was not pleased with what he found there: a six-pack of Heineken, a box of Ritz crackers, and an aerosol can of Easy Cheese.

There was no bottle opener, and the Heineken caps did not twist off. While Schoppe and his guests sat in the living room, the warrant officer grabbed the six-pack and disappeared into the bedroom. "He's not using his teeth, is he?" Schoppe asked.

The warrant officer was indeed prying off the bottle caps with his teeth.

He returned the open bottles to Schoppe's guests, who were attempting to snack on Ritz crackers and Easy Cheese. Jim depressed the cheese can nozzle over a cracker and watched cheese snake out very slowly. Very, very slowly. It took a good thirty seconds to cover the little cracker.

Schoppe reached for the can, which the warrant officer had stored in the suite's refrigerator. "If you don't want to be a warrant officer forever," Schoppe said, "this better not say, 'Do not refrigerate.' "

It did.

As distinguished visitors, MacNelly, Jim, and Gary were given a tour of the base. Schoppe drove them around, past lockstep marching groups of shaved-head recruits, past the close combat training area, the confidence course, and the bayonet-assault course. They passed the rifle range, where one group of recruits stood in a circle around their instructor aiming their rifles at him while he looked back to check their aim. Other recruits, their shooting practice finished, were standing with their arms in the air, being searched, Schoppe's warrant officer explained, "so no one can smuggle bullets back to barracks and shoot themselves or a DI."

The visitors stopped at a neat and hyper-clean brick barracks and marched inside. Jim and Gary were both wearing trim beards and expensive suits. MacNelly, a big man with prematurely gray hair, was dressed nattily in a tweed sport jacket over a red chamois shirt, corduroy pants, tassel loafers, and argyle socks. The recruits looked like a different species.

In skin-short haircuts and camouflage fatigues, sixty of them in one squad bay were working with intense concentration. Several were at ironing boards: one was ironing his hat; another was ironing his belt. Most were sitting on footlockers at the base of their double-deck iron bunks (to which their personal rifles were padlocked), pouring polish onto their boots and rubbing it in small tight circles.

A young lieutenant led the visitors into the bay, and the recruits leapt to attention as if stung with cattle prods. "SQUAD BAY, TEN-HUT!" they shouted. "SIR! GOOD AFTERNOON! SIR!"

While the recruits stood tautly, the lieutenant told the visitors that this was their daily hour of free time. "They can do what they want to do."

MacNelly, who was twice as big as the lieutenant but seemed cowed by the atmosphere, ventured a question: "Do they really all want to spend their free time polishing their boots?" (Despite his Marine-themed cartoons, MacNelly was not a military man himself. Out of Major Schoppe's earshot, he told Jim and Gary he had tried unsuccessfully to join the reserves to avoid going to Vietnam and ultimately escaped by drawing a high number in the first draft lottery.)

"Final inspection is coming up," the lieutenant explained, "and this may be the last free time they have to polish them."

Right, said one of the visitors, but why are they all sitting on their footlockers in the same position, facing the same direction?

"Even during free time, it is the responsibility of the DI to maintain good order and discipline," the lieutenant said. "Sitting the same way may be part of good order and discipline."

MacNelly took another good look at the scene. Eight months later, it appeared as a gag in "Shoe."

The tour moved on to the barracks that house new recruits during their first days on the base. The recruits come in on buses that arrive at 1:00 a.m., and they are kept awake all that first day until bedtime at 6:30 p.m. The recruits that the visitors saw looked listless and distracted. They sat on their footlockers with their eyes cast down, making eye contact with nobody, not even when a drill instructor led the Lin-Tex group in and the recruits leapt to attention shouting.

The drill instructor described the orientation program to MacNelly, Jim, and Gary. "Each recruit has a bag of personal effects in his footlocker," he said, "and we never touch those. Those are private."

Nobody asked, but he decided to demonstrate. He turned to one recruit, a muscular but scared-looking black man, and ordered, "Come here now!" The recruit raced over. The DI told him to get his personal effects bag. He raced to get it. "Open it up," the DI ordered. Rushing to comply, the recruit fumbled with the bag and dropped it. The gaping visitors, their hearts with the recruit, gasped silently.

The recruit picked up the bag and opened it. The drill instructor, to everyone's immense relief, ignored the fumble. He nodded as the recruit displayed the bag's meager contents. "Go away," he ordered. The recruit raced off.

The base exchange was featuring cologne for men.

A flyer being distributed near the exchange entrance bore the headline "Happy Birthday Marines!" over a large photo of a bottle of Calvin Klein's "Obsession," which was, the flyer said, available in the Beaufort area "only at the cosmetic counter at Parris Island Marine Corps exchange."

The "Marine Corps Birthday Bash" sale that Major Schoppe had scheduled to lure people to see MacNelly also included specials on tennis balls, lightning rods, and crystal glassware. Bali bras were 20 percent off.

All of those items and thousands more were displayed in the exchange, a large open emporium with the ambience of a discount drugstore that served the staff (male and female) of Parris Island, their families, and military retirees in the area. It sold inexpensive khaki pants and Hummel porcelain figurines, *Gung Ho* and *Soldier of Fortune* magazines, and Macintosh computers.

In the back, opposite an aisle of cigarettes, was the "Marine Gift Shop." It featured T-shirts with the Marine Corps insignia and bulldog mascot and, now, a brand-new display of "Shoe" T-shirts from Lin-Tex. There were seven designs, all with the skinny bird Skyler in his Marine uniform. In one, he asked, "Have you hugged your sergeant today?" In another, he counseled, "Your weapon is your best friend (it's the only thing around here that doesn't yell at you)." In a third, he was pictured arriving at Parris Island to be greeted by a drill instructor screaming, "Up against the wall, yew maggots!" The "maggots" design was displayed as prominently as the others, but base authorities had already decided that it would under no circumstances be reordered.

Jeff MacNelly sat amidst racks of T-shirts at a table with a laundry pen, facing a long line of Marines who had bought shirts and wanted him to autograph them. Despite Schoppe's worries, the event was a success.

Among those waiting patiently in line were several officers, some in camouflage fatigues, who had become fans of the Skyler strips while they were stationed in Beirut with the Marine contingent that was decimated by a suicide bomber.

"We heard someone was drawing something about the Marines," said Captain Mark Johnson as he stood holding a "maggots" shirt for himself and an "I Love a Marine" design for his fiancée. "Our first reaction was, 'It better be good.' Then relatives began sending them. They were good"—he searched for the right words—"comic relief."

The teen-age son of a colonel stepped up with a shirt for MacNelly to sign. "You want one of those?" MacNelly asked, pointing to a stack of Marine Corps anniversary souvenir cards he had designed.

"Yes, sir," said the teenager. " 'To Dan.' "

" 'To Dan'?" asked MacNelly.

"Yes, sir."

While MacNelly signed, Major Schoppe showed Jim and Gary around the store. "We gross nine million dollars a year," he said. Jim and Gary were impressed. "I have mostly civilian employees but some are military. If we go to war, the civilians aren't going to want to go, but we're still going to need exchanges. Of course, we wouldn't sell T-shirts."

But Jim and Gary weren't worried about World War III. The nation was at peace, and the T-shirts were selling. "I have big hopes for these shirts," Schoppe said. He promised to introduce Jim and Gary to the managers of exchanges on other bases.

Back in the line, a woman Marine sergeant asked MacNelly to autograph her "Have you hugged your sergeant today?" shirt.

"Were you ever in the Marines?" she asked.

"No," said MacNelly. "If I had been, I might not have thought it was so funny."

# "The Prince of Saudi"

THE PRESIDENT HAD SIGNED the new tax bill, but no shares in Universal II had been sold. Trudy Cass was making phone calls and sending prospectuses to brokers all over Texas, but no buyers had turned up.

The investor group Lundelius had been speaking with back in September had invested in something else. The Australian rancher who had inquired about buying frozen Senepol embryos had not been heard from again. The Granada semen collector had come out to the ranch and looked around, but he never collected any semen.

Pete would have been depressed if he hadn't been working on a big export deal to Sri Lanka.

The deal came in through Lundelius, who knew an Arab businessman in Houston named Ravi Vora who was said to have connections with the Saudi royal family. Vora told Lundelius he was working with some money people who wanted to develop a herd of cattle on Sri Lanka to export beef to the Middle East. He said they might be interested in buying their cattle from Pete.

Pete and Trudy Cass had a preliminary meeting with Vora, at which Trudy explained the concept of implanting Senepol embryos in the wombs of Holstein cows (Vora's group was also interested in buying dairy cattle). Ah, Vora said, so the resulting calves would be Senepol-Holstein crosses. No, said Trudy, the embryos are full-blood Senepols that are flushed from pregnant Senepol cows and then inserted into Holsteins. As she described the flushing and inserting, Vora, blanching, cut her off. "No, no," he said, "that's enough. You must be a very brave girl to work on a project like this."

But the meeting went well, and a follow-up session was convened with Ayoub Farah, a Saudi businessman from London who, as Trudy understood it, worked with Prince Mohammed al-Fassi, who had become famous in the United States a few years before for having pubic hair painted on the Grecian-style statues ringing his Beverly Hills estate. Al-Fassi had since been sued by his wife for divorce in an American court and now avoided traveling to the United States.

Pete wasn't quite sure who these people were. He referred to Ayoub Farah as "Abdul Farah" and described him as "the prince of Saudi." "Supposedly the king can't enter America," Pete said. "That's what Lundelius told me. I don't know how many kings they have over there." Trudy kept track of who was who—"My hairdresser does the hair for the Saudi royal family when they come to town, so I hear the names from him," she explained—and the meeting with Farah went well. The next step was for Pete to draft a proposal describing how Senepols would work on Sri Lanka; it would be submitted to the Sri Lankan government and the U.S. Agency for International Development, which was expected to help fund the deal. Pete told Vora he would need some information to write the memo, and he submitted a list of questions about climate and ranching conditions on Sri Lanka, which Vora sent to his associates there. As soon as the answers came back, Pete was going to whip out the proposal. "Keith is already working on it," he said. "We'll use his brain and mine." Pete planned on following up the memo with a research trip to Sri Lanka with Dr. McCall. He figured they would go in mid-December. A bloody civil war had recently erupted on Sri Lanka, but Pete paid it no mind.

In early December, two weeks after Pete had submitted his questions, he was still waiting for a reply. He now figured his trip to Sri Lanka would have to be put off until January.

In mid-December, Pete finally got a letter from Vora (dated the day after twenty-five people were killed in a battle between rival Sri Lankan rebels). It contained some disturbing news: "We

under-stand [sic] that the Government of Sri Lanka is pursuing a
project based on stock from Pakistan which is thought to be more
suitable to Sri Lankan condiitons [sic] than that from the Northern
climate." The letter also reported that there was no local market
for beef because most Sri Lankans are Buddhist. But it advised
Pete not to be too concerned by this "initial feedback," and it
requested specific information about the Senepol and the "back-
groung [sic] and qualifications of MB Universal and how do they
compare to the industry leaders."

Pete was a little discouraged to hear about the Pakistani cattle,
but he thought he could still salvage the deal. He knew he could
give the Sri Lankans satisfactory answers to their questions about
the Senepol. But he figured his trip to Sri Lanka would have to
be postponed again, at least until February.

Meanwhile, Pete was forging ahead in his search for investors
among readers of the *Wall Street Journal.* His advertisement ran
on December 16:

> **Individual Cattle Ownership**
> **\*Income Deferral**
> **\*Profit Potential**
> **\*Individual Business Opportunity**
> **MB Universal Programs Inc.**

The address and phone number of Hopes Creek Ranch were
printed at the bottom of the ad. By 5:30 p.m. on the day it ran,
Pete had received five calls from people who were looking for a
way to reduce their taxable incomes in the year that was about
to end. "Federal Express me an agreement," one caller said. "I
have a hundred and fifty thousand dollars, and I've got to put
it somewhere."

The deal Pete was offering investors was this:

For $35,000, MB Universal Programs (a partnership of Pete
and Dr. McCall) would lease an investor three Senepol cows
from which MB Universal Programs would flush twenty Senepol
embryos. MB Universal Programs would implant those embryos

in the wombs of twenty non-Senepol recipient cows (leased from MB Universal Programs). All the calves that resulted (MB Universal Programs estimated a 60 percent birth rate) would belong to the investor, who could take possession of the animals, sell them, or pay MB Universal Programs a fee to maintain them.

Basically, that meant each investor would be buying twelve Senepol calves for $3000 apiece. That was a lot of money for a calf, but the tax breaks involved could make it worthwhile.

When the first inquiries poured in, Pete had nothing on paper to send out. So he sat down for a couple of days—"working full blast, brains churning"—and produced an offering memorandum. He made copies, dispatched them, and waited for investment dollars to come back. He was actually glad, he said, that Universal II had not succeeded. This new individual investment program could bring in all the money he needed while giving him more flexibility in his operation than the limited partnership would have allowed.

While Pete waited to hear from the *Wall Street Journal* crowd, his plans were also moving forward on the Guatemala deal. He now planned to ship four animals in April to a cattle show in Guatemala City.

And he was thinking about buying a meat-processing plant in Burnet that he'd heard was for sale for $175,000—a bargain. The plant had fallen on hard times when its previous owners, who used it to process deer shot by hunters, had mixed up a large quantity of deer sausage using pork fat that happened to be rancid. "It ruined every deer that went through there," Pete said.

Pete had a new idea for the plant: he would use it to process Senepol beef in accordance with Islamic dietary law and export to the Middle East. This business had been suggested to him by the Sri Lanka deal. It looked like there was a reasonable chance it could work. Everything was fitting together.

# "Everything Is Selling"

I
T STARTED RAINING two weeks before Christmas, cheerless drizzle from a gray sky, and it never stopped.

Fortunately, the malls were enclosed.

Songs about Santa flying over the Rio Grande were on the radio. Festive lights hung everywhere. And Lin-Tex Marketing was offering the good people of Austin the opportunity to purchase T-shirts as gifts for their loved ones.

The citizenry was responding.

"Ears pierced cheap!" chortled one young shopper, reading the words off a sign in a cartoon panel on a "Neighborhood" T-shirt; the sign was posted next to a man and his long-fanged Doberman pinscher.

"Look at that cat!" said a woman nearby, pointing to a T-shirt featuring Bill the Cat in a cloud of fleas, retching.

It was two days before Christmas, and these amused shoppers had paused in their peregrinations through the Highland Mall to admire the wares in a Comic Collectibles kiosk, one of a dozen established by Lin-Tex for the holiday season. It was set up in a busy aisle between a Sheep Seats kiosk (selling sheepskin auto seatcovers) and a Simply Divine Designs kiosk (selling dinosaur T-shirts). Shoppers coursed around them, obscuring marks on the floor that indicated distance measurements for the benefit of "mall walkers," Austinites who took their exercise in the Highland Mall during quieter hours.

Jim had stopped by to see how things were going, and he watched as a young man and woman took a T-shirt shopping break from their duties as clerks in the mall's Petland store. The woman held up a "Momma" shirt with the legend: "This is my son. Be nice to him and see that he eats." "This would be good for Allen," she reflected, "only he might get mad." Her companion bought a "Hagar University—Tappa Kegga Brew" shirt for himself. Next to the cash register, a Mexican-American woman was working full time refolding shirts discarded by browsers. The kiosk manager, beaming, reported good news to Jim: "Everything is selling except 'Rex the Dog.' " And that shirt was a notorious turkey.

Elsewhere in America, Lin-Tex T-shirts were being sold in more than a thousand stores. The outward flow of merchandise had never abated, thanks to the late-season infusion of $180,000 from two last-minute loans. One hundred thousand dollars had arrived from Dave Teal, Jim's older brother, who, as the teen-aged assistant manager of a Kentucky Fried Chicken store in Columbus, Ohio, had distinguished himself by recruiting Jim to the fast-food industry. Dave, like Jim, had moved on to Wendy's, where he had risen to a senior executive position. Now he was an independent Columbus restaurateur and gourmet butcher. Responding to his brother's plea for help, he had borrowed $100,000 from his bank in Ohio and turned around and re-lent it to Lin-Tex.

The second loan had a more dubious provenance. After being rejected by Greater Texas and a string of other banks, Jim had continued to shop his package of personal collateral around the woebegone Austin banking scene. He took it to a small suburban institution called North Central National Bank, which duly turned him down. But an acquaintance of Jim who had an unspecified relationship with the bank informed him that, for the payment of a $5000 fee, the situation could be retrieved by going outside normal channels. There was something not kosher about this, but Jim needed the money too badly to play bank examiner, a role to which he was not disposed in any case. "Let's put it this way," he said later. "They told me they weren't making the loan, and when I called my friend, he said, 'The loan's being made. Just make sure I get my five grand.' I gave him the five grand. We got the loan."

The $180,000 from the two loans whizzed through Lin-Tex's

checking account in about fifteen minutes. Actually faster than that since Gary, playing the float as usual, had spent the money before it arrived.

But he kept the T-shirts flowing. Days before Christmas, Lin-Tex was still shipping emergency reorders of "Sold My Soul To Rock n' Roll," a hot-selling new "Bloom County" design featuring Opus the penguin as a punk rocker. Business was good. The banks that had turned down Lin-Tex seemed to have made a mistake.

Jim Akins thought so. He was the officer of Lamar Savings who had engineered the granting of a $500,000 loan to Lin-Tex a couple of years before and thereafter, as Lamar tumbled into hard times, had been unable to lend an additional cent. Lamar's troubles were deepening still; in this holiday season, it had announced companywide layoffs. Akins was fired. He asked Jim and Gary for a job, and they put him to work, for $300 a week, managing the Comic Collectibles kiosk in the Barton Creek Mall.

"We did thirty-eight hundred yesterday," Akins told Jim, when Jim stopped by to check how things were going. Akins was wearing a brown sweater and growing a beard; he had vowed never to wear a necktie again. He wasn't crazy about his new job—"I hate malls. I hate crowds. I hate Christmas," he said—but he liked it better than banking.

While he spoke to Jim, Akins was repairing some wire baskets that hung off the front of the kiosk and were used to display Opus dolls. "I've put off doing this right," he said. "I'm afraid it might fall and crush a child."

Behind him, teen-aged employees were selling T-shirts, or what T-shirts they had left. The kiosk had sold out of many sizes of the most popular designs.

Jim didn't say anything to Akins, but he was disgusted. "He's got his priorities all wrong. He's wiring together baskets when he's out of stock on items we have in the warehouse. Here's a guy who was a banker, who loaned us half a million dollars. He should be on the telephone to the warehouse right now instead of fucking around with that wire. This shows that bankers don't have the slightest idea what makes a business go."

Jim didn't want to make a scene with Akins. "Why get everybody all upset for maybe a couple hundred dollars?" But, as he drove away from the mall in his new burgundy Mercedes 420 SEL, he picked up the car phone and dialed his warehouse manager. "If Akins doesn't show up there in the next half hour," Jim told him, "take a ride to Barton Creek. Don't make a big deal about it, but ask Akins if he needs anything. Tell him you're in the mall doing some Christmas shopping."

Perhaps it was fatherhood that made Jim so mellow ("Last year Jim would have got Akins down and banged his head against the wood," Gary said when he heard about the situation at Barton Creek). On December 6, Frances's water had broken while she was at the beauty shop. She got to the hospital in plenty of time and had a relatively easy delivery, the old-fashioned way, with a lower-body anesthetic. She and Jim watched the birth of a seven-pound, fourteen-ounce son in a mirror.

In Frances's room afterward, she and Jim waited for the baby to be brought up. It didn't come, and it didn't come, so Jim went looking for it. A nurse told him that there was "a problem." And it suddenly hit Jim for the first time—watching the baby in the mirror had been like watching a show on TV—that he was a father, that he had a son, and the son had a medical problem.

The baby had been born with low blood sugar, which had promptly put it into convulsions. The infant—named J Carroll Teal (with no period after the J)—was admitted to intensive care, where he spent several days until his body adjusted.

On December 23, the only remaining sign of the baby's illness was a bald spot where the front of his scalp had been shaved for the insertion of an IV needle. In every other way, little J Carroll was happy and healthy. When Jim arrived home from his visits to the malls, he found his son swinging in a bassinet between the pool table and the backgammon table. Lights were flashing on a twelve-foot Christmas tree next to the crap table. In a stack of baby photos on the bar, there was a picture of J Carroll in a tiny Santa Claus suit, a gift from Gary and Dayna.

Jim picked up his son and kissed him. "How ya doing?" he asked. The baby didn't answer, but he looked comfortable with his dad. Every morning at 7:00 a.m., Jim would get up and place the fussing infant on his own ample stomach, and J Carroll, feeling the warmth, would go back to sleep.

Jim and Frances, Gary and Dayna, made two handsome couples at a celebratory dinner that night. Jim dressed in a muted Louis Roth sport jacket, Frances in an embroidered white coat, and, leaving the baby in the care of a Mexican woman, they drove to an upscale downtown restaurant in the Mercedes. Gary arrived with Dayna in *his* new company car—a Cadillac Fleetwood Di-Elegance. He wore an Italian tweed jacket; Dayna (who was now managing the travel agency Jim and Gary had bought) was in a slinky yellow cocktail dress. Both Jim and Gary wore gold rings set with diamonds; Frances wore five-hundred-dollar white leather boots.

They weren't exactly *rich,* not yet. To meet current expenses— including baby costs, repairs on the house and the swimming pool, and a $2000 string of pearls for Frances for Christmas—Jim had just had to sell six thousand shares of his Wendy's stock—at 10⅛. In retrospect, he wished he'd sold it two months before, at 14, or five months before, at 15, or six months before, at 17.

As the year drew to a close, however, there was no cause for complaint. Sales weren't quite as good as Jim and Gary had projected, but it looked like they would have a $600,000 December. At the dinner table, Gary pulled out some figures he had written on the back of a business card. They added up to $2 million in sales for the last six months of the year. Gary wrote down the figure .15 and circled it. That was their profit percentage. "Not bad," he said, "for a couple of hoods from Linden."

# "**I** Got What I Want"

**O**N CHRISTMAS EVE, Keith Newbill and a friend of his from Texas A&M climbed on their horses and rode to the back of Hopes Creek Ranch to round up three cows and their calves. These were above-average Senepol cows and calves; Pete had selected them to represent his herd at upcoming livestock shows in Houston and Guatemala. He wanted to take them off grass and put them on feed so they would look their best.

The rain that had been falling for two weeks had finally stopped—the sun was even shining—but Hopes Creek was high. When Keith and his friend got to its bank, driving the cattle before them, the cattle looked at the flood and decided they would prefer not to swim across. They could not be reasoned with. Keith and his friend had to get down off their horses, grab the cows' tails, and push the animals, hard, putting their shoulders into it, to get them into the stream.

When the cowboys and the cows finally reached the pasture by the house, everybody was covered with mud. Keith had mud on his shirt, on his hat, on his chaps, on his boots, on his spurs. He tracked mud into the kitchen when he came in to get an ampule of penicillin from the refrigerator (it was on the door next to the margarine). One of the calves had navel ill (an infection) and needed a shot. Armed with a hypodermic needle, Keith remounted his horse, which he had hitched to the handle of his pickup truck, and took off after the calf. He whistled to Meg, his New Zealand eye dog, and, diving at crazy angles, she cut the calf away from its mother. Keith twirled his lasso and snagged it. He leaped down and injected the penicillin. As the calf ran off, Keith gathered up his rope, accidentally snaring one of his horse's back feet, marring an otherwise perfect performance. He tried to act as if it didn't bother him and went back to the house to join the holiday festivities.

The first batch of relatives due for a ranch Christmas had arrived. Pete's older brother, Guy, a chief master sergeant at an Air Force base in New Mexico—"They say it's the largest electronics repair facility in the Free World," he said—was reading a paper in the living room. Becky was showing his wife Louise around the house, which had been cleaned up for company. "I already got what I want for Christmas," Becky said. "It stopped raining."

Louise was looking out a window. "Those cows are so pretty," she said.

"Well, thank you, Louise," said Becky.

A Christmas tree was set up by the front door, and presents were piled beneath it. The mantle was decorated with Christmas candles and a plastic nativity scene. The plastic cradle had been lost, so the infant Jesus nestled in an upside-down cowboy hat.

Pete, in the dining room, was handing Wendell a neatly typed letter to take to town to drop at the Federal Express. It was another last-minute, year-end rush dispatch of a tax-advantaged MB Universal Programs investment proposal to a *Wall Street Journal* reader eager to spend some money before December 31. "Whoa," Pete said as Wendell was walking away. "What's that?" He took a hard look at a brown smudge next to the letterhead. It might have been mud or, since he and Wendell had been walking back and forth through the cattle pen that lay between the house and the office in the barn, it might have been a blend of mud and something more pungent. Whichever, this was not the kind of thing some rich investor wanted to see when he opened his mail.

"We can't send it with that smudge," Pete decreed. "Take it back to the office and have Lisa retype it."

Pete hadn't got any money back yet in response to the proposals he'd sent out, but there were still seven days left in the year, and he was offering a non-tax-advantaged version of the deal that he figured should appeal to investors even after January 1. As far as he was concerned, the thing was still full of promise. He was already thinking about a letter he would have to write soon to his banker at First Bank & Trust in Bryan, which had lent him $55,000 a year before and needed to be reassured periodically that the cash was flowing in the right direction at Hopes Creek Ranch. When he wrote the letter a few days later, Pete made a point of mentioning that he had shipped out twenty-five proposals in response to requests from *Wall Street Journal* readers and that he was "working towards agreements with several individuals who want expanded programs."

He noted, moreover, that "Lundelius & Associates are still marketing Universal Two" (he did not go out of his way to mention that zero shares had been sold), that "we are in the process of developing Universal Three," that he had signed up a Senepol sales representative in Central America, and that "we are currently working with Gulf International Enterprises to develop a cattle breeding project in Sri Lanka." No actual sales had yet resulted from any of these ventures, but that was no cause for alarm. All of them were solid prospects; if only *one* of them came through, Hopes Creek Ranch would be in good shape. "We are looking forward to a year of growth and expansion for Hopes Creek Ranch and Universal Programs," Pete wrote to his banker. "Thank you for your support."


Wendell took the retyped letter into town, and Pete took out the horseshoes set. Keith, still wearing his spurs, pounded in the stakes by the electric fence behind the house. This was a relatively new fence, the building of which had nearly cost Wendell part of a finger. He was twisting a rod to tighten the wire when the rod slipped and the wire snapped free and whipped into him. "Shit," he called out. "It cut my finger off." In fact, the tip was hanging on by a thread. Pete paid to have it sewn back on, and Wendell walked around for weeks with the biggest bandage anyone had ever seen on a single finger.

Now, a Senepol bull on the other side of the fence looked on as the men started a round-robin horseshoes tournament.

Pete pitched his shoes with intense concentration. Bryan turned out to be a horseshoes natural (there was some speculation that his smooth delivery owed something to his weekly bowling); he quickly threw two ringers. The game came to a halt several times when shoes bounced into tall grass and disappeared or landed in puddles and got buried in muck. Then a shoe took a bad hop and rolled under the electric fence. Pete called over little Mollie, who was playing in a hammock between two trees. He rolled a cut tree stump over to the fence, took Mollie in his hands, stood on the stump, and hoisted her over. "Lift your legs," he told her as she passed over the electrified wire. He put her down near the bull, which ignored her, and she him, as she retrieved the shoe.

The game resumed, and Guy threw what he thought was a ringer. Pete, on the other team, granted that it was certainly *close* to a ringer but wasn't entirely convinced that it actually *was* a ringer. He pulled out a horseshoes rule book that came with the set and read that a ringer was accomplished when a straight line drawn between the heel calks of the shoe enclosed the stake. That was fine, but nobody was exactly sure which part of the shoe was the heel calk.

The ensuing discussion, entirely amicable, was interrupted when Pete was summoned to the phone. He came back with word that it had been "a depressing Christmas call." A Senepol calf on Dr. McCall's ranch had died. "It's the one out of four-eleven," Pete said. Keith shook his head. "The sad thing about it," Keith said, "is four-eleven's such a personable cow." "It's the first one we ever lost," Pete said.

The Christmas Eve meal seemed to cheer him up. The women laid out a spread of grilled steak, baked potato, salad, rolls, and Rice Divinity, a recipe of Lisa's that involved rice, whipped cream, chopped apples and pineapples, and miniature marshmallows.

While the food was being served, Keith looked through a telescope set up on the patio at some Senepols a few hundred feet away. He liked to look at cows when they didn't know they were being watched. When they did know they were being looked at, he explained, they got self-conscious and acted differently. "When they know you're looking," he said, "they go like. . . ." He impersonated a self-conscious cow by turning his back, dipping his head, and looking backward around his shoulder.

Then Keith joined the rest of the men with a plate of food on the patio in the sun. He mentioned that, the day before, he'd been knocked out of the saddle when his horse ran too close to a tree limb. Keith's spur caught in the side of the saddle as he fell, leaving him upside down and still attached to the horse, a potentially fatal situation.

"Did you get dragged?" one of the ranch visitors asked.

"I was fixin' to," Keith said. "I was looking up, figuring what I could do to avoid the melee, when my foot came right out of the boot. I powdered my boots yesterday morning, and I don't do that more than once a month."

"If you hadn't, would you be here today?"

"Part of him would," said Pete.

"There'd have been some salvage," Keith said.

Pete nodded.

"Pete'd be wearing my hat," said Keith.


It was almost 5:00 p.m. when the meal was done. Pete decided it was time to do some Christmas shopping.

He got in his pickup and drove to the Post Oak Mall, where he walked into a jewelry store to find a gift for Becky. He liked to give jewelry, because you knew it was actually worth something.

A sharp-dressed salesgirl with a remarkable amount of energy for the last shopping hour before Christmas sat Pete down at a counter and showed him a $799 set of gold and diamond earrings. "Refresh my memory," she said. "Did we already talk about the full-value trade-in and the lifetime diamond guarantee?"

Pete said she'd mentioned it, and he stared at the earrings. "I wouldn't mind getting them," he said, "but they're too much."

Unfazed, the salesgirl inquired politely what his price range might be.

"It should be under five hundred," Pete said, "and, to be practical, under two fifty."

The salesgirl nodded. "What's your wife's coloring like?" Pete said it was blond. "Well," said the salesgirl, "topaz would look nice on her. I like topaz myself. It's a very beautiful stone." She laid out a $199 pair of topaz earrings with single tiny diamonds and a matching $219 pendant. Pete looked them over.

He said he'd take the earrings and that he'd come back for the pendant in March for Becky's birthday.

"Fine," the salesgirl said. She walked off with the earrings to get them gift-wrapped. Then she turned around and walked back. "I just thought of something," she said. "When you come back, there's no guarantee that this particular pendant will still be here, and every one is a slightly different tint. You may not be able to match the earrings. I'm not trying to push you, but you can put it on layaway for twenty dollars."

Pete thought about it as he reached in his pocket to pull out his checkbook. There was a ten-dollar bill stuck in it.

"I'll take that ten dollars," the salesgirl said. "That will do it." Pete handed it over. "You're doing a good job," he told her.


Meanwhile, back at the ranch, more family was gathering. Pete's mother arrived from South Texas with her third husband, a retired official with the Immigration Service. Pete's sister Mollie drove up from Houston with her husband and son. The family sat around the Christmas tree talking all evening.

Christmas morning dawned cool and misty, with the boom of duck hunters' shotguns echoing over the pastures.

The sun was breaking through, burning off the mist, when the Binion kids—Mollie, Wade, and Pauline—started ripping into their presents under the tree. All three of them got watches. Wade got a toy rifle that fired plastic darts. Mollie and Pauline got dolls. Pauline protested that she was too old for a doll.

Pete got a tan leather briefcase and a fish-scaling board with a clip on the end to hold the fish.

Wade tore open a package and looked puzzled. "That looks like bases," Pete told him. "You know how when we play baseball, we always have to get hay or a dry cow patty?"

Pauline opened a plastic, battery-operated microphone, set it up, stood behind it like she'd seen singers do on TV, and started to sing:

> On the good ship Lollipop.
> On the good ship Lollipop.

Mollie leaped up and joined her in a duet:

> On the good ship Lollipop.
> On the good ship Lollipop. . . .

# "It's a Fun Business"

**T**HE WIND WAS BRISK, and the hookers in Times Square were wearing short fur jackets over their short dresses. Jim and Gary, walking south on Broadway at 10:00 p.m., were working off a heavy French dinner and a day of drinking that had begun twelve hours earlier in an Austin airport VIP lounge. They were in New York to attend the annual Toy Fair.

"Do you want a date?"

Jim turned to see a prostitute with curly hair and a big nose standing by a building wall, illuminated by the glare of streetlights. He considered her question briefly. "*He* wants a date," he replied helpfully, pointing to Gary, who was walking a few steps ahead.

The hooker stuck with Jim. She put her arm around him, real friendly, and they strolled along together.

"Let's just go over there," she said, pointing to a side street.

Jim pretended to be puzzled. "You want to date me over there?" he asked, loudly.

"Shhh!" said the woman. There were a couple of policemen nearby.

Jim decided to be a nice guy and not waste any more of her time. "Forget it," he said. "We're just going to fuck with you for twenty minutes."

"Really?" she said, misunderstanding.

"You'd better just go walk the streets."

"*Shhh!*"

"*Sweep* the streets," Jim said loudly, for the benefit of the cops. "*Sweep* the streets."

Not amused, the prostitute moved on. Jim and Gary turned the corner onto 42nd Street and headed east toward their hotel.

"Smoke."

It was a young black man in a wool cap.

"Smoke," he repeated.

Gary started to talk to him, and the drug dealer suddenly developed second thoughts. "You might be cops."

"Yeah!" Jim shouted. "I'm *the* cop!"

This drunken outburst removed any doubt the dealer had about Jim's status as a civilian, but he still didn't seem like a good prospect for business. The dealer fell in step beside Gary.

Gary chatted amiably with him as they walked along to the New York Helmsley, outside of which the dealer was joined by a colleague in a worn khaki jacket. Jim went inside and up to his room to sleep. Gary invited the two drug dealers in for a drink.

They sat at a table in the lobby bar, Gary and two young black men in shabby clothes, surrounded by gray-suited white business travelers. Nobody looked askance. The man in the wool cap, who said Gary could call him Joseph, ordered a Budweiser. The man in the khaki jacket ordered a Remy and Coke.

"Do you read the comics?" Gary asked them. He pulled out a Lin-Tex brochure promoting a new "Shoe" design. "You know the birds that live in the tree?"

Joseph looked at the picture. "Yeah," he said. "Are you the artist?"

"No," said Gary, "we license the rights. We take the characters and put them on T-shirts. It's a fun business."

Joseph looked almost interested, but the man in the khaki jacket didn't want to talk about birds in trees. He assumed Gary had invited him inside to conduct another kind of business. He had no way of knowing how much Gary loved to talk about Lin-Tex, how frequently he regaled taxi drivers, strangers in airports, and women at bars with unsolicited reports on the progress of the company. The dealer could not have imagined that his colleague had accosted the only wanderer through Times Square that night who, a little drunk and not ready for sleep, would invite two drug dealers into the New York Helmsley to have a fresh audience for T-shirt talk.

The dealer tried to seize control of the conversation. He offered Gary a special price on some excellent merchandise. He was wasting his breath.

"I'll send you a couple of shirts," Gary volunteered, sensing the dealers' disappointment. "Just give me your addresses."

The dealers looked at him.

"I guess you don't want to give me your names and addresses. Well, call me. Say that it's Joseph, and I'll send you a couple of large, extra-large, whatever."

He gave them his business card.


Gary didn't go into quite every detail of it with his guests in the bar, but business was good. December sales had finished at $575,000. January sales naturally dipped—they would be just over $250,000—but they were triple the sales of the January before. Jim had managed to pull enough cash out of Christmas receipts to repay the loan from his brother (the loan from North Central National Bank was still outstanding). The only troubling note was that Lin-Tex's inventory was high; Jim and Gary were sitting on $400,000 worth of T-shirts. If they'd had $200,000 in shirts and $200,000 in cash, everything would have been perfect.

Being short of cash was, by now, just business as usual, and it didn't deter Jim and Gary from pursuing a new venture. The morning after their Times Square ramble, they took a taxi through heavy wet snow to the Toy Center on lower Fifth Avenue, headquarters of the Toy Fair. They maneuvered their way through a lobby packed with toy manufacturers, retail buyers, trade journalists, a man in a Snoopy suit, and several costumed dwarves to an elevator that carried them to the fourth-floor showroom of R. Dakin & Company, the world's largest manufacturer of stuffed animals. The showroom shelves were filled with plush replicas of every beast that crawls or swims on the earth, from gorillas to lobsters. An entire section was devoted to Garfield, the comic-strip cat (whose T-shirt rights Lin-Tex did not own). There were twenty-four different stuffed Garfields—Garfield on a surfboard, Garfield pulling a rabbit out of a hat, Garfield wearing slippers made of stuffed Garfields, and the enormously popular Garfield with suction cups on his feet. Jim and Gary were gratified to see that the second-largest display devoted to a single personality belonged to Opus, the penguin from "Bloom County." Gary looked it over and remarked that he was thinking of introducing a line of T-shirts for stuffed Opuses.

That was not the project that had brought Jim and Gary to Dakin today, however. Lin-Tex wanted to do dolls. The Marines, who had enjoyed moderate success with their Skyler T-shirts, wanted to buy a Skyler doll. Mike Peters, creator of "Mother Goose & Grimm," Lin-Tex's second most popular strip, was eager for someone to market a doll of Grimm (a fat, yellow, bug-eyed dog). Jim and Gary, who saw the sales of their "Mother Goose & Grimm" T-shirts increasing from month to month, thought a Grimm doll was an idea whose time had come.

The Dakin showroom was mobbed with buyers when Jim and Gary sat down with Harry Nizamian, the company president. They had been pursuing him for weeks. On a visit to Dakin headquarters in San Francisco, they had discussed a Grimm doll deal with other executives (Nizamian had been on the road), but everything hinged on Nizamian's approval. He was a middle-aged man with curly hair and an embroidered yellow rose on the lapel of his suit. Buyers swirled around him, but Nizamian was calm. He focused his attention on Gary and Jim.

Gary started to talk. As usual, he covered his and Jim's biographies—"All we've ever done is sell T-shirts and fry hamburgers" ("Is that right?" said Nizamian)—and the current prosperity of their company. He said that Mike Peters's syndicate had granted Lin-Tex the Grimm doll rights. "They'll license us, and we'd like to do it with you. We've agreed that we'll put the money into Grimm, really because we want to start a long-term relationship with Dakin."

If Nizamian was flattered, he didn't say so. "What type of construction would the doll be?" he asked. "All textile? A plastic head?"

"All soft," said Gary.

"We'd like you to do the design research," Jim added.

"It must sit up?" Nizamian asked. "The doll must sit?"

Gary said yes.

Nizamian nodded. "Now who *is* Grimm?"

Gary showed him one of their "Mother Goose & Grimm" T-shirt designs. The yellow dog was standing over a pair of red shorts and two yellow shoes scattered on the floor near a mouse-hole. He was saying, "Burp."

"Okay," said Nizamian. "I see him all over. We'll probably have to use plastic to get the eyes."

Gary said Mike Peters's wife had made a mockup using Ping-Pong balls.

"We did that with Garfield when we started," Nizamian said. He looked at the picture of Grimm again. "They call him Burp?"

"No," said Gary. "He's just saying burp."

"He ate Mickey Mouse," Jim explained.

Nizamian nodded. "We can do it on a special-item basis. We'd need a firm order from you. But we'd pull some out, maybe fifty dozen, and test market it. If it goes, you could sublicense us."

Jim and Gary had to restrain themselves from kissing him. This was exactly what they wanted. If Dakin tested the Grimm doll, and it sold, Dakin could place it in fifty thousand retail outlets. The prospect of Dakin selling Grimm dolls everywhere and sending Lin-Tex Marketing a royalty for every one was a beautiful thing to consider.

# "We're Going to Put Embryos in Cameroon"

"**S**HHH!" SAID PETE. "We're in enemy territory."

A friend had just asked him about his still pending possible sale of Senepols to royal Saudi investors on Sri Lanka, but Pete didn't want to talk about it, not *here,* not on the veranda of an old St. Croix estate house where he stood with a drink in his hand looking out over a cow pasture at the Caribbean shimmering in the twilight, not while he was surrounded by a dozen other Senepol breeders.

It was by no means certain that one of his fellow breeders, who were gathered on the island for the annual meeting of the Virgin Islands Senepol Association, would attempt to cut in on Pete's Sri Lanka deal if they happened to catch wind of it. But why take a chance? The Senepol breeders cooperated completely in promoting the general fame and popularity of the Senepol, but when it came to the sale of individual Senepols, it was every breeder for himself.

Some of those lingering on the veranda, where a cool sea breeze rustled pleasantly through the heavy tropical air, had already made significant sales. Frank and John Niceley, the lanky ranching brothers from Mascot, Tennessee, from whom Pete had obtained *his* first Senepols, were pleased to report that they'd sold ninety-nine Senepols to Honduras, where they would be bred with Holstein dairy cattle. "They improve the udder characteristics when they're crossed with another breed," Frank Niceley said. "They provide firmness and good tit formation."

Two bland-looking young men named Owen and Bill who had recently begun marketing cattle for American Senepol Limited, the largest mainland breeder, were not shy about describing what they had achieved.

"We know how to sell," Owen said. "Bill has sold embryos to the Yucatan state government for five hundred pregnancies. I went to Africa in November—Nigeria, São Tomé, Cameroon. I met the president in São Tomé. We're going to put embryos in Cameroon."

Mario Gasperi, the host of the cocktail party, listened and smiled. With his wife Caroline, he was the second-largest Senepol breeder on St. Croix. He liked to hear Senepol success stories. The more the Senepol prospered in the world, the more his own herd, one of the foundations of the breed, would be worth.

"We have excellent prospects for a sale in Kenya," Owen said. "One private businessman there would buy more embryos than the entire breed could produce in six months—if we can lick bluetongue."

"It's a big problem," Mario said. Bluetongue, a virus that causes a disease in sheep, is often carried by cattle without affecting them; the importation of cattle that test positive for the virus is barred by many countries.

"It's called a disease but it isn't," Owen said.

"It's used as an excuse to keep foreign cattle out," Mario said.

Pete, who had spent a relaxing day looking at bulls and snorkeling with Becky, grew attentive. This bluetongue problem was news to him.

"Taiwan wants us to load up a hundred and ninety heifers on a seven-forty-seven," Frank Niceley said, "but they have to be bluetongue-free. They did get two thousand Santa Gertrudis from Texas, bluetongue-free."

"From Texas?" said Mario. "It's impossible. All Texas cattle carry bluetongue. Maybe they pulled some strings on the tests."

Pete's face darkened. He was still waiting for his own Senepol business breakthrough. No foreign governments were ordering hundreds of embryos or dispatching 747s to Hopes Creek Ranch. The initial promise of the responses to his ad in the *Wall Street*

*Journal* had so far come to nothing; no investment dollars had been received. Universal II looked dead. Sri Lanka was still hanging up in the air. The only deal that was definitely progressing was Pete's plan to send some cattle down to Guatemala. The last thing he needed was a bluetongue monkey wrench messing up his exportation.

It was weighing on his mind when Mario pulled him aside for some other troubling news. Owen and Bill, Mario said, had arrived on the island with a list of proposals from American Senepol Limited (ASL) to be considered by the association. If adopted, some of them would change the way the association was run; others might change the shape—literally—of Senepol cattle. If the proposals were rejected, well, Cecil Horne, the money man in American Senepol Limited, had already signaled that he might break off and start his own Senepol association.

Cecil Horne had not yet arrived on St. Croix, but his shadow preceded him. He was easily the richest man associated with Senepol cattle. Unlike the other breeders, he was a businessman first and a rancher second. "I doubt he pats his cows on the head and knows who every one of their great-grandmothers were," another breeder said. Horne's talk of splitting the association was not an idle threat; several cattle breeds were already represented by competing associations, their members having split over the merits of differing breed characteristics or the pedigrees of prominent bulls.

Pete didn't say anything about Horne's proposals. He would think hard before picking sides in what was shaping up as a political fight. He got another drink and looked out at the Senepols in the pasture. Mario had some good ones.

The next morning, waiting for the start of the tour of St. Croix Senepol herds that is the highlight of every annual meeting, Frank Niceley leaned against a fence at Mario's and reflected on the difficulties of breeding cattle. Frank was a conservative Republican from East Tennessee and something of a humorist; he enjoyed telling Pete that a Texan was a cross between a Tennessean and a Mexican. "Some people spend their whole life improving a cattle herd and end up with worse cattle than they started with," he said now. "The important traits aren't always things you can see. Performance is what matters, but performance averages don't mean anything. You can shoot a foot in front of a duck and then a foot behind a duck. On the average, you killed it, but you won't eat much duck."

These reflections by Niceley, who had once been but was no longer a partner with Cecil Horne in American Senepol Limited, were prompted by one of the proposals ASL had brought to the meeting: that, to publicize and promote the breed, the association start to run cattle shows for Senepols. Niceley was against it. Cattle shows handed out awards to animals based mostly on how they looked, not how efficiently they produced beef. The current trend in judging shows was to honor large animals, which Niceley thought encouraged cattlemen to do precisely the wrong thing. "Big cattle might have more meat per cow," he said, "but you'd probably do better raising a larger number of smaller cows. That doesn't sound very glamorous, but it appeals to people who've just about gone broke the other way."

Pete agreed. He liked some of the ASL proposals, such as moving association headquarters to the mainland and buying Senepol ads in beef cattle publications. But he hated the idea of cattle shows, and he was suspicious of another proposal for a classification system that would reward all Senepols, not just those in shows, that possessed "superior breed characteristics." Pete wanted to know what characteristics ASL had in mind. As far as he was concerned, a cow that produced a healthy calf once a year was a terrific Senepol, even if she was undersized or had a patch of white or black on her coat of Senepol red.

The tour of the herds began on Mario's spread and then moved to the rainy side of the island, where sharp-rising hills intercept drifting clouds. This was the domain of the Lawaetz family's Annaly Farm. In a cattle pen next to an abandoned sugar cane cutters' barracks, overgrown with vines and overrun with lizards, the breeders stopped to look at a group of sleek heifers. Dr. Nelson Pott, a veterinarian from Kentucky, was transfixed with admiration. "They sure put a fella's wishin' britches on," he declared.

"There's Cecil Horne," said Pete, gesturing toward a stocky, gray-haired man. Horne had just arrived from the airport. Pete looked him over respectfully. "I never met a rich man who wasn't mean and tough," he said.

Pete wanted to talk to Horne, and he caught up with him half an hour later at an Annaly Farm bull pen where a historic tableau assembled. The pen was bounded by a gently sloping pasture and a steeper slope that climbed into rain forest. Half a dozen handsome bulls trotted arrogantly around the pen, snorting and whinnying, the red tips of their penises extending from their heavy sheaths. A dozen men stood among them, representing the past, present, and future of the Senepol breed. Compared to these humans, the bulls had nothing to do with it.

The brothers Cedric and Henry Nelthropp were there. Nephews of Bromley Nelthropp, the Cruzan cattle visionary who singlehandedly created the Senepol, Cedric and Henry were in their sixties, tall men with weathered faces. They owned the third-largest Senepol herd on St. Croix, but it was an open secret that their ranching venture had passed its profitable days; they were selling their back pasture to a resort developer; they were looking for a buyer for their herd.

Old Frits E. Lawaetz was there. It was he who, in 1949, by persuading his then-employer to purchase the bulk of Bromley Nelthropp's herd, had guaranteed that the breed would survive. He tended it with care and, a few years later, gave it its name (previously, Senepols had been known as "Nelthropp cattle"). His sons Hans and Frits T. had long since taken over management of the Annaly herd, but Frits E., now eighty, was proud of what he had accomplished. Wearing a pith helmet that made his head look small, moving with a heavy limp (his right leg was amputated in a bout with cancer in the 1950s), he walked to the fence and looked into the pen, where his sons were showing the bulls to potential buyers.

The Niceley brothers were there. Pete was there. And Cecil Horne was there, standing in the pen wearing gray wool slacks and black wingtip shoes.

A few months before, veterinarians working with Horne had flown down to St. Croix carrying portable freezers, extracted two hundred embryos from island Senepols, and carried them north to Tennessee. There were at this time about 4400 Senepols in the world. Nearly three quarters of them still grazed on St. Croix, but an irreversible shift in the balance of power in the breed had begun. The island breeders had foreseen this years before. When they first decided to market Senepols to outsiders, they had debated whether to sell bulls only or to sell animals of both sexes. If they sold only bulls (as the King Ranch had done when it first developed the Santa Gertrudis breed), it would take those who bought them several years to develop their own near-pureblood Senepols (they could have half-bloods in one year, three-quarter-bloods in two years, and so on). If the Cruzans sold both sexes, the buyers could start breeding pureblood Senepols immediately—and compete with the islanders in selling them. The islanders would be at a disadvantage compared to mainland breeders when it came to selling to other mainland ranches; it would be a lot easier for new mainland buyers to buy locally than to traipse down to St. Croix and have to deal with quarantine requirements and the cost of airmailing cows.

The Cruzans decided to sell both males and females nonetheless. They took their money and they took their chances. "We had no choice," Hans Lawaetz said. "It doesn't do us any good to be sitting here with a herd of cattle, and no one is going to see it, and we have to sell them to the butcher."

The Cruzans took solace from the fact that mainland ranchers with money and connections could promote the Senepol in ways they could not; moreover, some new buyers would always prefer to buy from the breed's foundation herds, repository of the greatest genetic variety and some of the finest animals. (The islanders never sold their very best animals to Cecil Horne or anyone else; during tours of their farms they hid them in the hills.)

In the long run, it did not appear that St. Croix was destined to remain a cattle center no matter what the island breeders did. The Lawaetzes' animals had grazed for years on leased land around a nearby golf course (that had gained notoriety in 1972 when Cruzan black militants had murdered eight white golfers there); every morning young Frits would check the course and chase errant cattle off the greens. Now that same land was being divided into $100,000 lots for vacation and retirement homes. At Davis

Bay, just beyond the course, where an old Cruzan named Dan-Dan (who had given Hans Lawaetz rides to school in his oxcart in the 1940s) had once set up an improvised entrepreneurial barrier and charged tourists one dollar to use the beach, Rockresorts had just opened a $385-a-night luxury hotel. Hans had gone to work for the development company himself. "I knew I was going to lose the land," he said. "I figured I might as well join them."

The tenth annual meeting of the Virgin Islands Senepol Association of St. Croix convened the next day in a high-ceilinged conference room at the College of the Virgin Islands. The breeders began by reporting what was new with their Senepols. Pete went first. "Basically," he said, "we're trying to increase our cow herd. We're talking to a couple of different countries concerning exporting. We held an open house, and a TV crew came out and did a three-minute piece that went out on CBS's Southwest feed. We feel like it did us some good."

John Niceley said his Senepol yearlings had gained 1.7 pounds a day during the driest summer in Tennessee history. Dr. Nelson Pott said he hadn't sold many of his Senepols yet but he had high hopes. Mike Todd, a breeder from Kentucky, said he'd put a Senepol bull out with his commercial cows and every one got pregnant. Cecil Horne said, "We're still trying to expand our herd. We're putting a lot of emphasis on trying to create a market." Somewhere along the way, the discussion turned to cattle and horse-trading tricks, and old Frits Lawaetz volunteered that he'd once stuck pepper up a worn-out mare's ass so she'd act frisky and fetch a better price.

The keynote speaker was Don Vaniman, a wide-sideburned Montana rancher who, ten years before, when he was executive secretary of the American Simmental Association, had helped the Senepol Association get started. Vaniman was still bullish on the Senepol. "I have no doubt that it can replace the Brahman worldwide," he said. But he warned that its success was not guaranteed. "The Senepol is on the threshold of either becoming a great breed or just another breed that didn't make it."

Its fate, he said, would be determined by decisions the Senepol people were now facing. "Are we a family-type performance breed, or a rich man's exotic breed?" Would the breed be influenced by "those who are worried about functional efficiency or those who care about 'breed character'? Is it those who want to breed elephants or those who breed for reproductive performance and good working cattle?"

John Niceley underlined Vaniman's point with a post-speech question: "What do you think the effect of the show ring would be on this breed?"

"I'm anti-show ring," Vaniman declared. "It helps a few breeders." Heads turned toward Cecil Horne, who sat in the front row stroking his upper lip. "Judges are paid to see and not think," Vaniman said. Caroline Gasperi laughed approvingly. "Who needs a two-thousand-pound heifer?" Vaniman asked. Pete nodded. "The show ring has probably torn more breeds apart . . . the show people versus the performance people."

When the ASL proposals came up, the association decided not to decide. They were referred to the board of directors, which, meeting immediately after the general meeting, tabled them for consideration "in the near future." Pete asked Cecil Horne point-blank, "Will you divorce yourself from this association if they are not acted on?" Horne said he didn't want to but he might.

The group did act on one matter. A consensus had developed, even among the islanders, that the name "Virgin Islands Senepol Association of St. Croix" was a little provincial for a group representing a breed that everybody hoped would sweep the world. The board of directors had recommended switching to "North American Senepol Association" or "International Senepol Association." Hans Lawaetz, who was chairing the meeting, favored the former himself, provided that St. Croix was generally considered to be part of North America. He wasn't sure if that was the case, and no one else in the room was either. After some discussion, the group voted to rename itself the "American International Senepol Association" (with the subtext, added at old Frits Lawaetz's insistence, "Founded in St. Croix, U.S. Virgin Islands"). Pete voted against the new name. Just as he'd once rejected "World" as too limited a name for his own company, he now thought "American" was too restrictive; it didn't sound right for a breed that was going to be sold in, say, Sri Lanka.

Pete and Becky had one more day on St. Croix, and their plan was to spend it sailing. Young Frits Lawaetz had arranged for half a dozen of the Senepol people to go out on a thirty-eight-foot trimaran owned and sailed by Walt Frazier, a slim, self-possessed black man who from 1967 to 1979 was one of the finest players in the National Basketball Association. A member of the 1970 "dream team" world champion New York Knicks, Frazier, known by the nickname "Clyde," distinguished himself on the court by the intelligence and seemingly effortless grace of his game and, off the court, by his luxurious wardrobe, pink Cadillac Eldorado (the "Clydemobile"), and supremely cool personal style. When Frits told Pete they were going sailing with his friend Clyde, it never occurred to Pete, a serious sports fan, that Frits could mean *that* Clyde. By the time the Senepol party boarded the trimaran in a morning drizzle, Pete had learned whose boat it was; he was amazed and impressed.

Frits, a quiet man (but not always so; in his younger days he had gained renown for riding his horse into bars), neglected to introduce his guests to their host, and the moment never seemed right for them to introduce themselves. Frazier managed the interesting feat of ignoring them without being impolite. He smiled back when smiled at, but he didn't have much to say, not even when, tacking back and forth near the beach a couple of miles from where they had started, his steering mechanism failed and the boat crunched aground on a bed of coral. Frazier pulled down the sail, and Pete and Frits jumped into the water to push the boat free. Frits wore sneakers; the spiny coral jammed into Pete's bare feet.

He leaned hard against the boat despite the pain, but he and Frits, soon joined in the water by the other male guests, were hampered by a lack of direction from Frazier, who had occasionally displayed a passive streak even as a basketball star. Pete, a former member of a College Station sailing club, had some ideas about what should be done, but he didn't presume to take charge. He just pushed to no avail as the boat gradually washed up on the beach.

For the next few hours, a variety of rescue attempts were undertaken. Frazier summoned the Coast Guard auxiliary on his radio, and a boat appeared crewed by fat men in orange life vests. They carried a tow rope to the trimaran in a dinghy, and Frazier tied it on. The rescue ship moved forward, and the rope snapped almost immediately. The auxiliarymen announced that they were low on fuel and motored away, never to return.

The male members of a Cruzan family that appeared to be living in tents on the beach waded into the water and started pushing. So did a party of tourists on a picnic. A vacationing northern business executive came down from his hillside condo and started issuing unsolicited instructions. There was a great deal of pushing and winching, much of it involving mutually canceling forces. Pete kept pushing long after it became clear that the boat was hopelessly stuck. He knew it was hopeless, but he would not be the first to quit.

The trimaran was freed at last by a renewed bout of pushing and a tow from a passing motorboat called *The Stink Pot,* which proceeded to tow the damaged sailboat to a marina for repairs. The Senepol party, left behind on the beach, watched it go. Now that there was no more work to be done, Pete hoisted a gallon jug of rum punch salvaged from the boat and swigged deeply. "That was the least organized rescue attempt I ever took part in," he said, "and that includes stuck cars, stuck trucks, stuck cows. . . ." He drank again and decided things could have been worse. "I killed a couple of cows trying to rescue them, and we all lived here."

"Clyde ought to sell that thing and buy a motorboat," Frits said.

"He ought to buy a truck," Pete declared. He had another drink. He could see it clearly:

" 'The Walt Frazier line of sailboats! Four-wheel drive!' "

# "It's a Stupid Item But It Sells Out Everywhere"

**H**AVE YOU SEEN 'Farts Around the World'?" asked Jim. "It's a T-shirt line."

Scott Robinson said he hadn't. He'd seen the Canned Fart, and the Fart Bear, and Phineas Fart, and, of course, Fart: The Game, his own fart product, which he was displaying in his booth at the semi-annual New York International Gift Fair, a major trade show where Jim and Gary had stopped by for a visit.

Robinson, cheerful and boyish-looking, was a ten-year veteran of the gift industry. As a young stockbroker he'd had a dream, the same dream that motivated thousands of other would-be gift industry entrepreneurs: to be independent, to be creative, to come up with a clever idea and make a lot of money. Most such dreamers never act, but Robinson had translated his dream into reality by bringing to market Dirty Words, a game in which players scored points by rolling dice with words printed on them and forming sentences like "You tickle my deep moist loins." The game was a hit. Robinson followed it up with Deluxe Dirty Words and a variant called Juicy Words ("You taste my hot wet melon"). Then Spencer Gifts, a national gift-store chain where the Dirty Words line was a big seller, approached Robinson and his partner with a request: "Trivia is big now. Sex is always big. Can you do something with sex and trivia?"

Indeed they could. They produced a Trivial Pursuit imitator called Sexual Trivia, and it, too, was a success (at least as a game;

when Jim and Gary licensed the rights for a line of Sexual Trivia T-shirts, it was a spectacular flop—just one more inexplicable mystery of the vagaries of popular taste). Robinson's company grew, and he and his partner branched out into non-risqué games, importing a line of chess sets, dartboards, dominoes, and similar items from Taiwan. The display in the booth where Jim and Gary stopped to see Robinson featured one of his most successful new products—a miniature pool table that unfolded from a briefcase. "We've sold fifteen thousand since last Father's Day," he said. "We found it in Taiwan and were the first ones to import it." He pointed to a mockup of another unfolding briefcase. "That's going to be an air-hockey table, and we're going to do a miniature golf course in a briefcase."

But Robinson never forgot where he came from. His display included a board game called Lifestyles of the Poor and Disgusting and a drinking game called Party 'Til You Puke. "The only thing we can't do are drug games," he said. "It's real touchy stuff. No store will buy them except for a few little head shops. I had a guy submit a great game called Trafficking. It had one of the most beautiful boxes I've ever seen, and packaging is everything for a party game. It doesn't matter what's in the box. The game was okay, too. But I couldn't touch it."

The market had no such sensitivity about farting. On the contrary, the origin of Fart: The Game had been another call from Spencer Gifts, which had noted the growing popularity of flatulence-related novelty items. "The fart category is huge," they told Robinson. "Can you come up with a game?" He devised Fart: The Game himself. It called upon players to fart on demand and included a game board with penalty and bonus squares, e.g., "Farted on a terrorist. He fainted and you saved the airplane. You get five gas coupons."

"We've sold thirty-five thousand since last fall," Robinson said.

Jim looked it over and just shook his head.


Compared to many of his colleagues in the gift industry, Jim was Thomas Edison. Not that comic-strip T-shirts were unique or even particularly ingenious. But they were *useful.* You can wear a T-shirt.

By contrast, most of the items marketed through the multi-billion-dollar American gift industry—ceramic kittens, say, or the legendary Pet Rock—are not very functional. In fact, to a significant degree the gift industry is *defined* by the uselessness of its wares.

The gift industry operates through a series of national and regional trade shows and hundreds of independent sales representatives, each of whom sells the products of many different manufacturers in a specified territory on a commission basis. This structure is similar to that of several other industries that operate in parallel, including the housewares industry, the toy industry, the gourmet foods industry, and the stationery industry. The decision where to market a given product is usually fairly straightforward: hot mitts are housewares, notepads are stationery. The gift industry includes many products that are also marketed elsewhere, including hot mitts (especially those that are shaped like crocodiles or Marilyn Monroe) and notepads (especially those that bear headings like "In the event of nuclear war, disregard this message"), but its *raison d'être* is products that fit nowhere else. If an item isn't a houseware or a toy or a tool or useful in an office, and you can't wear it or eat it—if it has no discernible function of any kind—it is a gift.

And so the endless aisles of New York City's Javits Convention Center, where Jim and Gary strolled for an afternoon among 2200 exhibit booths displaying the wares of tens of thousands of manufacturers to 45,000 visiting retail buyers, were crammed with ceramic ducklings, seashell mobiles, wind chimes, limited-edition statuettes of Kris Kringle, plaster cats, and decorative wine bottle recorkers.

Those were among the traditional wares. Novelty products on display included mock urine specimens, inflatable Richard Nixons, and lawn signs (complete with stakes) with the message "The Divorce Is Final!"

Jim and Gary had arrived in New York directly from Los Angeles, where Lin-Tex had just participated in its second MAGIC

apparel show. Lin-Tex was still a very small player in the apparel
industry, however. The bulk of its sales were made through gift
industry channels.

So Jim and Gary roamed the aisles, looking at what was new
and greeting old friends. After Scott Robinson, they stopped to say
hi to Wood Huntley. Years before, Huntley had followed *his* entrepreneurial dream out of a promising career as a lawyer (he was
part of the defense team at Maurice Stans's Watergate trial) to
produce Singin' Sam's Shower Songs, waterproof lyric cards for
singing in the shower. He sold fifty thousand sets. Unfortunately,
he had produced eighty thousand. Huntley ultimately found success with Cleans & Dirties, paired dishwasher magnets used to
inform all the members of a household of the status of the contents
of its dishwasher. The success of Cleans & Dirties had inevitably
provoked a mob of "knockoff artists," gift industry cutthroats who
produce low-cost imitations of any successful product. Huntley
had moved on to a wider line of refrigerator magnets and decorative
plastic boxes, and he was doing fine.

Jim and Gary found him in the booth of a New York rep named
Kenny Bookbinder, who had once been approached by an entre-
preneur from Normal, Illinois, who was producing small busts
sculpted of dried manure. "He called the product Shithead," Bookbinder said. "He was very surprised when I turned it down." (Another New York rep took it on.) Strong-selling items in
Bookbinder's booth included Betty Boop pens, the world's smallest
wooden jigsaw puzzle (a 2¼ inch by 2½ inch puzzle of the Statue
of Liberty with ninety-nine pieces), and the 15% Tip Table, a
wallet-sized plastic card listing the appropriate 15 percent tips for
restaurant bills from one to one hundred dollars. "It's a stupid
item," Bookbinder said, "but it sells out everywhere."

Jim and Gary moved on to their final stop of the afternoon—
the booth of New World Sales, their own New York rep. Like all
manufacturers, they relied on commissioned sales reps to sell
their products. All reps, including New World Sales, handled the
products of more than one manufacturer. All manufacturers, including Jim and Gary, tended to believe that their reps put too
much effort into selling the goods of other manufacturers and not
enough effort into selling theirs. Jim and Gary had come to New

York to see what their rep was doing—and to let him see them seeing him.

The New World booth had three Lin-Tex T-shirts mounted on its walls, two with Opus the penguin and the strong-selling "Shoe" design, "I'll have what the gentleman on the floor is having." The Lin-Tex shirts were surrounded by shirts from other companies. There was "Big Fred Kahuna" (Fred Flintstone on a surfboard), a baby-sized T-shirt with the legend "Caution—I Brake for Nipples," and a hot new Buckwheat design called "Yupwheat," which depicted Buckwheat as the BMW-owning head of a yuppie family. There was also a "Fitnessaurus" shirt with a picture of a dinosaur lifting weights. For the past few seasons, dinosaurs had been an extremely popular design motif on all kinds of giftware. The present show still displayed dinosaur sponges, cocktail napkins, toys, and inflatable rafts. But the dinosaur as a big-selling gift item was now generally considered to be on the verge of extinction, and exhibitors and retailers throughout the hall were wondering what would be next. (Some were betting their businesses on their guesses.) "A lot of people say ants are the next dinosaurs," Wood Huntley reported. Others guessed bunnies, or spaceships, or Marilyn Monroe.

Jim thought it should be anything licensed by Lin-Tex. He thought New World Sales, at least, should have had more than three Lin-Tex designs on the wall, and he muttered as much to Gary, who ignored him and turned smiling to a young salesman working the booth. "How's the show been?" Gary asked.

"Pretty decent," the salesman replied. "We're doing very well with your stuff. The Hagar stuff is selling, and Pavlov."

This was a pleasant surprise, sort of. Hagar, the comic-strip Viking, and Pavlov, a playful dog whose strip ran in a handful of papers, were soft spots in the Lin-Tex line.

"What about 'Mother Goose and Grimm'?" asked Jim.

"Sleazy is selling," said the salesman, referring to the design in which Snow White is flashed by a dwarf of that name. The owner of New World Sales, a thirtyish man with a beard and modish sweater, finished writing up an order and walked over to Jim and Gary. He wanted to talk about "Bloom County," the heart of their line.

"Do a Deathtöngue shirt," he said. "That's going to be big. A lot of people are asking about it."

Deathtöngue was a parody heavy-metal rock band that was appearing regularly in the "Bloom County" strip. Lead singer Bill the Cat bit the heads off roadies between songs like "Pimples from Hell," "Leper Lover," and "Let's Run Over Lionel Richie with a Tank."

Jim assured the rep that a Deathtöngue shirt was in the works.

The rep wanted more. "Is anybody doing 'Bloom County' calendars?"

Sorrowfully, Gary said no. He and Jim knew they could sell a carload if cartoonist Berke Breathed would authorize them, but Breathed, still resisting overcommercialization, had drawn the line at T-shirts and the Opus doll.

"How many of *these* could you sell?" asked Gary. He raised his wrist to show off a prototype Bill the Cat watch he and Jim were hoping Breathed would authorize.

"They'd be good," said the rep.

A gift-shop owner leaned into the booth and interrupted. "What's new?" he asked.

"New Buckwheat designs," said the rep.

"Hey!" said Jim. "New Bill the Cat!"

He and Gary walked off down the aisle, their mission accomplished; they had put in their appearance. The booths they passed by were crowded with hundreds of products, but one caught Jim's eye. It happened to be a representative of the trend that many in the gift industry considered a frontrunner to be the next dinosaur.

It was a cow.

"From Fashion to Furniture, Bovines Boom" was the headline over the *New York Times* account of the gift show. The article cited the cow emblem of Ben & Jerry's ice cream, a Lord & Taylor sweater adorned with a Holstein, a line of cow clothes from Fiorucci, the popular cow cartoons in "The Far Side," and a multitude of cow tchotchkes—place mats, potholders, pillows, bookends—that had surfaced at the gift show.

"The ubiquity of the cow in the gift business may be a recognition of its increasing presence in art, fashion, interior design, cartoons and dinnerware," the *Times* reported. ". . . The cow is an icon deeply rooted in history. It has been the subject of Greek myth and religious worship, of elegant verse and classic paintings."

The item that caught Jim's eye was Roly Poly the Friendly Calf, a mechanical animal that walked and did flips.

"I've got one of these," Jim said enthusiastically. "It scares the shit out of the dog."

# "The Best Cow in the Show"

**F**OR MOST OF TWO WEEKS, Pete sat in his booth at the world's largest cattle trade show, the Houston Livestock Show and Rodeo. Pete's booth was at the edge of the cavernous Astrohall in an area set aside for exotic breeds. His display consisted of a 2000-pound Senepol bull, two heifers, and a cow with her calf, all of them tied to a metal rail. Pete had put up a sign that said: "Senepol—The Cattleman's Edge."

Across the aisle was a booth with the sign: "Charbray—The Cowman's Breed." The next booth down was "Bralers—America's Beef Breed."

Around the corner, there were other booths with other breeds, most of them European breeds newly introduced to the United States or "synthetic" breeds (like the Charbray and Braler) created by crossing European breeds with Brahmans, the testy but hardy breed of Indian origin that was a staple of hot-weather ranching all over the world.

All of the booths had animals on display, many of them as sleek as Pete's Senepols. They had slogans, too. And everybody was passing out literature explaining why their breed was just the thing to make life easier and more profitable for commercial cattlemen, who were passing through the hall by the thousand:

"Charbray bulls are fertile, they range well and will add height and length to old conventional-type cattle."

"Bralers display superior calving ease. The breed's typically smaller calf head size and a more streamlined shoulder profile facilitate calving."

"Few breeds can match the average retirement age of Red Brangus."

"The docility of the Normande cow is well known. Many Americans who served in France in World War II remember seeing Normande cows being milked by women in open pasture."

And so on.

Pete's brochure boosted Senepols for their hornlessness, their heat tolerance, their insect resistance, their sunny disposition, their fertility, and other virtues. It included a price list (semen was $20 a unit; frozen embryos were $500; pregnant cows were $2500— or $2300 in quantities of ten or more). Finally, because he was up to date, Pete had put up a sign saying Senepols had the "lean and tender beef consumers prefer."

The cattle industry had taken several years to respond to consumers' concern about fatty beef, possibly because it was so unexpected after at least six thousand years of consumer preference *for* fatty meat. When Abel sacrificed sheep to God, the Bible reports, he offered up "the fat thereof," and God was pleased. In modern times, the association of fat with taste and tenderness was institutionalized in the American beef-grading system—prime beef has the most internal fat. When the Houston Livestock Show started in the 1930s, it was called the Houston Fat Stock Show.

Now, suddenly, fat was taboo. The beef industry banished old advertisements that pictured inch-thick steaks topped with pats of butter and had just launched a new ad campaign featuring actress Cybill Shepherd posing sexily and wondering if people "have a primal, instinctive craving for . . . something hot and juicy and so utterly simple you can eat it with your hands"—like hamburgers.

The Shepherd ads were a topic of conversation at the livestock show. An article in a women's magazine on beauty secrets of the stars had just quoted the highly paid actress/endorser as saying, "I've cut down on fatty foods and am trying to stay away from red meat." Mortified, Shepherd insisted those words had never passed her lips (the magazine had obtained them from her publicist). But

Pete, among others, was not assuaged. "For a million bucks," he said, "she should walk around with a hamburger in her mouth all the time."

Despite the Shepherd flap, the ad campaign appeared to be succeeding, and the cattle business (which had always been cyclical even in the absence of health concerns) was beginning to enter a profitable phase. But the hard years were so fresh that it was a difficult time to be peddling something new. Pete was additionally handicapped by the fact that most ranchers had still never heard of the Senepol, which was, by any standard, a very minor breed. (The total world population of Senepols was smaller than many individual Texas herds of other breeds.) On first seeing it, cattlemen often assumed that the Senepol was some kind of Brahman cross. Most new breeds that had caught on in Texas *were* Brahman crosses; it was considered important to have some "ear" (Brahmans have enormous ears) in any hot-weather breed. The Senepol had no Brahman in it. It was an *alternative* to the Brahman. And Pete had to explain that, to browsers stopping by the booth, over and over and over again.


Keith was a little overwhelmed by Houston. The city had seen more prosperous days—the collapse of oil prices had cut off the local economy at the knees and "Move in for $1" signs were posted in front of apartment complexes all over town—but it was still a lot of city for someone accustomed to country life. "At home," Keith reflected as he drove to the Astrohall one morning, "everybody knows *something* about you. If I go in a store, they know, 'Oh yeah, that's the guy who works south of town.' All those rooms. . . . " He gestured at high-rise office buildings by the side of the expressway. "There're probably five people in each one of them I'll never know anything about." He drove by a police car parked on the shoulder. "Houston has *five thousand* police officers," he marveled. "A whole city of police officers!"

When Keith got to the Astrohall, Pete was off at a meeting about his Sri Lanka deal. A burly A&M student named Barry was working the booth. He had just finished washing the cattle. Now he was using a rake to scoop manure out of the wood shavings the Senepols were standing on. The task was complicated by the fact that the Senepol calf had diarrhea. Barry had a bottle of Kaopectate for it.

Keith was taking Sine-Aid (the dust in the Astrohall was stirring up an allergy). He took a walk to the show ring, where three hundred people were sitting in bleachers watching gray Brahman bulls being judged. The bulls stood still in the ring, each accompanied by a handler with a long "show stick" that resembled a backscratcher. The handlers used the sticks to prod the bulls' feet, to get them to stand in the most handsome position. They poked the large bunched muscles in the bulls' humps, to get them to lower their backs. They gently stroked the bulls' stomachs, to relax them. The judges made their choices, citing the show-ring criteria Pete hoped would never be inflicted on the Senepol: "This bull is especially straight and correct in his lines. . . . That bull is not as stretchy as the bulls I placed above him."

There were money people in the stands, big-time Brahman breeders with thousands of acres and private planes and landing strips behind the house. They watched the judging attentively. The winning owner would receive a silver tea service, presented by the All-American National Junior Brahman Queen, a teenager in cowboy boots and a rhinestone tiara. The owner and the bull and the queen would have their picture taken together. And there were higher stakes involved—money and prestige.

Looking at these people made Keith annoyed. "They turn up their nose at the Senepol," he complained, "and say, 'Just another exotic.' They forget their own background. Eighty years ago the Brahman faced the same opposition. They should be looking at something new. If we could just get one or two of them to switch. . . . "

Keith spotted someone he knew, a short, pudgy, bearded rancher in a fine leather jacket. "How did the sale go?" Keith asked him. "Not bad," the rancher said, "considering the times."

The rancher did not seem interested in lingering with Keith. He turned his attention back to the show. He was Fernando Somoza, nephew of the deposed and assassinated Nicaraguan dictator. He was married to the daughter of a prosperous Texas rancher, now deceased, for whom Keith had once worked. Keith used to see him on the ranch. He always carried a machine gun.

"It would be great if we could get Fernando interested," Keith told Pete back at the booth. "He has a lot of influence in Central America."

Pete nodded. His sales trip to Guatemala was coming up.

"Sin-a-Pool?" An old rancher in overalls was standing in front of the Senepol booth, looking at the bull. "What are these?" he asked. "They've got some Brahma in them. I can see that."

"No," Keith said.

"Santa Gertrudis," said the old man's son.

Keith shook his head. "It's Red Poll and N'Dama. It's not considered a crossbreed. It's been breeding true for sixty years, in the Virgin Islands."

"Pretty," said the old man, and he walked away.


Keith and Pete taped up flyers around the hall announcing a Senepol seminar, which convened late one afternoon in a large bare room with a concrete floor. Pete had a keg of beer brought in, and the event began with a cocktail hour. The turnout was sparse—fourteen people, and seven were Pete's friends or relatives—but Pete was excited, because one of those in attendance was Cas Maree.

Maree, a well-dressed and debonair man, was a professor of animal science at the University of Pretoria, South Africa. He was an internationally known cattle authority. He had influence over the cattle industry in South Africa and some of its neighboring countries. And he was very impressed with the Senepol.

Maree had come to Houston to speak at the International Stockmen's School that preceded the livestock show, and he had met Frank Niceley and young Frits Lawaetz there. They had told him about the Senepol and led him to Pete's booth, where he looked over the animals and announced to Pete, "I've walked all through this place, and this cow is the best cow in the show."

Pete fell in love with the man.

His ardor increased as Maree commenced to bring potential customers to the booth. He brought a friend who was a leading breeder of Texas Longhorns; the Longhorn man said he wanted to try a Senepol bull on his cows. Maree showed up next with a young white Zimbabwean who said he wanted to buy fifty straws of semen (but had to check with his father-in-law first). Maree himself told Pete that he would suggest to South African agriculture authorities that they buy some Senepol semen or embryos and try the breed out. During the beer cocktail hour preceding the seminar, he told Pete the Senepol had sales potential elsewhere in Africa as well. "I'll be talking to people in Swaziland as soon as I get back. They have access to money that we do not, big money, from Canada, the EEC, the Nordic countries. . . ."

Pete calmed himself and delivered his talk, which was illustrated by slides of Senepol bulls. "As you can see," he said, "they have a nice tight sheath. Some bulls have a problem with their sheaths dragging in the cactus. . . ."

Two days later, Maree was guest speaker in a beef cattle class at Texas A&M and Pete drove up from the show to hear him. Maree showed the class some slides of Senepols. "I just saw Senepol cattle for the first time in my life last week," he said, "and I was so impressed. . . . I have a feeling that someday all cattle will look like this."

"We think so much alike," Pete said to Maree during the drive back to Houston. Maree was his passenger. "I always thought smaller and medium-sized cows were more reproductively successful," Pete said.

Maree nodded in agreement.

Pete said he was planning a sales trip to Africa in the fall.

Maree said he had a friend in Botswana Pete ought to see.

Pete asked about the situation in South Africa. "According to the papers," he said, "South Africa is a nonstop riot. But I don't believe anything I read in the papers."

Maree assured him the situation was generally calm. His campus had never been affected by any kind of riot, he said, nor had the gas station he owned on the side.

Pete nodded thoughtfully. He asked Maree about getting travel documents to visit South Africa. Maree asked Pete if he could help him find instructional books on clawhammer banjo technique for his son. They were hard to find in Pretoria.

Back at the booth, in between fielding inquiries about what

kind of Brahman cross the Senepol was, Pete started calling music stores. "Do you have any claw banjo lessons?" he asked.

He continued his quest the next morning on a visit to the office of his sister Mollie, a Houston accountant. He and Mollie got out the phone book and made half a dozen calls.

"Do you have any hammerclaw books?" Pete asked on one line.

Mollie was on another phone. "I'm looking for bearclaw material," she said.

Pete found a store that had it. He drove over and bought three books and gave them to Maree a few hours later, when Maree stopped by the booth to say goodbye. "You did us a lot of good," Pete said.

"Keep it up," said Maree. "I wish you success."

He left Pete feeling jubilant. Pete stepped out in front of the booth, as if he were a visitor, and declared: "These are the most beautiful cows I've ever seen! I have ten thousand Charbray and I'm going to get rid of every one."

He was still happy at dinner in a Mexican restaurant with Becky and a friend. He ate half a dozen enchiladas and drank several Margaritas and said he might name the cow he'd brought to Houston "Cas Maree."

The check came and Pete looked it over. "Do you need help with the tip?" Becky asked, reaching into her purse. "I got this in a bookstore in College Station." She pulled out a small plastic card—a 15% Tip Table.

# "**B**ut Our Sales Are Great"

**J**IM HAD A BAD DREAM.
A baby was floating face down in a swimming pool. "That's my son," Jim said, in the dream.

Jim was having money troubles. For seven years, he had received $2500 every month from the sale of his Wendy's restaurants to Charlie Ogle. The payments had continued even after Ogle, a race-car enthusiast, was killed in a crash at the Daytona Speedway. But now the people administering Ogle's estate had suddenly cut Jim off, for no reason he could discern except that they were "fucking scumbag lawyers." Jim continued to draw $1500 a week as a salary from Lin-Tex, but the missing Ogle payments made a difference in what he could afford. He had to explain this several times to Frances, who liked to take her girlfriends out to lunch and pick up the tab. Jim sat in his office one afternoon looking at a $2000 American Express bill and talking to Frances on the phone. "On this card," he explained in a low, clear, deliberate voice, "I have to pay this all now." Frances said something. Jim spoke again, very slowly: "Frances, we don't physically have the money."

As usual, the company was short of cash. Post-Christmas sales were up sharply from the year before, but so were expenses. The "Shoe" Marine shirts were still selling at Parris Island, and Gary had gotten them into four other Marine bases on the East Coast, but the military business was not yet the bonanza Jim and Gary had foreseen. Their travel agency was losing money. There was no money to pay R. Dakin & Company to manufacture a Grimm doll.

A guy with whom Jim and Gary played golf expressed interest in investing in Lin-Tex. Jim thought he was a good prospect; he had a three-million-dollar house—paid for. Thinking they might get $200,000 for 10 percent of the company, Jim and Gary opened the books to him. "Why would I want to buy into this deal?" the man asked after he'd seen them. "You don't have anything on your asset sheet."

"We know," Jim said. "But our sales are great."

The man shook his head. "If I did this, I'd worry all the time," he said. "It would ruin my golf game."

# "Islamic Slaughter? Is That a Problem?"

THERE WAS NO WORD FROM Cas Maree, but Pete and Becky did hear from Walt Frazier, who had been elected to the Basketball Hall of Fame twelve days after the St. Croix sailboat fiasco. Pete and Becky dropped him a note and enclosed some snapshots of what Pete referred to as "the shipwreck." Frazier called the ranch to thank them.

Meanwhile, Pete was absorbed in a series of meetings with Ravi Vora about the cattle deal for Sri Lanka, where the bloody civil war was getting worse (Becky was clipping articles about ambushes and massacres). Vora assured Pete that the fighting was not where the Senepols were going to go. He told Pete that the Saudi royal family was out of the deal and some private Sri Lankans were in. He negotiated with Pete for a 10 percent commission on any sales Pete made to the island. Pete waited for word on his planning trip there, which the Sri Lankans were supposed to pay for. He'd once figured to go in December; now April looked like a good bet. He expected to hear any day.

Meanwhile, he learned from Vora of an opportunity to export beef and butter to Egypt. The quantities required were enormous—1.1 million pounds of beef and 1000 tons of butter, every month—but Pete was not fazed. He and Keith spent hours on the phone in the office in the barn calling butter producers and meat packers. "I'm looking to get some beef, with five percent maximum fat, about 3400 head a month," Keith said one afternoon in a call to a Palestine, Texas, packer. "I want to know if we could work something out with you all . . . 1.1 million pounds a month . . . in quarters. . . . It's going to Egypt. . . . I think that's no problem." He cradled the phone on his shoulder and called over to Pete: "Islamic slaughter? Is that a problem?"

"No," said Pete.

"No," said Keith.

Pete was looking to make two or three cents a pound on 1.1 million pounds of beef a month, but he never could find beef cheap enough. ("He says people call all the time wanting massive quantities of meat for some low price," Keith reported after his talk with the Palestine packer. "He talks to them, then they disappear.") The butter deal, on the other hand, continued to look promising. Pete would buy part of the load from a butter maker at the world price. Then the government would chip in some butter for free from its stockpile.

Meanwhile, Pete was trying to raise $500,000 to take over a dairy he had been offered and turn it into a feed lot. He sent letters to the respondents to his *Wall Street Journal* ad; they hadn't come through with any money for Senepol embryos, but Pete thought they might be interested in this.

He still needed some cash flow. He had just bought Hopes Creek Ranch from his father-in-law, which mainly involved taking over Billie's land payments. Assuming he could keep them up, Pete had some new ideas for developing the back section, which he didn't need for cattle. He was thinking of building an old-age home there, or a summer camp, or a golf course.

# The First-Ever Sometimes-Annual Comic Cotillion and Rodeo

ITH CASH FLOW TIGHT, Jim and Gary did what came naturally —they threw a $25,000 party. The "First-Ever Sometimes-Annual Comic Cotillion and Rodeo" they called it, and they invited all their cartoonists and a smattering of sales and syndicate people to a gala weekend in Austin. While they were at it, and since they were having company, they expanded and remodeled the Lin-Tex offices.

The cartoonists, most of whom worked at home alone, were pleased to be invited out, and a *Who's Who* of the funny pages descended on the Austin hotel where Lin-Tex had booked a bloc of rooms: Mell Lazarus ("Momma" and "Miss Peach"), Johnny Hart ("B.C." and "The Wizard of Id"), Mike Peters ("Mother Goose & Grimm"), Jeff MacNelly ("Shoe"), Jerry Van Amerongen ("The Neighborhood"), Bill Rechin and Don Wilder ("Crock" and "Out of Bounds"), Michael Fry ("Cheeverwood"), Art and Chip Sansom ("Born Loser"), Sam Hurt ("Eyebeam"), and Bob Thaves ("Frank and Ernest"). (Berke "Bloom County" Breathed was cruising off Florida on his yacht, *Penguin Lust,* and did not show up; he generally tended to avoid gatherings of cartoonists.) In the generously stocked hospitality suite and lounging by the pool ("Is this what the Old Cartoonists' Home will look like?" Van Amerongen wondered), the cartoonists renewed old friendships and talked shop. Van Amerongen complained that his original artwork came back from his syndicate with coffee stains. Don Wilder said that *his* syndicate had liked "Fonda" as the name of a new "Crock" character until he announced that her last name would be "Peters." Johnny Hart's business manager mentioned that Hart sometimes sent in "Wizard of Id" strips "with the king's dick hanging out," to keep the syndicate editors entertained. Mike Peters said he'd had trouble with his "Sleazy" gag in "Mother Goose & Grimm": "You can't flash Snow White in a family newspaper." His usual strategy when submitting a risqué strip, he said, was to accompany it with an inoffensive strip so editors would have a choice—and make sure that the inoffensive strip had no humor whatsoever.

Bob Thaves, a white-haired comic-page veteran, said he'd worked overtime on "Frank and Ernest" to get a few days ahead of his deadlines so he could come to the party. But being ahead made him nervous: "Virgil Partch . . . who drew 'Big George' . . . his eyesight started to go, so he worked like crazy and got five years ahead. Then he was in a car crash, and he and his wife were killed. I think there's a lesson in that."

And the cartoonists talked about their syndicates, with which they maintained uneasy alliances. Traditionally, syndicates (which distribute comic strips to newspapers, license the rights for commercial uses—including T-shirts—and share the proceeds with the cartoonists) required new cartoonists to sign over ownership of their strips as a condition of being taken on. For hungry newcomers, this was an unhappy choice: give away their strip or draw it solely for their own amusement. Some of the cartoonists gathered in Austin had managed to retain ownership of their strips, and some had not. But all had noted with interest the recent launch of a new syndicate, Creators, which did not even attempt to take ownership. Creators had announced its arrival with ads in the cartoon trade press picturing a broken ball and chain. In interviews, the syndicate's founder compared himself to Lincoln freeing the slaves. A representative of Creators had shown up in Austin for the Comic Cotillion. Johnny Hart had already moved "B.C." to the new syndicate.

This was an area in which Jim and Gary did not wish to get involved. They valued and enjoyed good relations with the cartoonists, but they relied on good relations with the syndicates. Their

T-shirt licensing agreements were signed with the syndicates, not the cartoonists. (Generally, the syndicates received an 8 percent royalty on Lin-Tex's sales and split it with the cartoonists.) It was syndicate executives who could give them a crack at new properties and syndicate executives who they could rely on to be businesslike. Cartoonists could be a little unpredictable.

But Jim loved them. He'd always enjoyed reading comic strips, and now it was his job. When he spotted one he liked, he dispatched Gary to try to sign it up. "Basically," he said in a welcoming talk to the cartoonists, "I come in, I read the comics, I read the rest of the paper, watch a little bit of 'Leave It To Beaver,' and let Gary do all the work." Jim got a kick out of associating with cartoonists; he got a kick simply out of seeing their strips before they appeared in the paper. When J Carroll was born, Mike Peters had drawn the birth announcement, and Jim enjoyed being able to tell people that it had been created, for him, by a Pulitzer Prize winner.

So it was Jim's pleasure to accomplish one of the goals of the weekend—to see that the cartoonists had a good time. He cooked barbecue for them and escorted them to a Mexican restaurant, a lakeside café, and the Austin Livestock Show and Rodeo. He drank with them and told them jokes and laughed at their jokes.

Gary dangled the dollar signs in front of them. In a half-hour speech, he announced some good news—that "Bloom County's" share of Lin-Tex sales was decreasing and that all of their shares were going up, or could. Lin-Tex sales had grown from $1.5 million to more than $4 million in one year, he said, and annual sales of $15 million were within reach. "That's great for us and super for you, if you care about money." He described the Marine program Lin-Tex had run with "Shoe" and the extra sales it had produced. "You've got a lot of fans in the military." He told them to think about designs for polo shirts, which were going to be Lin-Tex's entree into the department-store market. (Art Sansom said he wanted to design one with a little green alligator.) He said Lin-Tex was about to launch a line of comic-character dolls.

Some of this was a little exaggerated. Sales were a bit under $4 million. The Marine program was only a middling success. The dolls weren't going to happen until Lin-Tex came up with some cash. But these were small points. With enthusiasm and cooperation (and, most important, a flow of good new designs) from the cartoonists, Lin-Tex could flourish.

The cartoonists listened. Mike Peters, an enthusiastic and sociable fellow with an air of childlike simplicity (he usually greeted Jim by rubbing his belly), sketched during Gary's speech and afterward displayed what he had drawn. All of the sketches had his characters in Marine uniforms. In one, a uniformed dog was pledging: "Today Grenada. Tomorrow King Features." In another, a uniformed pig was driving a tank and firing its cannon. The pig was saying: "Eat lead, Garfield!"


The other cartoonists responded as well. Bob Thaves and Johnny Hart, who had been slow to deliver promised designs, now vowed to get them out. Art Sansom (who played footsie with Thaves's wife one afternoon until Thaves told him, "She has a new metal leg. She probably doesn't know") had come to Austin without a Lin-Tex contract. He approved one while he was there.

And all the cartoonists participated in a press conference in a brand-new showroom at Lin-Tex headquarters, posing for pictures, signing autographs, and answering the usual questions. (Johnny Hart told one reporter that, frankly, he couldn't say where he got his ideas.) Mike Peters sat on the floor under TV lights drawing sketches of Mother Goose and Grimm. "I wanted Grimm to be a real dog," he said. "You never see Snoopy chasing cars. The first time I drew Grimm drinking out of a toilet, I lost Philadelphia."

The cartoonists and reporters were standing amid kiosks and racks that displayed Lin-Tex shirts under signs that said "Comic Collectibles." This was Lin-Tex's new selling concept, developed largely by Gary, who was tired of selling T-shirts to stores design by design and strip by strip. Instead of selling a store ten dozen "Bloom County" shirts and five dozen "Shoe" shirts, Gary wanted to sell it twenty dozen—or forty dozen—assorted shirts packaged collectively as "Comic Collectibles" in a permanent Lin-Tex display. As an incentive to the retailer, Lin-Tex would promise to replace slow-moving shirts with other designs. (This was actually a great opportunity for Lin-Tex to unload old and obscure designs that no retailer would ever order but random customers might buy if they saw them on display.) The concept freed Lin-Tex from relying on a retailer's familiarity with a given strip. "We realized that if we go into a buyer's office and they don't know the strip, we're fucked," Gary explained. "So we're selling the concept, not the designs. We say, 'Give us eighty square feet and we'll show you how to make money.'"

Lin-Tex was going all out to push Comic Collectibles. It had already sunk money into the displays and a beefed-up marketing department (headed by Mitch Tucker, who had begun his professional career frying hamburgers for Jim and Gary at Wendy's). The Cotillion weekend was part of the campaign. It was intended to show the cartoonists that their shirts were being promoted, to show the sales reps the new product they were selling, and to show the syndicate people that Lin-Tex was on the move.

"We needed to make a major statement in the industry," Gary said later. The T-shirt business was becoming more competitive. Other companies had recently beat Lin-Tex to the rights for promising new strips. Non-comic-strip designs like Spuds MacKenzie and cows were competing for shelf space. Lin-Tex didn't want to be left behind.

To finance the Cotillion and the launch of Comic Collectibles, Jim and Gary had skimmed money out of cash flow, money which more conservative businessmen might have used to pay bills. This was a risky course. "Other companies our size would never have dreamed of doing those kinds of things," Gary said. But Lin-Tex didn't want to stay that size. Jim and Gary were going for the big time.

# Aggies Abroad

AT 8:00 A.M. on an overcast morning, an unmarked white plane appeared in the sky above the Guatemala City airport. An old DC-6 with heavy black smudges from engine exhaust under its wings, it angled over the airport once, made a wide turn, and came in for a landing. It taxied to a stop in front of the customs warehouse and its cargo door swung open. A Senepol cow looked out. In a tiny window over the wing, Pete's face appeared. He looked out, too.

Two days before, he and Wendell had left Hopes Creek Ranch in a pickup truck hauling a trailer with the Senepol cow, a calf, and two heifers. They drove nonstop to Miami, a tiring and expensive trip. The truck was getting terrible mileage; gas and meals cost Pete nearly $500, far more than he had budgeted. In Miami, he'd gotten a few hours sleep before rising at 4:00 a.m. to be loaded onto a cargo flight of Bellamy-Lawson Aviation. The fare from Miami to Guatemala City was fifty-seven cents a pound, for him and the cattle. It came to $2360.

He spent the trip in the cargo bay, shivering, worrying that the crates stacked all around him might topple, sleeping fitfully. He had a dream: the plane crash-landed in Millican, Texas, a few miles from Hopes Creek Ranch.

But it didn't. Pete was on the ground in Guatemala with four Senepols. Unless border guards came out and shot them, he had accomplished something: Senepol genes would soon be improving

Central American cattle stock. First Texas. Now Guatemala. The Senepol was spreading all over the world, and Pete was its instrument. He was doing good, and he was hoping to do well. Senepol sales in Central America looked like his brightest prospect. He still had no sales anywhere else.

Cargo handlers rode up to the door of the plane on a forklift, and one of them patted the cow on her head. They hoisted up a ramp and led the Senepols onto a gaily painted Hino truck decorated with decals of Jesus Christ and Woody Woodpecker.

Pete climbed down a ladder from the cockpit carefully carrying a silver semen tank that contained, frozen in liquid nitrogen, 140 straws of semen from two fine Senepol bulls. Roberto Perdomo was waiting on the tarmac to greet him. A bearded young man with a happy-go-lucky attitude, Perdomo was the son of a former Guatemalan minister of agriculture. He worked for the agricultural attaché at the American Embassy in Guatemala City. He was Pete's business partner in Central America. And he was an Aggie (and the son of an Aggie). He wore a maroon Aggie cap.

Months before, a German resident of Guatemala who was studying at Texas A&M—a favorite school for the sons of Guatemala's upper class—had come out to Hopes Creek Ranch with a Brazilian friend of Pete's to go fishing. The German Guatemalan had picked up some Senepol brochures, which he gave to Roberto, a friend of his, over summer vacation. Looking back at this chain of circumstance made Pete marvel at how one thing could lead to another. A friend brought a friend out fishing, and now Pete was standing in Guatemala with four Senepols and a business partner.

Roberto was holding a fistful of official documents, including a Licencia de Importacion for "135 ampollas de semen, raza Senepol . . . que se encuentra in buenas condiciones sanitarias." That one covered the semen tank, more or less, but the documents for the cattle were not complete. Pete figured it didn't matter, that once the cattle were actually landed no one was going to bust a gut examining their paperwork (or *his*, for that matter; he hadn't brought a passport). And he was correct. "We just have to pay the import tax," Roberto told him.

"Import tax?" said Pete.

"The import fee," Roberto explained. "Twenty-nine hundred."

"Twenty-nine hundred?" Pete looked poleaxed. He had just about gone broke getting this far. Nobody had said anything about an import tax.

"Quetzales," Roberto said. Twenty-nine hundred quetzales was almost $1200. "It's based on the value of the cattle," Roberto said. He pointed to the airplane's bill of lading. "You put seven thousand dollars."

"I thought I was doing that for the insurance," Pete groaned. "I should have put three hundred dollars. Is there any point in my going over there and arguing?"

"No," said Roberto.

Pete didn't have 2900 quetzales. (For that matter, he couldn't even pronounce "quetzal"; during a week in Guatemala, despite intense effort, he never mastered it.) Nor did he have $1200. So, leaving the Senepols behind as hostages, he climbed into Roberto's old Volkswagen bus, which was decorated with Aggie stickers, and held on tight as Roberto rocketed out of the airport and into the city, honking constantly and darting into any gap that opened before him. Pete's attention was momentarily diverted from Roberto's driving by the heavily armed soldiers he saw posted along an old Spanish aqueduct by the side of the road. He asked if it was a military base. Roberto shrugged no.

At a stoplight, Pete was surprised again. Students wearing red and yellow peaked hoods over their heads were passing out flyers and asking for money. "They're collecting money for a march," Roberto explained.

"Why are they wearing masks?" Pete asked.

"I don't know," said Roberto. "It's the custom. It's going to be a messy march. Like the March of Roses, but messy. There will be drinking. They will be saying things against the government."

Pete was surprised once more when Roberto pulled up in front of the American Embassy. The place was like a fortress, surrounded by walls and gates and Guatemalan guards carrying automatic rifles and shotguns. A gardener working on a small lawn bounded by high fences looked like a man in a cage. To enter the building, Pete had to pass through a metal detector, open his bags for a search, and be buzzed through a second locked door. And he was an American citizen. It didn't seem right.

Inside, Roberto led him to an office maintained by a local bank, and Pete glumly cashed a check for $1250.

Back at the airport, he and Roberto waded into the tumult of the customs shed, where ragged lines funneled toward a dozen document-stamping clerks. Roberto procured the services of a round-faced customs broker whom Pete distrusted at first sight, and the broker led them through line after line. Pete handed over the import duty—2978 quetzales. Roberto said it would have been one third less if Pete had brought documents proving the Senepols were purebreds. Pete didn't have the documents. Nobody had told him to bring them.

Other fees and surcharges and taxes were demanded. Pete counted out a hundred quetzales here, two hundred quetzales there. "They found the semen," Roberto said. "You have to declare its value and pay a duty."

"Okay," Pete grunted. "A penny a straw."

Roberto said the duty was 500 quetzales. The customs broker said they could skip the duty if they gave a customs guard 250 quetzales. Pete said he'd pay 50. The broker disappeared into the warehouse and returned with word that 200 would do. Pete gave him 200. The broker asked for his own fee of 125 quetzales. Pete gave him 25 and said he'd pay the rest later. Roberto said he needed 90 quetzales for the truck driver. "I don't mind paying for the truck," Pete said as he handed the money over. "He's *working* for it."

Eventually, Pete and Roberto made it out of the airport with the cattle and a couple of quetzales. They drove to a fairground at the edge of the city where EXPICA, the Central American cattle show, was under way. The cattle on display—mostly Brahmans— were overwhelmingly from Guatemalan ranches. No Nicaraguans had registered. Some Costa Ricans had wanted to come but they didn't want to drive through Nicaragua. A couple of Salvadorans had registered too late. There were a few Hondurans.

Pete guided his Senepols down a ramp from the truck and tried to slip halters over their heads. The cattle were skittish; one knocked Pete backward into a pile of fresh manure. With help from Roberto, he hired an elderly stable hand with a dapper mustache and swollen, shoeless feet to feed and watch the animals.

Pete instructed the man in Spanish, which he spoke to a limited extent. As a boy, Pete had worked side by side with Mexicans on a ranch on the Rio Grande. (Every morning the manager would tie flags to a tree on the riverbank indicating the number of workers he needed that day, and that many Mexicans would wade over.) Pete was pleased that his Spanish seemed to work with the cowhand, but he had a setback soon after, when Roberto took him to lunch at a Mexican restaurant and Pete ordered three *ensaladas* (salads); he wanted three enchiladas.

After lunch, Roberto drove Pete to see Max Stern, the German Guatemalan who had brought them together, at Max's family's hardware store in the busy district by the bus station. Pete was impressed by what he saw of the city. It looked clean and full of free enterprise. Pizza Hut delivery motorbikes scooted through traffic; sidewalk vendors hawked orange juice and shoe shines. In the street outside the hardware store, there was a row of eleven consecutive shoe-repair stands. Indian women from the countryside debarked from buses carrying baskets of vegetables and chickens, and peasant men walked along with enormous sheathed machetes hanging from their belts.

The hardware store, a major supplier of rural ranches, stocked a bewildering variety of machetes and a large selection of American tools. Max was in the back, in an office where his Texas A&M diploma hung on a wall along with several Mayan stone figures and a sign that said: "I'm the Boss—That's Why." Max's father, who had come to Guatemala as a hardware salesman in the 1960s, was speaking on a two-way radio to the manager of the family's thirty-square-mile ranch in a northern province. A topographical map of the region was on the wall. "Those maps are now prohibited," Max said. "The guerrillas were using them."

Max, slim and serious, asked Pete how his trip had been and how the cattle were. Pete said the cattle were at EXPICA and seemed to be all right, although they had lost a lot of weight traveling. "I'll have one of the boys from the house spend the night there," Max said, "and sleep with the cattle."

Pete was to stay at Max's family's house, and now Max drove him there in his Daihatsu Rocky. As he turned left at a fortress (now an army computer center, Max said) in the center of the

city, Pete looked out the window at armed soldiers sweeping cigarette butts out of the gutter. Max warned Pete not to photograph
them or any other soldiers. They didn't like to have their pictures
taken. "They got a bad deal from the press," Max explained.

Max was referring here to innumerable press reports that the
army, engaged for twenty-five years in a sporadic war against leftist
guerrillas, had routinely massacred unarmed peasants and had,
with the police, kidnapped, tortured, and murdered unionists, students, professors, agronomists, lawyers, politicians, and anyone
else deemed to be a "subversive." Most accounts put the number
of victims of official violence between 100,000 and 200,000. A
recent report by Amnesty International had painstakingly re-
counted dozens of individual atrocities, including one incident, not
all that unusual, of an Indian village where the army "reportedly
forced the entire population into the courthouse, raped the women,
beheaded the men and battered the children to death against rocks
in a nearby river." According to the Amnesty report, several kidnap
victims, since permanently disappeared, had last been seen in
secret cells in the very building outside which Max now told Pete
of the soldiers' "bad deal."

At the time of Pete's visit, Guatemala's first civilian president
in a generation had been in office for fifteen months, but the army
retained effective power. Political violence had abated but not disappeared; a local human-rights group counted 169 political mur-
ders in the two months before Pete arrived. And the structure of
the country was unchanged. A small oligarchy owned most of the
land; they used it to grow crops for export—and to raise cattle—
while Indian peasants lacked land to grow corn and beans. (In
neighboring El Salvador, guerrillas had on occasion machine-
gunned cattle to make a political point.) Malnutrition was
widespread.

Pete didn't know anything about any of this—he generally kept
up with current events and even wrote his congressman when
something bothered him, but Guatemala didn't get much coverage
in the College Station newspaper—and Max didn't mention it. He
drove into a quiet residential neighborhood at the edge of the city,
pulled up to a closed gate, and honked. Two servants opened the
gate and Max drove through.

From the street the property had looked unimpressive—just a short wall with a gate in it. "My parents built it that way," Max said. "They didn't want to attract attention." Specifically, they had not wanted to attract the attention of criminals who kidnapped wealthy Guatemalans for ransom. Inside the gate, the house and grounds widened like a wedge of pie. The house was modern and austere, large and airy. It opened onto an enormous patio, overflowing with plants, that hung on a hillside with a view of the volcanoes that ring Guatemala City.

Max led Pete into a small guest suite as servants descended upon it, dusting lampshades, laying decorative strips of embroidered cloth over the wooden furniture, and setting out a single lavender orchid on a table between the leather couch and two leather chairs. Max's father raised orchids in a greenhouse out back.

"Did they bring that tree in just for me?" Pete asked as a servant deposited a potted tree in a corner of the room. Before Max could answer, another servant walked in, carrying another tree.


Pete returned that afternoon, and at least once a day thereafter, to EXPICA, where his Senepols were not officially in the show but had been established, thanks to string-pulling by Roberto, in a rough-hewn outdoor pen beneath tall eucalyptus trees. Pete was surprised to see soldiers in camouflage fatigues patrolling the grounds, and he was displeased one morning to find a mound of human shit in the dirt beside his pen, but much of EXPICA was familiar. There were the cattle, and hand-holding schoolchildren marveling at the size of the bulls. There were even Texans, a contingent flown in by Guatemalan Brahman breeders to judge the EXPICA Brahman show. Pete could hear their comments on the animals over the public address system from the show arena— "She shows a lot of femininity. . . . She stands on her legs real good." Pete snorted. "Did you ever see one fall down," he asked, "unless it stepped in a hole?"

Most comforting to Pete, there were Aggies. At a cocktail party one evening, held beside cattle stalls where peasant workers were unrolling their beds for the night, Pete met half a dozen Guatemalan Aggies, including Eduardo Castillo, whose family owned several large ranches and the country's leading brewery. Castillo said he was in the market for some Red Brangus semen. Pete said he used to be in Red Brangus himself until he'd switched to the Senepol because it was gentler and more fertile. Castillo stopped by to see Pete's Senepols the next day, and he returned the day after that with his father. How much? he asked Pete. Nine thousand dollars for the four, Pete said. Castillo said he would probably want to buy some semen.

Roberto spent his days at his job at the American Embassy, while Max took time off from the hardware store to drive Pete around Guatemala City, calling on more prospects. Pete chatted about Senepols with a rancher whose office walls were decorated with photos of his helicopter and a Charolais bull he'd bought for $22,000; the rancher said he'd been an active organizer of EXPICA until guerrillas burned his ranch house and coffee processing plant and he decided to adopt a lower public profile. Pete spoke to wealthy young men in the offices of a coffee export firm and an insurance company. He dropped Senepol brochures at the office of a rancher named Leonowens, who Max said was the great-grandson of Anna of *Anna and the King of Siam.*

Pete took in the city as Max drove him around. The air was cool and bright and occasionally enlivened by the scent of roasting coffee. There was activity at every red light—girls in Pepsi uniforms selling bottles of Pepsi, boys selling oval cans of sardines, a fire-eater performing for coins, a woman begging with a baby (Max said she rented the baby; it never got any older). Pete was only uncomfortable once, when Max drove him smack into the demonstration he'd seen students soliciting for, and they were stuck in traffic next to a float with hooded students and an angry caricature of Uncle Sam.

Every night, after a final check on his Senepols (two of them had developed runny noses and Pete was feeding them antibiotics), Pete met Max and Roberto at El Establo, a bar popular with young "garchs" (pronounced "garks"), the children of the oligarchs. The bar was run by a skinny long-haired German who looked like one of the Fabulous Furry Freak Brothers; its slogan was "So what?" Leaving the bar one night, Pete was accosted by a small boy begging. "Get a shoeshine box," Pete advised him. The boy seemed not to understand. "Shoeshine box!" Pete said. "Shoeshine!"

The next night Pete attended a bull auction at the EXPICA show arena. Guatemalan and American ranchers were socializing as bulls were led to and from the auction ring. Pete was introduced to Fernando Somoza, who had a Red Brahman operation in the country. "You're a friend of Keith Newbill?" Pete asked. Somoza corrected him: "He used to work for us."

A boy peddling sticks of sliced cucumber dashed across the floor and vaulted a fence into the stands, and people all around were suddenly running. Pete turned to see a big gray Brahman bull that had broken loose from its handlers. The dictator's nephew was gone. Everybody was scrambling to get out of the animal's way.

Pete stood stock still. The bull ran by him, tossing its horns, missing him by inches. Pete remained still as the bull turned around and ran by him again. The bull trotted off, and two cowboys subdued it. Only then did Pete move. He hadn't wanted to run like a coward. He didn't want to give these foreigners a bad impression.

After three days in Guatemala, Pete's prospects looked good. Castillo had declared his interest in Senepols. A soft-spoken American named Bronson who ranched in Guatemala had stopped by Pete's pen several times, and Max's friend Leonowens had sent word he was planning to visit.

Pete was looking forward to making more contacts as he dressed at Max's for a cocktail party at the home of the U.S. Embassy's agricultural attaché. Pete didn't have a shirt that wasn't dirty or ripped, so he borrowed one from Max. He tied a red tie around his thigh and transferred it to his collar as Max entered the room carrying Pete's boots, which had just been polished, for the second time that day, by one of the family servants. Pete slipped them on. "Another hard day on the ranch," he said.

Pete rode to the party with Max and his fiancée Dolores, the sheltered daughter of a wealthy family who worked for an American advertising agency in Guatemala City. They arrived at the attaché's home in a suburban neighborhood and found a crowd gathered around two bars and a buffet table. The Texan Brahman judges were the guests of honor. Fernando Somoza was there.

Pete and Max met the attaché, and Max raised an issue that was bothering him. Under pressure from the United States, which was worried about the northward spread of the Mediterranean fruit fly, Guatemala was conducting an eradication campaign against the insect that included aerial spraying with a cancer-causing pesticide that was banned in the United States. Max was concerned that the spraying was damaging coffee plants. The attaché, a fat man, had no interest in discussing the subject. He said the problem was being studied and turned away. Pete was irritated by this evasiveness, and he was outraged by the attaché's total lack of interest in Pete's Senepol sales mission. "Don't we pay him to promote American exports?" Pete demanded.

A couple of drinks put Pete in a better mood, and then he and Max and Dolores left the party. "Would you like to hear some mariachi music?" Max asked. Pete said sure.

Max drove to a busy intersection where mariachi bands assembled every night, waiting to be hired on the spot for a party or a song. His car had barely pulled to a stop when a dozen arms, gaily clad in embroidered coats, were thrust through the open windows proffering the business cards of mariachi bands. Dolores shrank back with a little cry. "Does anybody want a beer?" Max asked. More arms were thrust into the car with bottles of beer for sale. Pete saw Dolores's dismay. "Out! Out!" he shouted. But no arms retreated.

Max bought a round of beers as several mariachi bands gathered at the curb, their members in brightly colored uniforms with floppy bow ties. Max called out that he'd hire the band that started to play first, and, with the strum of a guitar and the wheeze of an accordion, one commenced a love song. "I want to kiss your lips," Max translated for Pete. "A woman is like a rose."

A cool breeze blowing in the car windows carried the scent

of a bonfire around which some of the unemployed musicians were gathered. Fireworks exploded nearby. A taxi pulled up behind Max's car and bumped it, gently.

Pete was getting into the spirit of things. He drank his beer and yelped along with the music. In simple Spanish he requested a song in honor of Max and Dolores's engagement. The band played "Where Is My Engagement Ring?" The trumpeter, a little old man in a Panama hat, carefully wrote down the name of every song the band played, in case there was a dispute about the bill. The charge was five quetzales per song.

The band played for twenty minutes. Pete, Dolores, and Max never got out of the car. It was a drive-in mariachi band.

Afterward, Max drove toward Dolores's home. "Look!" she said.

She pointed to the horizon, where the black sky was illuminated by what appeared to be a string of red Christmas tree lights. It was molten lava flowing from Pacaya, a volcano twenty miles from the capital that had been erupting for three months. Ordinarily, it was obscured by haze, but not tonight.

Max looked at it solemnly. "I'm a Lutheran," he told Pete, "and I'm not religious. But somebody took a picture when the volcano erupted. You've seen how the Virgin Mary looks in pictures? You can see that in this photograph. It hasn't been doctored. You don't have to draw lines. You just see it there. . . .

"I'm not religious," Max repeated. "But it makes you think."


"Is *Cats* still playing?" asked the beautiful Guatemalan woman. She was young and fragile and dressed in silk and pearls. She had a slight but constant tremor. "I was going to see it in New York, but my friends saw it and they told me, 'It is people dressed like cats.' Dressed like cats!" She dismissed it. "Pffft!"

At the other end of a table in an elegant seafood restaurant, Pete was speaking to the woman's husband, a rancher at least twenty years her senior. Roberto had arranged this luncheon meeting. He told Pete that the rancher was seriously interested in investing in Senepols.

"The last time I was in New York, I took my daughter to Macy's," the rancher's wife was saying. "We took a cab back to the hotel, with an Iranian driver, and he took us out of the way. I said, 'Where are we going? I know New York.' The driver got angry. He said I talked too much. At the hotel he locked the doors so we couldn't get out. I opened the window and yelled, 'Help! Help!' He let us out and I threw some coins at him. He came running into the hotel after us. He was saying, 'You go fuck yourself! You go fuck yourself!' "

At the other end of the table, Pete was discussing irrigation and cattle diseases and the role of cattle in agriculture. "Cattle are pioneers," the rancher said. "Cattle go in first when a country is being developed. . . ."

Pete nodded and pushed his appetizer around on his plate. It was ceviche—marinated raw fish—ordered for him by Roberto. Pete thought at first it might be a vegetable, but he got suspicious when he stabbed it with his fork. ("I didn't know if I was killing it," he explained later.)

"From raising cattle, people learn which land is the most fertile," the rancher said. "Then they plant crops on the best land, and the cattle end up on the poorest land. This causes cattle people to become psychologically unbalanced. They think, 'What can I do that will make more money?' They try all kinds of things. My cousin sold his cattle—sixteen thousand head—and started raising shrimp. He lost twenty million. Dollars."

Pete was impressed. If *he* ever managed to accumulate $20 million, he would never put it at risk. (He'd more likely "put it in the bank and let it draw interest and have somebody massage me all day.") He continued to listen as the rancher told him how his family's sausage factory was the most advanced in Latin America, how he had discovered a legume that was miraculously rebuilding the soil on his ranch, how the family farms had had no trouble with guerrillas because they treated their employees so generously.

It was beginning to strike Pete odd how people always told him how well they treated their peasants.

The rancher invited Pete to visit his ranch, and Pete accepted.

There was good news back at EXPICA. Bronson and Leonowens were at the Senepol pen, and they said they were interested in buying some bulls.

They didn't make a definite offer, and Pete didn't have any
bulls with him anyway. But he could get bulls. "We didn't have
anything special to do today," Max said happily, as he drove Pete
home, "and things really happened."

"It's like the climax to a movie," Pete exulted. "I'll ride off
into the sunset with a hundred thousand quit-zollies."

Before dawn the next morning, Pete rode out of the capital
with the rancher from the seafood restaurant. Roberto sat in
the back seat with the rancher's twelve-year-old son. Pete was
looking forward to seeing the ranch, which the rancher had
described as a paragon of efficiency. ("He's the god-king of agriculture," Pete said, "according to what he was telling me.")

After their lunch meeting, Roberto had told Pete that the
rancher wanted to buy one hundred units of semen for $2000.
Roberto also said that he, with the rancher's backing, wanted
to establish a herd of Senepols in Guatemala as a joint venture
with Hopes Creek Ranch. It was not made clear, however,
whether Roberto or the rancher intended to put any actual cash
into this venture.

Pete was already having second thoughts about Roberto. He
was far more impressed with Max, who since Pete arrived had
asked if *he* could join Pete in the Senepol business. They had
made no arrangement, but Max had hustled nonetheless to introduce Pete to several live prospects. Roberto had brought him
only this rancher, who talked about everything but business as
he sped south on Highway 9 past sugar cane fields being cleared
by burning.

He told Pete that, as the head of an industrialists' association,
he had been a target of the left; that, as the head of another
group that had commissioned a study of Guatemala's problems
and found that corruption among the military was one of them,

he had become unpopular among some of the officers. He denounced Jimmy Carter, who had cut off military aid to Guatemala in 1977 (it was restored by Ronald Reagan). "The people he sent! The ambassador from the United States was like the ambassador from Russia!"

Pete didn't like Jimmy Carter either; he'd thought he was weak. "I think he personally set the United States back ten years."

"He interfered in our internal affairs," the rancher complained.

"Was that because of the human-rights violations?" asked Pete. "Wasn't that the approach he took?"

"I will tell you about that," the rancher said. "General Romeo Garcia became the president. He had a very strong will. There were criminals who were committing fifteen or twenty crimes, and the judges were afraid to send them to jail, because of fear of retaliation. So Romeo Garcia organized groups of"—he paused, hunting for the word—"something like soldiers. They were . . . they *were* soldiers. And they started to eliminate these people. They killed thirty or forty some days. They killed maybe one thousand in all. And some people started to say Guatemala was violating human rights, and the country got a bad name. They killed two thousand criminals. They didn't kill just *anybody*."

Pete was silent.

"There," said the rancher, pointing, "is the sugar cane factory my grandfather started. It is the biggest in Central America."

They turned west, toward the Pacific Ocean and Mexico, and the climate changed, from the fresh sunshine of the highlands to the steamy heat of the coast. Roberto nodded off in the back seat, as did the rancher's son, whom he called, affectionately, "Juanito bonito."

In a village near the ranch, everyone transferred to a Land-Rover, which the rancher drove directly onto his fields, bouncing over ruts and ditches. He showed Pete his herd of purebred Brahmans and paused on a hilltop to show Pete the view. In one direction lay large grassy mounds—buried Mayan pyramids, the rancher said, which he was preserving from excavation. The pastures of the ranch stretched off to a distant forested slope. "Twenty-five years ago," the rancher said, "all of this was tropical forest. I worked for five years to clear it."

It was immense. "Did you use bulldozers?" Pete asked.

The rancher shook his head. "I brought in Indians from the highlands. I told them they could grow corn here for clearing the land."

"How long did they do that?" Pete asked.

"Five years," said the rancher impatiently. Hadn't he just said it took five years to clear the land?

"I meant how long did you let them grow corn," Pete explained.

"Five years," said the rancher.

The rancher was an Aggie, and his son was looking forward to becoming one. On the drive back to the city they swapped Aggie jokes.

"You know how you can tell Aggie wives?" asked the rancher. "They have tattoos on their navels that say, 'This side up.' "

"You know why Aggies don't have hemorrhoids?" asked Juan. "Because they're perfect assholes."


Pete thought the ranch was a mess—the pastures were over-grazed and the cattle looked sickly. He didn't like the rancher either. He didn't want to do business with him.

This was, for the moment, a moot point, since the rancher left Guatemala City the next day for the Holy Week holiday without making Pete an offer. EXPICA came to an end, and everybody left town for the holiday. There was no business to be done.

No one had made Pete an offer, but Max expected one from Leonowens soon, and other ranchers seemed seriously interested. Pete was thinking of coming back in sixty days with a truckload of Senepols. He would drive them through Mexico.

In the meantime, he needed somewhere to store the four animals he had in the country while Max and Roberto arranged their sale. Roberto located a dairy farm owned by his cousin about thirty miles from the capital. On Palm Sunday, Pete loaded the cattle on a hired truck, which he and Roberto followed in a rented Jeep.

They were blocked by a religious procession in the center of the city. Purple-robed worshippers marched down a street that was covered with a mile-long mural, made with colored sand, of abstract designs and faces of Jesus. Waiting for it to pass, Pete relaxed in the car with a beer and a Guatemalan newspaper that carried American baseball box scores. Then Roberto drove out of town on a dirt road that rose into mist-covered hills. It twisted up and came down into an idyllic narrow valley, where peasant men walked with enormous loads of wood that were suspended in slings from their foreheads and rested on their backs. Roberto turned down a long dirt track that led to his cousin's farm. The cattle truck, still ahead of them, had stopped halfway down the track, just before a bridge over a little river.

The truck driver said he wouldn't cross the bridge. He was afraid it might collapse.

Pete took a hard look at the bridge. Its roadway was wood, but it was supported by concrete. "It's rated ten tons easy," he said. He didn't see any problem.

The truck driver wouldn't budge. He sat in his truck with his helper and three small children who had come along for the ride and said he would unload the cattle where they were, and Pete could walk them over the bridge.

Pete didn't think he could. Both sides of the road were unfenced, and there was a lot of grass around that would look attractive to a cow. It would be difficult to persuade the animals to walk straight across the bridge to the gate of the dairy.

The Senepol cow was already off the truck; the driver had put her off because she was bumping around. Pete tried to grab her halter, and she bolted, brushing Pete aside, and, in an amazing demonstration of Senepol climbing prowess, dashed straight up a steep slope.

Without further consultation, the driver put the other three animals off the truck, and they raced up a gully beside the hill the cow had climbed. All four animals disappeared. Pete stood helplessly on the road. "We may never see them again," he said.

The driver asked to be paid. And, Roberto said, "He wants a tip."

"No tiene vacas," Pete protested. We don't have the cows.

He paid the driver anyway.

It was getting toward dusk, and Pete walked over to the dairy and talked to the manager about hiring a couple of his men to round up the Senepols. The manager said they could do it in the morning. Roberto suggested to Pete that they borrow a couple of horses and do it themselves. Pete didn't think they could do it.

He got into the Jeep with Roberto and drove in the direction the cattle had fled. A bone-rattling ascent took them to a high pasture half a mile from the dairy where the Senepols were grazing contentedly. Their red coats looked beautiful against the lush green grass.

Pete relaxed. "It's a nice place to show them," he said. He asked Roberto to speak to his cousin about keeping the Senepols right there.

Pete got out of the Jeep with a camera and walked toward the animals. They looked so pretty he wanted a picture. "Oooooo," he called in a high-pitched voice, to make them look up. "Oooooo."

They looked at him, and he looked at them, as the sun set over Guatemala.

# III. SMALL FORTUNES

# "Y'all Need a Bunch of Money Right Away"

"**F**UCK," SAID JIM, "we gotta come up with the cash."

He was sitting in his green leather chair behind his big wooden desk, talking on the phone with Gary, who was in California selling T-shirts. Gary was doing a pretty good job of it, but it looked like he was on a fool's errand. Lin-Tex's main supplier, a Kansas company called Dyco that manufactured and printed most of the T-shirts Lin-Tex sold, had cut off Lin-Tex's supply. Inventory was dwindling. Orders were piling up, and Lin-Tex was running out of shirts to fill them.

The T-shirt business was more competitive than ever—Spuds MacKenzie, the Budweiser dog, was at the height of his popularity and Spuds shirts were soaking up buyers' dollars—but demand for Lin-Tex product was still growing. Several cartoonists had gone home from the Comic Cotillion and produced good new designs. "Bloom County" was still hot—it had just won the Pulitzer Prize for editorial cartooning and, moreover, been denounced by the National Federation for Decency for introducing a character whose last name was the Yiddish word for excrement. Berke Breathed had just delivered a T-shirt design featuring Bill the Cat's heavy-metal band that Jim and Gary were convinced was going to be their first million-dollar shirt. In California, Gary had attended a meeting of Marine Corps base exchange officers and walked away with a fistful of orders, including one from the exchange at Guantanamo.

But it was far from certain that Lin-Tex would be able to deliver shirts to Cuba or anywhere else. After years of dancing around the edge of a terminal cash-flow crisis—all the "playing the float," all the last-minute deposits and wire transfers—the game appeared to be up. Payment for the T-shirts Lin-Tex sold simply arrived too long after bills from its suppliers were due. The more successful Lin-Tex grew, the farther it fell behind. Dyco had finally lost patience with Lin-Tex's promises and bounced checks. No cash, no more shirts.

Ordinarily, a company holding orders for merchandise it couldn't pay to produce would turn to its bank for a loan. But it was clear that Lin-Tex might as well ask Bill the Cat for a loan as an Austin financial institution. The local banking scene had actually deteriorated since Christmas. Lamar Savings, which held a $440,000 Lin-Tex loan (paid down from $500,000) was operating in technical insolvency—its net worth was approaching a negative quarter of a billion dollars—and could not lend another cent. North Central National Bank, from which Jim had arranged a last-minute Christmas loan, had been shut down by federal regulators in April. United Bank, which had once been Lin-Tex's bank and still held a $325,000 personal loan to Jim (secured by the last of his Wendy's stock, its value declined to $250,000) went belly up in June.

"Are you in L.A. now?" Jim asked Gary. "Before you leave, why don't you walk into a couple of those banks cold and introduce yourself and see if they have any interest in doing business with a Texas company?"

It was not likely that they would; most small business loans are made locally.

A few minutes later, Ray Bicknell, the president of Dyco, called. Jim decided to play it light.

"Hello," he said. "What's going on? I'm just sitting here trying to figure out how to pay the bills. Every time Dyco's name comes up, we put it on the bottom of the list."

Ho-ho-ho. This was not the best approach. Lin-Tex was $50,000 over its $100,000 credit limit with Dyco, and Bicknell seemed fixated on that fact. Unreasonably so, Jim thought. He thought Dyco should simply give Lin-Tex a higher line of credit; $100,000 was low for the amount of business they were doing.

He and Gary had already invited Bicknell down to Austin to meet and talk things over.

"Two of the banks we've been dealing with just failed," Jim explained on the phone. "There's not a bank in this town that's got a cent. Can you go into your bank and ask if they're interested in dealing with us? . . . I understand it's not too great to go into a bank that you've been bouncing checks off of, but it's because of our growth. . . . If we're in bed with you, and you're in bed with your bank. . . . Sure, we've bounced some checks, but we've made every payment on every loan. . . . I would think you *would* give a shit about the $1.2 million we did send you last year. . . . Okey-doke, we're doing *our* planning for next year, too. . . . One way or another, we're going to do eight million dollars next year. . . . No, that's not a threat at all. . . . We totally recognize that we have a hell of a relationship with you. That's why we invited you down. Name the day. . . . Okay, bye."

The conversation ended abruptly and not well. Jim called for Rudi Garnett, the ordinarily self-possessed young woman who managed the office and served as his and Gary's girl Friday. "He said," Jim reported, "'If you clear the fifty thousand dollars in checks, we'll come down and see you. If you don't, we don't need your business.'" Rudi nodded grimly. It was she who received and dispatched checks, who screened all important phone calls. She didn't like some of the calls she'd had to screen lately.

An hour later, things got worse. Lin-Tex had a second T-shirt supplier, an Austin company run by a man named Harlan who bought blank shirts wholesale and printed them for Lin-Tex. Naturally, Lin-Tex owed Harlan money. It was *normal* to owe a supplier money. But now Harlan called and said he needed $51,000 to pay the manufacturer from which he bought shirts. No cash, no more shirts. First Dyco, now Harlan. It was a double whammy.

Rudi had written a couple of checks that morning to pay other urgent bills (one to a sales rep, one to the IRS), nearly depleting the Lin-Tex account. But now she asked Jim, "Would you like me to go over to the bank right now and get a ten-thousand-dollar cashier's check for Harlan while that can be done, before the other checks go through?" That would mean bouncing the morning checks, but it might be enough to placate Harlan for the moment.

Jim thought it over. He called in Rick Chapman, who ran Lin-Tex's warehouse and shipping operation and was the son of Norman Chapman, a wealthy Chicago businessman for whom Gary had once worked in the restaurant business.

"Rick," Jim asked, "if you had the choice, what would you do with fifty thousand dollars, give it to Dyco or to Harlan? Which would do the most good?"

"Harlan has white blanks," Rick said, "and Dyco doesn't. He can supply most of the designs we need. Dyco can't do us much good right now."

Jim digested the information.

"Does Norman do loan sharking?" he asked. "Will he do a straight loan-shark deal, where we'd pay five thousand cash up front for a hundred thousand at whatever points over prime he needs?"

"He could do it," Rick said. "I think it would be best for Gary to call and present it as a straight business proposition. If I called and asked for a hundred thousand dollars to buy part of Lin-Tex, he'd react differently. . . . "

*Buy?* Nobody had said *buy*.

Jim gave it up.


But he and Gary were ready to sell part of the company. They didn't know what else to do. The unrelenting tension from juggling not enough cash was making Gary ill. He was constantly exhausted and lacked an appetite. He suffered from stomach pains and nausea.

Ray Bicknell of Dyco, who was bankrolled by his brother, a Kansas Pizza Hut magnate and former gubernatorial candidate who was best known outside Kansas for financing and co-starring in a movie in which Vanna White appeared bare-breasted, had proposed one solution to Lin-Tex's problem. Lin-Tex would close up its Austin operation and let Dyco take over shipping and billing. Jim and Gary would move to Kansas and travel from there, selling shirts. Lin-Tex and Dyco would in fact combine, with Dyco supplying all the shirts Jim and Gary could sell and owning 51 percent of the joint venture. Jim and Gary said no thanks.

They had recently begun looking into raising money on the penny stock market, a murky arena in which low-priced shares are aggressively peddled by commission salesmen. A University of Texas professor with whom Jim played golf one afternoon advised him against it. The penny stock market would taint Lin-Tex forever, he warned. "Fuck 'taint,' " Jim replied. "I'm in the T-shirt business." He continued to explore the option.

The other obvious alternative was to sell a minority interest in Lin-Tex to a venture capital investment group. Jim and Gary worried that such a group would take too much for too little, that it might even end up owning Lin-Tex. But they hired a consultant from an Austin venture capital firm to investigate the area. He arrived at the Lin-Tex office for a meeting the morning after the phone call from Harlan.

"I'm desperate for cash," Rudi told him as they sank into white leather couches across from the bar in Jim and Gary's office. "More than any other day, I am desperate."

The consultant, a fresh-scrubbed young man in a gray pinstripe suit with a heavy Texas accent, nodded sympathetically. "Y'all need a bunch of money right away," he said. "But the equity market is such that you can't get a bunch of money without putting together a well-thought-out plan." He described the business plan that Lin-Tex would have to write. It needed to trace the history of the company, make projections for the future, and accentuate, with charts, every single positive trend they could think of. "You want to show the number of customers you've got, the number of telemarketing people you have, sales per telemarketing person, the space stores are giving you. . . . Tell them sales per store and number of products carried. Last year you had shirts; now you have shirts and caps. . . . "

Jim and Rudi nodded.

"When we start writing the plan," the consultant said, "you're going to miss sales appointments. You'll be spending all your time on this plan when you should be out selling."

"They're out right now," Rudi said, "writing thousands and thousands of dollars of orders, and we can't fill them."

The consultant shook his head. "You're going to start alienating customers. You've got a bad problem."

"How much do you think we could raise?" Rudi asked.

The consultant made a quick and dirty calculation. For the fiscal year just ending, Lin-Tex was going to show operating earnings of $200,000 ($150,000 net profit plus $50,000 paid out in loan interest). Companies were generally considered to be worth some multiple of their operating earnings, perhaps five times earnings for a company in a stagnant field or twenty times earnings for something very trendy. The consultant pegged Lin-Tex's value at nine times earnings, or $1.8 million, minus the company's $500,000 debt. Net value: $1.3 million.

If an investor bought in with $1 million, say, that would immediately add $1 million to the value of the company. So, to that hypothetical million-dollar investor, Jim and Gary should expect to give up 43 percent of Lin-Tex. (One million dollars is 43 percent of $2.3 million.)

"We need two million dollars," Jim said, "for ten percent of the company."

The consultant ignored the joke. "People need to understand that you understand your business," he said. "These venture guys are pretty tunnel-vision. They're going to have a hard time believing that two hamburger guys can manage this company."

The phone rang and Jim took it at his desk. "I like Jim and Gary," the consultant confided to Rudi. "I find them interesting. Their character comes out, the way they act and dress. But they're not the Ivy League types investors are used to dealing with."

Jim, in jeans and ostrich-hide cowboy boots, hung up the phone and walked back from his desk, which was a twin of Gary's. When he and Gary were both in town, they sat side by side, at identical desks, in identical chairs, running their company. The wall behind them was decorated with mementoes of their non-Ivy League lives: a floor plan of the original Wendy's restaurant; a photo of Jim, with Wendy, presenting a check for charity to Danny Thomas. From Jim's first boom years there was a framed check he had written to the IRS for $33,000; from Austin, the trophy they had won in the Sugar's golf tournament.

"Once you get the plan out," the consultant was saying, "I'll get it to ten groups the next day. Then it may take me a couple of weeks to get them on the phone. I have a whole lot of confidence in y'all and this whole deal. But it's going to be a long, slow climb."

The mailman arrived with $8000 in checks. Not enough to resolve the immediate crisis.

A cashier's check sat on Rudi's desk, made out to Harlan for $11,000. She had gone and gotten it the previous afternoon, knowing the other two checks would bounce as a result. "I'm not going to give it to Harlan unless he'll be back in production," she told Jim.

Then Gary called and asked about the royalty payment due the syndicate from which they licensed "Bloom County." "We need to Federal Express them twenty-two thousand dollars tomorrow if they're going to get it by the fifteenth," Rudi said. "You know how pissy they get if it's late. . . . Okay. . . . Hold our breath till Monday and wire it in."

Harlan called and said he would start printing shirts again if he got the $11,000 and a promise of the other $40,000 in a week. Rudi was getting ready to take him the check when Gary called again. He said he thought it was more important to get some money to Bicknell at Dyco in an effort to persuade him to come to Austin for a meeting than it was to get a week's worth of printing out of Harlan.

So Rudi went back to the bank again, cashed in the check for Harlan, got a new one for Dyco, and dispatched it by Federal Express. As for the "Bloom County" payment, she'd put it out of her mind. That one wasn't due for four whole days.

# "**F**ixin' to Come a Gullywasher"

**I**N THE MUDDY PEN outside Pete's office sat a cow with a broken hip. She had broken it giving birth to a calf that was too big for her. As part of a venture unrelated to the Senepol business, Pete had had several mixed-breed cows implanted with embryos sired by a Brahman bull. The bull had a history of siring enormous calves, but no one had taken notice of that until the embryo calves started being born—killing their surrogate mothers in the process. Pete had taken action in time to save one cow by hiring a veterinarian to perform a Caesarean section; the recuperating cow now wandered in a pen by the house displaying big stitches on her flank, her healthy calf beside her. The calf of the cow with the broken hip was likewise prospering, but the cow was in a bad way, sitting splay-legged in the mud. She had sores on her body and flies on her sores. Whenever a human walked near, she tried to stand up but succeeded only in toppling forward and banging her head on the ground.

Inside the office, Pete got a call from his banker with more bad news. Pete had managed to pay down his operating loan from $55,000 to $40,000, and he expected the loan to be renewed, as it had been routinely several times before. But now, the banker said, the bank (which was financially shaky, although the banker didn't mention that) did not care to renew the note any longer. It would be due, in full, on July 27. That was seven weeks away.

Pete didn't have $40,000. All he had was a lot of nothing new.

The Sri Lanka deal, despite one final flurry of phone calls and assurances, had never come through. Nor had the export beef deal, nor the butter deal, nor the feed lot. Some of the partners in Universal I, enmeshed in the gears of the collapsing Texas economy, had failed to remit scheduled payments that Pete had been counting on. The tank of semen he had left in Guatemala, hoping for a quick sale, had somehow defrosted and gone bad.

Most disappointing, none of the cattle he'd left in Guatemala had been sold. After listening to the banker, Pete dialed Max at the hardware store in Guatemala City to see if anything was happening. Max reported that Leonowens had, at last, gone out to look at the four Senepols on Roberto's cousin's dairy farm, and he had asked the price. Ten thousand dollars, Max had told him. Max was expecting a counteroffer at any moment.

"Well," Pete said, "I'd like to sell them. Let's try not to go lower than eight thousand, but if he'll buy 'em at seven we'll take it. . . . If he buys 'em, I'll come down there and bring you some more semen." Pete still thought Guatemala was his brightest prospect and was tentatively planning a second sales trip there for August.

He hung up the phone and sat silent in his chair in the little office in the barn. He was alone there now. Lisa, the secretary, had left two months before to get married. Keith had quit after Pete told him he'd have to lower his salary. (Keith was thinking of moving on to business school at the University of Texas; after that, maybe the movie business; he wanted to do "something creative.")

Pete picked up the phone and buzzed Becky in the house. "Is there any bad mail?" he asked. In fact, there was some good. A Louisiana rancher who'd seen the Senepols at the Houston Livestock Show wanted more information. Pete let out a little whoop. He tried to call the rancher immediately, but the man was out.

Pete needed to make a sale. He had this $40,000 due, plus big payments coming up on the ranch (which he had taken over from his father-in-law). He had two car loans, plus a loan on his computer, plus an equipment loan that had financed his cattle chute and the microscope he used for embryo transfer work. The only money coming in was what he got for selling hay, which he was cutting as frequently as the weather allowed. The only Senepol sale he'd ever made was still the sale of six embryos to a rancher named Louper, and that had been months ago; Louper's cows were nearly ready to give birth.

Meanwhile, two new Senepol herds had recently been established in Texas, which Pete thought of as his territory, and he'd had nothing to do with either one of them. A small rancher near Burnet had bought a cow and calf from the Niceley brothers, and a big operator in Throckmorton, a well-known Simmental breeder, bought seventy-nine animals directly from St. Croix, most of them from the Nelthropps, who were breaking up their herd. The Niceleys were promoting their Senepol sales effort with a full-page ad in *The Cattleman* ("Get the Tropical Punch of the Red-Hot Breed") and had established working relationships with both Annaly Farms and the Throckmorton rancher. Pete was being left behind.

Things had sunk so low that he had begun thinking about getting a job, but Dr. McCall made another suggestion: why didn't Pete open a feed store? Pete jumped at the idea; he could run a store with Becky and Wendell and bring in enough cash flow to keep things together until he started selling Senepols. He went out and found an empty lot on the south side of College Station— an area that needed a feed store and didn't have one—and arranged to rent it for $300 a month. He was looking for an abandoned oil field building to move there, and he was already planning his inventory. He would sell Purina feeds, and the hay he was currently selling wholesale to another feed store, and decorative shrubs, and imported saddles and bridles from Guatemala. He'd asked Max to find out if they made such things there.

When Pete walked out of his office to go to lunch, he could see some of his plans being realized. Using timber from the tree that had fallen on Pete and nearly killed him, Wendell was banging together a little plant nursery.

Seeing the frame go up was encouraging. This business was not going to rely on Saudi princes or *Wall Street Journal*-reading millionaires or anything else out of Pete's own control.

As Pete walked by, the crippled cow, trying to rise, banged its head into the mud. "When are you going to take it to the slaughterhouse?" Pete called to Wendell. If they got it there before the cow developed a fever, they could sell the meat.

"They can't take it till morning," Wendell said. "But I'm going to put it in the trailer now, so it'll be more comfortable."

Pete looked up at the sky and nodded. It had been pouring off and on for weeks, and clouds were massing up again. "It's fixin' to come a gullywasher," he said.


Max was supposed to call back in the afternoon with Leonowens's counteroffer, but Leonowens didn't make one. Eventually, he offered to buy two of the Senepols, but Roberto, operating beyond Pete's control, insisted on selling all four and the deal fell through.

The Louisiana rancher was never heard from again.

The price of beef for slaughter was rising, and Pete sold some animals to raise cash. He sold some mixed-breed cows that were surrogate mothers to Senepol calves and doubled up their calves on surviving moms. He hated to do it, but he sold a Senepol cow that wasn't breeding and some Senepol bull calves that were less than first rate, and Texas got its first Senepol hamburger.

With the proceeds, Pete paid the bank $9000 ($7000 principal, $2000 interest), and the bank renewed his loan after all, for a term of six months. The new balance, $33,168.20, was due on January 25. Collateral, as before, was all the cattle Pete owned.

Pete worked on setting up the feed store and anything else he could think of, and he took heart from his family. The kids were strong and happy. Becky was running what she called "Camp Senepol" for them and four of Pete's nephews and nieces from Houston. She drove them to swim and play baseball and led them in crafts projects and awarded merits and demerits for good and bad behavior and, every night over supper, had each child recite what he or she had liked best about the day.

She went to church every Sunday, and she told Pete she knew that things had to work out:

"Someone didn't take you out of the onion fields of South Texas and the rice paddies of South Vietnam for you to rot in College Station. There's got to be a purpose in there. And we'll find it."

# "We Can Almost See the Money"

**T**HE MEETING WAS so important that Jim and Gary didn't even drink on the plane, even though they had flown first class as usual and the booze was free. It was only 9:00 p.m. when they arrived at their hotel, but instead of going out on the town they went to bed. The meeting was set for 10:00 a.m., and they wanted to be at their best.

They arrived a few minutes early at the skyscraper at 40 Wall Street, checked the building directory, and stepped into an elevator. They were wearing suits and silk ties and matching pairs of $450 alligator-and-ostrich loafers. Jim wore a $1500 bracelet on which the word "Comics" was spelled out in diamonds and gold. Gary, who had lost his matching bracelet a few weeks before, was carrying a combination videocassette recorder and television in a bag over his shoulder. He pressed a button in the elevator; the door slid shut; and he and Jim rode up to see if Loeb Partners, a blue-blood investment firm with one of the most lustrous names on Wall Street, wanted to buy a minority interest in Lin-Tex Marketing.

Jim and Gary had been looking for cash nonstop since their dual supplier cutoff in June. They'd managed to convert their big Lamar Savings loan from a short-term to a long-term obligation, which made their balance sheet look less precarious but did nothing to improve their cash position. (In finalizing the transaction, they'd given Lamar a $10,000 check—drawn on their Lamar account—to cover current interest, and it bounced.) Jim put up one of his few remaining unpledged personal investments to get a $22,500 loan from a small Austin bank, but Lin-Tex needed much more than that. June came to a close with $300,000 in orders sitting on the table unshipped, because Lin-Tex didn't have the money to buy the product.

Jim called his brother Dave in Columbus and described his plight, and Dave suggested he call Jim Kirst in Florida. Kirst was an early Wendy's franchisee who had made millions of dollars in the fast-food business. He had at various times been involved with, and made money from, Wendy's, Burger Chef, Ponderosa, Rax, and Red Barn. He had frequently obtained financing for his ventures from Loeb Partners, with happy results for all. Jim telephoned Kirst, who remembered him and Gary from their Wendy's days. He suggested they call Loeb Partners, and he called the firm first himself to put in a good word for the boys.

By this time, Lin-Tex's situation had improved a little. Both of the suppliers that had cut off Lin-Tex had agreed to resume shipping directly to Lin-Tex's customers, provided they could collect the receipts directly and apply them to Lin-Tex's debt. Some of Lin-Tex's customers were paying cash in advance for their shirts in exchange for a discount; this enabled Lin-Tex to get the shirts produced but cut into the company's profit margin. Finally, Jim and Gary had found a third supplier to whom they did not yet owe a pile of money. All of these solutions to their problem were stopgap, however. Shipping shirts from three locations was in itself a logistical and accounting nightmare. Lin-Tex still needed an infusion of capital.

Jim phoned a principal at Loeb Partners named Peter Dixon, who said he was pleased to hear from Jim and asked for a copy of Lin-Tex's business plan. The plan wasn't ready, Jim said. He sent Dixon a brief financial statement, an Opus "Sold My Soul To Rock 'n' Roll" T-shirt, a Lin-Tex polo shirt with Bill the Cat embroidered on the left breast, and a Bill the Cat golf cap.

Gary threw himself into writing the plan and came up with a nicely laid-out sixty-five-page document crammed with charts and graphs and convoluted but enthusiastic prose. "Our retail reorders of the same designs," it stated at one point, "has proven that the shelf life of the majority of our products has an infinite selling season." Elsewhere: "The success of Lin-Tex to date has given its size of potential outlet of goods excellent recognition in the overall industry."

The plan explained Lin-Tex's new Comic Collectibles marketing concept and included a chart showing that the number of stores buying it had increased from 3 to 110 between January and June. Another chart showed the increase in total retail sales outlets from 159 to 1,755 over the sixteen months since Lin-Tex had switched from a mail-order to a wholesale operation. "The sales growth of the company," the plan declared, "from $225,000 [in its first year] to $3,700,000 [in the fiscal year just ended], was not accomplished with a trendy product or magical powers; it was the result of a gathering of critical knowledge of the market, the precise execution of a R&D plan, and some unbelievable luck."

The plan did disclose that Lin-Tex had been running in the red for several months, a result, it said, of funding stepped-up marketing efforts out of cash flow. Two color-coded sales history charts, showing steady growth month after month and year after year, went no further than May, when sales had topped $400,000; it was left to one small black-and-white graph to disclose that shipments in June had plummeted to $100,000 (the plan did not explain why).

The package concluded with some optimistic projections of future growth and a balance sheet that ascribed a value of $2.5 million to Lin-Tex's T-shirt rights to "Bloom County," "Mother Goose & Grimm," and ten other comic strips. The balance sheet did not include a disclaimer that Lin-Tex's accountant always insisted on adding when Jim and Gary valued their rights this high; standard accounting practice was to value such rights at the price paid for them (in this case, a small fraction of $2.5 million). Jim and Gary thought this rule was unjust, and the page with the accountant's disclaimer usually disappeared from their financial statements. "It's a collating problem," Gary once explained.

As soon as the plan was finished, Jim rushed a copy to Peter Dixon, whose first reaction was that it was "rough." He nevertheless invited the Lin-Tex partners to New York for the meeting which Jim and Gary now approached with a combination of ostentatious casualness ("We don't need this deal; we're shipping again, aren't we?") and high anxiety.

The elevator stopped on the thirty-fifth floor, and Jim and Gary got out. They walked down the corridor to the door marked Loeb Partners and stepped inside. From what they saw, it appeared a mistake had been made, that Loeb Partners ought to be seeking money from Lin-Tex Marketing, not the other way around. The reception area was a shabby little room with stained carpeting and two old chairs. Beyond it the firm's employees were conducting their business in ancient wooden cubicles. Compared to the Lin-Tex offices, the place looked like a bus station.

Loeb Partners was so established and rich it didn't need a nice office. It was a successor to the brokerage firm of Loeb Rhoades & Company (later Loeb Rhoades, Hornblower & Company), which had been purchased by Shearson in 1979; Shearson Loeb Rhoades had in turn been purchased by American Express in 1981. Several of the Loeb Rhoades principals had taken their substantial profits and regrouped as Loeb Partners, the main activity of which was investing the surplus cash of the principals and their relatives and friends.

One of their assets had been the building in which their office was located (a building which, upon its completion in 1930, had briefly been the tallest in the world). In 1984, the firm sold it to a company that turned out to be a front for Ferdinand and Imelda Marcos. A federal racketeering indictment of the Marcoses later charged that they had bought the building with stolen funds, and it was put in the hands of a court-appointed receiver. None of this affected Loeb Partners' sales agreement, part of which entitled the firm to rent its office (which had once been a Loeb Rhoades brokerage office) at a bargain rate. Peter Dixon, who worked in a cubicle not much larger than Jim's desk, considered it "a rather modest office of the old style," and he was as comfortable there as he needed to be.

Dixon, in his fifties, was thin and precise, with heavy black-framed glasses and an accent he had acquired at a private school in England. His father had been a partner in Rhoades & Company, which had merged with Loeb & Company in 1937 to form Loeb Rhoades. He greeted Jim and Gary and ushered them into the office of Thomas Kempner.

Kempner, sixty, the chairman of Loeb Partners, was the grandson of Carl Loeb, who founded Loeb & Company in 1931. Kempner's wife Nan was a leading New York socialite, endlessly chronicled in the society columns for sipping champagne with Baryshnikov at a benefit for the ballet or jetting to Paris with Ivana Trump to see the spring line by Christian Lacroix. Two months before his appointment with Jim and Gary, Kempner's New York apartment had been the subject of a fawning article in *Architectural Digest*, complete with photos of the Aubusson rugs, Ming porcelain, and Chippendale mirrors that filled "the two-story apartment the size of a country house."

As soon as he and Jim were seated in Kempner's office, Gary broke the ice by declaring, "We're just a couple of poor kids who never did anything but fry hamburgers and make T-shirts."

It was his standard introductory rap, and Jim joined in the chorus with tales of Kentucky Fried Chicken, including how he'd had to stand half in the bathroom at one store to bread the birds. Gary brought their story to the Lin-Tex years: how, in the early days, they'd sold armadillo T-shirts from the trunk of their car at venues like the Marble Falls Howdy-Roo. To bring the saga up to date, he plugged in the TV/VCR he'd carried up and inserted a tape produced at the Lin-Tex office. Gary's voice was on the sound track.

It began: "Down in Texas, we say, 'Howdy!' "

The tape showed smiling Lin-Tex employees answering phones, typing on computers, and stacking T-shirts on warehouse shelves. There were shots of sales manager Mitch Tucker, who, Gary narrated, "started frying hamburgers for us when he was sixteen," and internal marketing manager Charles Crowley, "who come to us by way of . . . the hotel business."

There were still shots of Gary in his Wendy's uniform and Jim with Colonel Sanders, and, of course, there was the Ur-Lin-Tex story:

"When people ask me to talk about Lin-Tex Marketing, I've got to go all the way back to the third grade, 1956, where I was placed next to a gentleman named Jim Teal. . . ."

Jim rolled his eyes.

Kempner and Dixon sat and listened to the tales of chicken breading and everything else. In the course of looking for investments, they and their venture capital associates investigated up to a hundred companies a year, and they had seen people like Jim and Gary before. They were glad to see them again. "If you've made any investments in the food field," Dixon explained later, "Jim and Gary are people that one is very comfortable with. The food field is not an area that attracts postgraduate students. The retail business does not attract many intellectuals. . . . We have gone with overeducated types who are involved in high technology and haven't the slightest idea how to make any money. We often have to bring in practical business managers. At the other end of the spectrum are people who know how to make money, who have been making money since age seventeen, the hard way, working ten to fifteen hours a day, who worked their way up the way Jim and Gary did. I'm more comfortable with those people. They've demonstrated they have the drive and the guts to make money."

Also working in Jim and Gary's favor were a strong initial endorsement from Kirst and the fact that the kind of money they were seeking was a small sum to Loeb Partners.

But the meeting did run into a few minor hitches.

Neither Dixon nor Kempner was familiar with "Bloom County," although Dixon was a big fan of "Andy Capp," and Kempner stated, to Dixon's amazement, that he read "Spiderman" every day. Gary and Jim assured them of "Bloom County's" popularity.

Dixon produced the "Sold My Soul To Rock 'n' Roll" T-shirt Jim had sent him. "We put it through our test laboratory," he said, "and the test laboratory reported some problems with deterioration of color." He held up the shirt, and it looked awful; the design was badly faded. "My wife washed it five times," Dixon explained.

Gary pounced. "She bleached it."

Dixon acknowledged she had.

"You can't bleach these shirts," Gary said.

"If you don't bleach them," Kempner asked, "do they get clean?"

"I don't do my own laundry," Gary said, "but when I wear my shirts they're clean."

Finally, Kempner indicated that the concept of wearing T-shirts as outerwear—the very root of Lin-Tex's business—was a little alien to him. He had served in the Navy, he said, where T-shirts were worn as *underwear,* and he had worn T-shirts as underwear ever since. Of course, he had noticed some people wearing T-shirts as outerwear, and he'd seen that the T-shirt Jim sent Dixon was large enough to be worn as outerwear. . . .

"Tell them what happened at your club," Dixon cued him.

One of his nieces, Kempner said, a middle-aged woman, had appeared at the country club the previous Sunday wearing a T-shirt with a humorous dinosaur design. (This "was not a deal-making occurrence," Dixon said later, "but it was a happy coincidence, another added influence. An elite gentlewoman comes in wearing something her daughter had given her for her birthday in one of the elite clubs in America. It reflected the acceptability level T-shirts have now achieved.")

Those hurdles passed, the meeting turned to the question of money. On the phone a few days earlier, Gary had told Dixon that Lin-Tex was looking for $500,000 for 20 percent of the company. "You wanted five hundred thousand dollars for twenty-five percent . . . ," Dixon now began.

Gary corrected him. "I said for *twenty* percent."

Jim jumped in with a gag. "No," he said, punching Gary in the arm. "You're giving away too much. Five percent."

Kempner and Dixon laughed, and moved on.

Dixon asked what Lin-Tex would do with $500,000.

Pay off $150,000 in debts, Gary said. Put the rest in certificates of deposit. Borrow against the CDs.

And that concluded the meeting. Dixon and Kempner said they would talk things over and be ready to meet again the following day around lunchtime.

Gary said they'd be there. He grabbed the ruined bleached shirt and stuck it in his bag, and he and Jim marched out of the office.

Gary didn't want to wear the same suit to meet Loeb Partners two days in a row, so he and Jim went shopping. At Paul Stuart,

Jim was amazed by the prices ($800 for a sport jacket) and amused by the company logo that appeared on the house-brand polo shirts. "It's a man sitting on a stick!"

He and Gary walked down the block to Brooks Brothers, where Jim inspected the logo with interest. Kempner had mentioned this logo during their meeting when talk had turned to the Lin-Tex polo shirt with its embroidered Bill the Cat. "All we see down here is the Golden Fleece," Kempner had said, "and we're tired of it." Neither Jim nor Gary was aware that the Golden Fleece was a mythological object sought by Jason and the Argonauts nor that it had been expropriated by Brooks Brothers for its logo, so they let the comment pass.

But now here, on a Brooks Brothers polo shirt, was the Golden Fleece (in the Brooks Brothers representation, a sheep hanging from a branch in a sling). "It's a sheep being hung!" Jim exclaimed. "It's fucking horrible! I wouldn't wear it in a million years."

Gary, browsing among the pants, announced that he was ready to leave.

"What's the matter?" asked Jim. "Couldn't find no pants with a pig being hung?"

At Saks, Gary bought a gray plaid suit on sale for $500.

Next stop was Yankee Stadium, for a summer evening's relaxation with a baseball game and large cups of beer. Jim was distracted temporarily by a young man in front of him who was trying to attract the attention of some women a few rows away. "Hey!" the young man called to them. "Hey!" They ignored him. Trying another tack, he pulled a few small bills from his pocket and fingered them so the women could see.

Jim tapped him on the shoulder. "Like this," he instructed. He pulled a hundred-dollar bill out of his pocket. He licked it. He stuck it on his forehead.

By 11:00 a.m. the next morning, Jim and Gary were in their suits and ties and ready to go. Jim was reclining on a bed in their hotel room watching "The Price Is Right" while Gary used the phone, attempting to reach Peter Dixon to find out what time he wanted to see them. Towels were wrapped around the base of the toilet, which had overflowed in the adjacent bathroom.

Dixon was in a meeting, and he had been in a meeting for a while. He had promised to call in the morning, and he hadn't done it.

A blond contestant on "The Price Is Right" guessed the price of a car wrong. She wasn't even close. Jim addressed her by the name on her name tag: "Dana, you dumb shit."

He turned to Gary. "Guess we already got our answer." If Dixon didn't call, Loeb Partners obviously wasn't interested.

Gary walked to the window, which looked south. He could see the Empire State Building. Beyond it, on Wall Street, the fate of Lin-Tex was being decided.

"Peter," Gary called into the distance. "When is lunch?"

"Peter," he called again, "we can almost see the money from here."

"The Price Is Right" ended and "Scrabble" came on. One of the clues was "Helps Dolly Parton keep her head above water." The answer turned out to be "Treading."

When the show was over, Gary dialed Dixon again, and this time he got through. "Yes," Gary said. "How are you? Okay. . . . Okay. . . . Okay. . . ."

Jim looked out the window. "Peter," he called, "we're trying to see your cash from here." Then he spoke softly, mimicking what Dixon might be saying to Gary: "There's no real need for you boys to come over and see us today. I don't think we're going to make a deal."

On the phone, however, Gary was saying: "Okay. . . . Okay. . . . Super. . . . All right. . . . How about this? I'm going to be in all next week. You can reach me any time in Austin. . . . To make sure I'm not reading anything into this, you feel there's room for some additional talk, but you think there's a proposal that can satisfy our needs and your needs too. . . . Right. . . . Right. . . ."

"Super Password" was on the TV now. Two of the clues were "Attractive" and "Kennedy."

"Caroline," Jim said. He was wrong.

"If you want to call him, fine," Gary was saying to Dixon. "He knows the business overall very well and can give you a good overview of the comics industry. He knows a lot of people and deals with important people."

"Don't oversell," Jim muttered.

Two more clues were up on "Super Password": "News" and "Schwarzenegger."

"Maria Shriver," Jim said. Correct.

Gary hung up. "Well," he said, "we don't need to meet today. He said they liked us both very much, felt we were sincere, honest. Tons of companies come through there, and they found our company very impressive. What they'd like to do now is start formulating a plan to sell to their investors and their key people. Peter said Kempner was so enthusiastic he started last night."

Jim turned off the TV, and he and Gary looked at each other. They had one reservation: they'd been led to believe that either Dixon or Kempner could pull out his own checkbook and write a check for $500,000. If they liked the deal so much, what was this stuff about consulting with investors?

But this certainly wasn't *bad* news. It might be the end of their troubles. Gary, still suffering physically from tension, had said a few days earlier that he felt the tension worse "the closer we get to the home run. There's just one more step between now and financial Utopia."

Was Utopia at hand?

Gary looked out the window. "Thanks, Peter," he called. "I blew five hundred dollars on this suit."

He picked up the phone and dialed Rudi at Lin-Tex.

"It's a done deal," he reported, "if they don't come back and try to rip us off."

# Plugging a Hole

**A** WOMAN PHONED PETE from a ranch in Texas and said she was working with some Venezuelans who wanted to buy eight hundred Senepols. The deal was going to be financed, she said, by a New York businessman whose office was at 80 Wall Street. Pete called the man to chat and was put off by what struck him as "a typical New York personality." He sounded "like he ate big meals and drank a lot of cocktails and has a lot of money and doesn't necessarily have a lot of morals." The man remarked that if the government didn't have a monopoly on them, he would be happy to trade in nuclear weapons.

Of course, by this time Pete would gladly have sold Senepols to the Ayatollah Khomeini, so the New Yorker's personality was not an issue.

Pete drove down to Houston to meet with the woman who'd called him and said he could supply eight hundred Senepols at $1900 apiece. One million, five hundred twenty thousand dollars. He figured he'd sell thirty out of his own herd and broker a deal with his fellow Senepol breeders for the rest.

The woman said the Venezuelans had decided they wanted only three hundred head. Fine, said Pete. In that case they'd be $2200 apiece. Six hundred sixty thousand dollars. His profit, he calculated, would still be more than $200,000.

Five days later, the president of a Venezuelan cattlemen's organization flew up from Caracas and Pete picked him up at Houston Intercontinental. He drove him and the woman to the ranch and showed them around.

Nineteen days after that, having heard nothing, Pete called the woman. She said the Venezuelans were interested in buying one hundred head if Pete could document that they were good milkers. Pete sent off some information.

And he never heard another word.

And then, like manna from heaven, descended Horace Mc-Queen from Lufkin, Texas. He called Pete and said he wanted to buy eight Senepols. He drove over and picked them up and gave Pete a check for $20,800. And the check was good.

This cheered Pete up considerably. He made a payment that was overdue on a loan he had taken out with the limited partners in Universal I. Then he turned his attention to $25,000 in payments that were overdue on Hopes Creek Ranch.

The ranch payments had been due on August 18, three weeks before the appearance of McQueen, and they had been heavy on Pete's mind. He'd had a quick and intense education in the obligations he had incurred by "buying" the ranch from his father-in-law for a token sum and a promissory note. There were, he learned, four separate notes payable to two different lienholders (not counting his note to Billie):

— On the fifteen acres nearest the road, which included the house, the barn, and the small house where Keith had lived, a payment of $510 was due quarterly to a man named J. S. Mogford, who had sold the ranch to the man who sold it to the man who sold it to Billie.

— On the remaining 185 acres that made up the front of the ranch, $5401 was due quarterly to Mogford.

— On the back 358 acres, $28,501 was due annually to Mogford.

— On the entire property (excluding the house and surrounding fifteen acres), $19,765 was due quarterly to a man named Boedeker, who had sold the ranch to Billie.

Billie had turned the ranch over to Pete when he could no longer make the payments himself; he'd been paying with money he'd been receiving from investors to whom he'd sold another million-dollar property, and those investors had gone broke and stopped paying him. Billie had already poured $300,000 into Hopes Creek Ranch. Now he advised Pete to walk away from it, to stop throwing good money after bad. "Why plug a hole with your finger," he asked, "when the dike is breaking?" Pete didn't need to own a 558-acre ranch to run his cattle business; he could lease grazing land somewhere else.

But Pete wasn't ready to walk away. Under any circumstances, he intended to stay in the house; he could pay $510 quarterly forever. And, for now, he wanted to keep everything, at least until the next round of payments was due.

The money due on August 18 had been the $510 (which Pete had paid), the $5401, and the $19,765. The $28,501 wasn't due until November, when the $510, the $5401, and the $19,765 would also be due again.

November seemed like a long way off. Pete accepted that he might have to give up the back section then, but first he wanted to try to sell it at a profit. Alternatively, he was going to look for partners to fund development there. He was thinking about catfish farming again.

The front he definitely wanted to keep. And it looked like time was on his side. The feed store would be open soon, bringing in cash. And interest in Senepols was on the rise. There was his sale to McQueen, and a slew of new telephone inquiries. The Simmental breeder in Throckmorton who had bought seventy-nine Senepols from the island was planning on showing them at a field day in October, which should stir up interest even more. Pete was planning his own third annual Senepol Stampede for October as well. (Becky wanted to cap the festivities by burying a time capsule; she was hoping to get mementoes from the governor and the A&M football coach.) Meanwhile, a man dropped by to see Pete's Senepols and Pete learned afterward that he was connected with the King Ranch. The King Ranch! A rancher in Burnet named John Hoover told Billie he wanted to buy some Senepols, and Pete was trying to set up a meeting with him. Things were definitely on the move. This was no time to cut and run.

So, when a deadline of September 18 was set for foreclosing

on the ranch, Pete mobilized. He began to negotiate with Boedeker, who was not pressing for immediate payment of the money owed him. It was Mogford who was forcing the issue, and Pete and Boedeker had a common interest in seeing that Mogford was paid; if he wasn't, the entire chain of subsequent sales of Hopes Creek Ranch would come undone.

Together, Pete and Boedeker raised $5401 in cash, and Pete drove through a rainstorm to get it to Mogford's lawyer's office by 5:00 p.m. on September 18.

He made it, and he felt pretty good.

He had saved the ranch.

# "I've Got Half a Million Dollars"

**A** WEEK AFTER Jim and Gary met with Loeb Partners, Gary flew to New York again and drove to Connecticut for a meeting with Walden Books. Walden was interested in buying the new "Bloom County" T-shirt featuring Billy and the Boingers (Bill the Cat's heavy-metal band, renamed from Deathtöngue, the strip explained, because "Deathtöngue is not particularly conducive to positive, Christian, all-American thought in our nation's youth") to sell side by side with a new "Bloom County" book. Gary walked out of the meeting with a $136,000 order. He picked up a phone in the reception area to call Peter Dixon and see what was happening.

Dixon had assured Jim and Gary that an offer would be coming soon, but none had yet arrived. Dixon had been doing some checking up on Lin-Tex. He called T-shirt retailers, syndicate licensing managers, and a lawyer who represented several prominent cartoonists. All spoke highly of Jim and Gary. Meanwhile, Dixon's secretary was washing and rewashing a Lin-Tex T-shirt—without bleach. It came out fine.

Dixon was in a meeting when Gary called from Connecticut, but Gary reached him when he got back to his hotel in New York. The deal was just coming out of the typewriter, Dixon said. A messenger brought a deal memorandum to the hotel a couple of hours later.

Gary did not respond to Dixon immediately. He didn't want to discuss the offer until he understood it, and he didn't understand it. Also, he wanted to talk to Jim. But the next afternoon he figured he ought to give Dixon a call anyway. "Did you get our document?" Dixon's secretary asked anxiously.

"Yeah," Gary said, "but I had to spend the day in the New York Public Library looking up the Latin words in it." (Gary always enjoyed playing up what he referred to as his "hillbilly" background in conversations with the cultured Dixon. At one of their meetings, when Dixon took orders for lunch to be brought in by a Wall Street delicatessen, Gary requested "a Moon Pie and RC Cola.")

The secretary put Gary through to Dixon, who told him how excited Loeb Partners was about the prospect of investing in Lin-Tex Marketing.

"This looks like the beginning of a good relationship," Gary said.

"They don't come along very often," said Dixon, "so grab it."

"Let me go home and tell Jimmy," said Gary.

One of the first things Jim did, when Gary told him, was to call a friend and chant, in the schoolyard rhythm, "Nyah nyah nyah-*nyah* nyah, I've got half a million dollars and you-oo don't."

The deal Loeb offered was complex, but it boiled down to this: in exchange for a $100,000 investment and a $400,000 loan, Loeb would own 25 percent of Lin-Tex Marketing. If, at the end of five years, Lin-Tex's annual earnings were less than $4 million, Loeb's ownership share would increase another 1 to 10 percent (depending upon exactly what Lin-Tex's earnings were), up to a maximum of 35 percent. Implicit in the arrangement was the promise of future backing and loan guarantees for Lin-Tex by Loeb. The big payoff for Loeb Partners—and for Jim and Gary—would presumably come when a successful Lin-Tex made a public stock offering and the owners' shares would be worth millions.

This offer was a little below what Jim and Gary had been seeking, and they did have other options. Orders for T-shirts were coming in strong (although there was still a $300,000 shipping backlog resulting from Lin-Tex's debts to its suppliers). Jim and Gary had been invited to present their business plan at a venture capital conference in Dallas at the end of August (but attending it would mean missing a golf tournament they wanted to play in).

Lin-Tex's sales manager's brother-in-law, who worked at the Equitable insurance company, said he knew a lot of investors who might be interested in Lin-Tex and offered to set up meetings. Jim and Gary were talking to the Austin economic development authority about getting a low-interest loan and job-creation grants to set up a Lin-Tex shirt manufacturing operation. A member of the fast-sinking Austin banking community said he wanted to lend Lin-Tex some money and asked Jim and Gary if they had any real estate they could put up as collateral. "Jesus Christ," said Jim, "isn't that what's putting you fuckers into bankruptcy?" "Well, yeah," said the banker, "but we *understand* land loans."

After several days of stewing things over, Gary called Dixon and made a counteroffer that adjusted the terms of the deal slightly in Lin-Tex's favor.

Dixon laughed. "The only counteroffer," he said, "is no offer."

In that case, Gary said, the original offer sounded just fine.


And then nothing happened. Jim and Gary expected their $500,000 to arrive in a matter of days; Jim was especially looking forward to paying off their debt to Dyco and starting over with a clean slate. But no money arrived. Nor did a final contract. Dixon called to say the paperwork was taking a little longer than he had expected.

Jim and Gary waited in Austin, and then Jim took off on a long-scheduled driving trip with Frances, the baby, and the dog in the "Banana," the Lin-Tex motor home that had been mobile headquarters for his bachelor party. The trip was to take them to visit friends and relatives in the Midwest and conclude in upstate New York in time for the B.C. Open golf tournament, a professional event linked to the popular caveman "B.C." comic strip, to which Lin-Tex had the T-shirt rights.

Since their marriage, Frances had taken to complaining that Jim didn't do enough things with her (a few days before their first anniversary, he'd told her, "I'm playing golf. What do you want to do?"), but, in the confines of the motor home, their togetherness was sorely tested. The baby, a sturdy and generally good-natured little boy, required attention. The dog had to be smuggled into motels at night. In Ohio, Frances got food poisoning from some ranch dressing and Jim had to rush her to a hospital. Jim and Frances squabbled at first, but they eventually fell into a relaxed routine. Jim was still driven mad by how long it took Frances to dress for the simplest outing ("Any human being can get dressed in two hours," he once complained, "but not Frances"), but traveling in the motor home diminished that problem. Jim could drive to a destination while Frances dressed.

The golf tournament offered a chance to decompress. Jim and Frances checked into a Holiday Inn near the En-Joie Golf Club in Endicott, New York, and Gary, who had just split up with Dayna, flew in to join them. In the pro-am that preceded the professional tournament, Jim and Gary were teamed with the defending champion and Johnny Hart, who drew "B.C." Hart, a native of the region who had created "B.C." in 1958, lived on a large estate in nearby Nineveh, which Jim and Gary had visited in 8-degree weather the previous winter to coax some T-shirt designs out of Hart and establish a friendship. On the first hole, Hart hit a bad slice into the refreshment area and clipped the ear of a woman serving ice cream. On the second hole, he beaned a member of the gallery. No one in the group played particularly well, and they finished poorly.

Jim and Gary were still in Endicott when they finally received a contract from Loeb Partners. They read it eagerly, and they didn't like what they read. The contract threw out several existing agreements between Jim and Gary, including a provision that Frances would get Jim's salary for a year if he died and another that Jim's brother Dave would run the business until it could be sold if Jim and Gary both died. The contract also specified that only Loeb had the right to buy Jim's or Gary's stock if one of them went bankrupt. "All of a sudden," Jim complained, "the remaining partner is a fucking minor leaguer. Loeb's an *investor*. They have no right to come in and throw out all our agreements. Maybe they can explain to us why these things are necessary."

If not, he vowed, there would be no deal.

# "Fifteen Dollars in Ten Hours"

A LITTLE GRAY NISSAN backed toward the front porch of the feed store, and Pete's heart was made glad. When they backed up to the porch, it meant they were going to buy something.

The driver was a young man wearing camouflage coveralls and a knife in his belt. "What kind of deer blocks you got?" he asked Pete. "Are they apple blocks?"

"This is what we've got right here," Pete said. He pointed to a pile of what looked like brown bricks. "You're welcome to read the label."

The label said the deer blocks were made of grain, molasses, salt, and minerals—all taste-tempting treats to a deer. (Deer blocks are set out by hunters as bait. Becky didn't think that was fair.)

"I'll take two sacks of corn," the hunter said, "and one of those blocks." The corn was used as bait, too.

"Where you hunting at?" asked Pete.

"By the racetrack."

Pete nodded. "Quite a few in that direction."

"Got one yesterday," the hunter said.

"Great," said Pete. "Bow hunting?"

"This time of year, better be."

The hunter paid for the corn and the block and carried them out to his car.

Pete, smiling, watched him drive away. "A customer!" he said. "What a way to start the day!"

It was a clear and sunny fall day, a football day (fans were pouring into College Station to see the Aggies play)—and the seventh day of operation of Texsen Feed and Supply, Pete's feed store. The vision of the summer had been realized two months behind schedule, but now (with financial support from Dr. McCall) it was finished and open for business.

The building was a triumph of Binion family construction. Thirty feet wide by forty-five feet deep, it had been hammered together in sections on the ranch and then hauled to the vacant lot on the south side of College Station and erected. A roof was put on and tin sheeting nailed to the sides, and there it stood, roughhewn but sturdy and thoroughly weatherproof, even if it lacked such niceties as a telephone, water, and plumbing.

It had electricity. Becky sat at a desk behind the chest-high wooden counter pecking away at the Apple computer, keeping the roster of Wade's soccer league up to date and creating a spreadsheet of the store's inventory with wholesale costs and retail prices. Piled all around were 25- and 50-pound sacks of Purina Dog Chow, Puppy Chow, Cat Chow, Catfish Chow, Rabbit Chow, Horse and Mule Chow, Nurse Chow (for calves), and Preconditioning Chow (for cattle in feed lots). Also Layena (for chickens), Pig Startena, and Omolene 100, Omolene 200, and Omolene 300 (all for horses). Also rat poison, fire-ant poison, horse-worming paste, horse shampoo, horsehair polish, bridles, hay, and deer blocks. There were as yet no decorative shrubs, but Becky had bought some seedlings at K Mart and was growing them at the ranch in the nursery Wendell had built.

The kids were in heaven, conducting a sort of feed-store Olympics. They crawled through boxes, leapt off piles of Chow, and raced up the aisles, chariot-style, on a metal cabinet on wheels until it hurled too close to Pete one time too many. He summoned the children to the counter and they stood silently before him. Wade, almost nine, and Pauline, seven, wore their soccer uniforms. Mollie, just turned four, was barefoot and streaked with dirt.

Pete pointed to the cabinet. "The next man or woman who sits on that is going to get a whipping." The children nodded solemnly and dispersed.

Pete turned his attention to a receipt from a sale made while he'd been out coaching Wade's soccer team in a game (they lost 2-1, which Pete had taken as a bad omen). "Eighteen twenty-six," he read aloud. "What was this? Rat pellets?"

"No," Becky said. "Calf scour boluses." To treat calves with diarrhea.

Pete nodded with satisfaction. Eighteen dollars and twenty-six cents in the till. God bless the sick little calves.

The store was working out just fine. Sales the first day had been $46.75. The second day they rose to $47.35. Then they soared to $117. Then dipped to $74.52. Then never dropped below $100 again. This was a lot better than going out and getting a job somewhere, which had been Pete's other alternative. In the store he could sit behind the counter and work on his agricultural projects and generate cash flow at the very same time.

Wendell liked the store, too. It was much more pleasant than chasing cattle around cold fields at dawn in the mud. And he enjoyed the contact with the public. Bryan wasn't one for waiting on customers, but he did a good job of hauling Chows around. The first couple of days, every time a car drove by, Pete had him walk out the front door with a sack of dog food on his shoulder to make the place look lively. The first time a customer drove in, Bryan got so excited he dropped the bag in the parking lot and ran inside, destroying the illusion.

Pete stood behind the counter now and watched a man in an orange T-shirt pick out twenty-five dollars worth of rabbit food.

"Rabbits, huh?" Pete commented.

"The kids got to have something to play with," said the man.

"It's cheaper than a horse," Pete said.

"I imagine."

A shout came from Pauline on the loading dock. "Train coming!"

Across the highway, on tracks parallel to the road, a freight train was just pulling even with the store. Pauline and Wade and Mollie ran out front frantically yelling and waving Aggie pennants.

The engineer waved back.

———

A man came in and asked what was the difference between Omolene 100, Omolene 200, and Omolene 300. Pete directed him to the labels on the bags. "They give you a little talkin'-to right here."

A man came in and bought some wild bird feed for his wife to set out. "Do we need to feed the wild birds?" Becky asked. She'd never noticed the Wild Bird Chow before.

The Aggie game was on the radio, but Pete didn't turn it on. "You can't be a sports fan and run a business," he explained.

Between customers, he was poring over a survey map of Hopes Creek Ranch. The map identified the property as part of the "James Hope League," land that had been granted to James Hope in 1824, at a turning point in Texas history. The granting of the land had itself been part of that turning point. In 1821, Moses Austin had won permission from the Spanish government to settle three hundred Anglo-American families in Texas, the beginning of a population movement that would eventually result in Texas's war of independence from Mexico and its joining the United States. Moses Austin died in 1821, but his son Stephen carried the project on. Eleven of the families settled in what is now Brazos County, and James Hope was the first of those to receive his official land grant. He was given 2¼ leagues (a league was equal to 4428 acres) and 2 labors (a labor was 177 acres). Some of that land had come down to Pete.

Pete was figuring out where to put catfish on it.

He identified 100 acres that would be good for ponds because of the drainage. He picked a corner of the land for his fish-processing plant. He had already gone up to A&M to get literature on catfish farming and other kinds of aquaculture; he was thinking of being broad-based and raising catfish and crawfish and shrimp and "specialty items for the Vietnamese" (there were a lot of Vietnamese refugees in Texas). He had a copy of "Farming Fresh-water Shrimp" on his desk and a brochure called "Cost Analysis for Texas Crawfish Production." Another brochure, "Direct Marketing of Fish and Shellfish," was filled with practical tips for the aspiring fish farmer:

*Be patient with customers.* The old saying "the customer is always right" must also be adhered to . . . even though complaints and pettiness may at times seem unbearable. It seems that women have a superior aptitude for dealing with customers and it is sometimes a good idea to let women partners handle customer relations while men produce the fish. . . .

*Be generous to media representatives.* Media people are human. They will enjoy, appreciate and always remember free fish. . . .

*When media does come to your farm* be completely cooperative and cordial. Do whatever they want regardless of how stupid it may sound or inconvenient it may be. Adopt a "your wish is my command" attitude. Such an experience may be demeaning but the cash in your pocket will quickly heal any ego infractions.

The next round of payments on the ranch was due in six weeks. Pete figured he would have to get his aquaculture project launched by then or give up the back 358 acres. He was looking for limited partners willing to invest $250,000.

Meanwhile, he had decided to postpone the third annual Senepol Stampede until the spring, when he would hold his first public auction of Senepols. The Senepol business still looked solid, at least for the long term, and the feed store fit into Pete's plans for it. "Texsen," the name of the store, was the name he'd always intended to use for his own brand of Senepol beef. He would sell it right here—or in a new store he would build next to the feed store since it was against health rules to sell meat in a feed store. This lot on Highway 2154 would become a two-store Binion family mini-mall, selling everything from kitty litter to filet mignon.

A customer walked in and Pete looked up from his map. She was a short-haired woman in overalls, and she paid for her purchase with another woman's check. A lesbian, Pete concluded.

The store had several lesbian customers. They tended to be very interested in horse nutrition.

She was the eleventh and final customer of the day. At 6:30 p.m., Pete shut the door, which had been opened at 8:30 a.m., and counted the money. Gross receipts were $154. The standard markup was 20 percent. Rent came to $12 a day. Pete figured electricity cost two or three dollars. He totaled it up. "We made fifteen dollars in ten hours," he announced. He was smiling. He looked happy about it.

Back at the ranch there were five hundred bales of hay lying in the meadow behind the house. More than a thousand had already been picked up and sold, wholesale, for $2.50 apiece. When Pete got home, Wendell and Bryan and Aleta were hauling in another load on a trailer hitched to an old Ford pickup. Pete met them in the hay barn, stripped off his shirt, and climbed eight feet up atop the hay already stacked there. Wendell and Bryan tossed bales to him and he slotted them together like building blocks. The pile grew higher and Pete climbed higher. Bryan, who never seemed to tire until he finally collapsed asleep, tossed the 65-pound bales to a height well over his head as if they were sacks of potato chips. But a couple of throws fell wide.

"Has your hay-throwing deteriorated?" Pete asked him.

"I ain't tryin' to be deteriorated," Bryan said.

When the trailer was empty, they went out for another load. Aleta drove the truck bouncing over the field. Wendell and Bryan picked up the bales, and Pete stood on the trailer and stacked them. As the trailer filled, the old truck spewed exhaust and struggled with the weight. Its headlights froze deer in the woods at the edge of the field. Their eyes reflected back like Christmas tree bulbs.

Afterward, Pete sat outside with a rum and Coke and hooted at the owls. They didn't hoot back. The harvest moon, just past full, was shining on his fields.

"This is what it's all about," Pete said. "You look that way and you can't see a light."

The trees cast moonshadows. Their upper branches were filigree against the sky. The only sounds came from crickets—and Pete.

"You carve out your land," he said, "and you try to hold it."

In the morning he noticed a cow in trouble. She was a Jersey-Hereford cross in labor with a Senepol embryo, and it wasn't going right. She stood in a pen behind the house, her back bowed. There should have been some sign of the calf. Pete was afraid it might be turned.

He moved the cow into the pen by the barn and went to look for a rubber glove. Wendell came out with a length of yellow rope, a bottle of Sunlight dishwashing liquid, and a blue plastic bucket that he filled from a tap at the trough. Pete came back without a glove; he couldn't find one.

Wendell got behind the cow and shooed her toward a chute. She resisted, sidestepping nervously, but Wendell got her in, and Pete dropped a bar in behind her so she couldn't move. "She's a little sore and a little wild," he said to Wendell. "Let's see what she does." He took off his shirt and grasped the cow's tail firmly with his left hand. He inserted his right arm, up to the shoulder, in her rectum.

His right hand pushed gently on the wall of her uterus, feeling for the calf. "It's upside down and backward," Pete said. He pulled out his arm and washed it at the tap.

Wendell washed the exterior of the cow's vagina with the dishwashing liquid and then Pete inserted his arm, reaching directly for the calf. If it was alive, it would kick.

The cow bellowed and started to buckle. "No, Momma," Pete said, his arm still inside her. "Don't go down."

He leaned into the vagina until he felt the calf. It didn't move. The cow thrashed in the chute. "Oh, Momma, easy," Pete grunted. His face running with sweat, he went down on one knee and leaned in deeper. The cow crashed against the sides of the chute and uttered a strange uncowlike moan. "Okay, baby, easy," Pete said. He withdrew his arm as the cow shat.

Pete knew the calf was dead, but he wanted to save the

mother. She was worth $500 for beef. He released her from the chute into the pen and prepared to try to pull the calf.

Wendell slipped a halter over the cow's head, and he and Pete tried to tie her to a post. They pulled her near and she broke away. They pulled her near again, got the rope around the post, and used it as a pulley to draw her in. She bucked and broke away again. Pete fetched a hypodermic needle and injected a muscle relaxant into her flank. Then he and Wendell tried once more and this time got her tied.

Pete wanted her down, so they looped a rope around her left front leg and tried to trip her with it. She danced over the rope and stayed upright. They tried again and again, but she always danced away. It is hard to trip a cow.

Switching from guile to force, the men tied her front legs together and tried to tip her by pushing on her side. She hobbled away. They wrestled with her, even got her down on her knees a couple of times, but she always managed to get back up. Men and cow were breathing hard. They finally tied her back legs together as well as her front and shoved with all they had and she went over and the men fell down with her. Pete sat on her side while Wendell tied her front legs to the post. She struggled still. Wendell sat on her head.

Pete lay on the ground behind her, sprawled in the dirt, and inserted his arm into her vagina. The cow pissed, drenching him. He ignored it. He was grunting and the cow was grunting. He pulled his arm out and put it back in, this time with the yellow rope in his hand. He tried to loop it around the dead fetus's legs but it slipped right off. A milky fluid spotted with blood dripped out of the vagina around Pete's arm. He tried for the fetus one more time and then decided it was beyond him. He would have to call a vet.

"We're gonna let her go," he called to Wendell, who was still sitting on the cow's head. They started to untie her and she bucked. Wendell was tossed three feet straight up. "Hold her right there if you can," said Pete, who was facing the other way and didn't see that Wendell was aloft.

"If you can't hold her, let her go," Pete added, just as Wendell came crashing to the ground.

# "It's Time for the Cosbys"

**W**AITING FOR THE PLANE from New York to arrive, Jim and Gary had a drink at the Austin airport bar. They were nervous and excited; Gary was unusually pensive. "At this time tomorrow," he said to Jim, "we'll be drunk and real happy. . . ." Jim finished the sentence: "Or drunk and real sad."

They walked out to the gate to meet Peter Dixon and the Loeb Partners attorney, Bruce Lev. Dixon walked off the plane wearing a pinstriped suit and carrying two enormous boxy briefcases.

Somewhere inside them, Jim and Gary hoped, was half a million dollars.

They all rode to a hotel called La Mansion in Jim's Mercedes. "Do you want a drink?" Gary asked. Dixon and Lev declined. "There's a couple of topless clubs near here," Gary said. Dixon and Lev did not respond. They got out of the car and said goodnight.

Jim waited all morning at the Lin-Tex office for the meeting to begin. The night before, he had asked Gary if they should wear shorts today to show Dixon their usual casual style. "Let's wear suits," Gary had suggested. Jim was wearing a suit. Rudi and the other women in the office were dressed in silk.

It was almost noon when Gary arrived with Dixon and Lev from a preliminary meeting with Lin-Tex's lawyer. Gary led the

New Yorkers into the office he shared with Jim and showed them the adjacent twin desks. "This way after I've had a phone call I don't have to repeat everything to him," Gary explained.

"A commendable idea," Dixon said. He perused the items hanging on the walls—Jim and Gary's Wendy's memorabilia, original artwork for comic strips, an autographed picture of George Hamilton. Lev stopped in front of the Sugar's trophy. "Is this the tournament you told us about?" he asked.

Touring the warehouse, Lev grabbed a shirt off a shelf and handed it to Dixon. "Peter," he said, "this is just the shirt for you."

"Is it Beethoven?" Dixon asked.

It was a naked woman in the arms of an oilman. "I love it when you talk crude," she was saying. The design was from the early days of Lin-Tex, when the company sold mostly armadillo designs and peddled its shirts from the trunk of Gary's car.

Dixon took the shirt.

The meeting convened in the conference room, which was decorated with Indian artifacts Gary had negotiated a good price on with a local dealer. Gary removed the steer horn centerpiece from the table and all were seated: Jim, Gary, Dixon, and the two sides' lawyers. For Loeb Partners, there was Lev, bearded and wearing a custom-made Alexander Julian suit (he was a personal friend of Julian); among Lev's other clients was a sex magazine for which he negotiated columnists' contracts with Marilyn Chambers, star of "Behind the Green Door," and Seka, star of "Inside Seka." For Lin-Tex, there was Hubert Gill, a smart Austin attorney who had argued before the Supreme Court of the United States and had also recently represented a woman who'd been stuck in a gas station restroom for several minutes and sued the oil company for $30,000 (she lost).

As the meeting began, most issues between Loeb and Lin-Tex had already been settled. Two weeks before, Jim, Gary, and Gill had flown to New York to hash out the points in the proposed Loeb contract that Jim and Gary had found objectionable. Dixon explained that the contract had come "off the shelf," and he adjusted or withdrew the distressing clauses. Although Dixon had seemed impressed that Jim and Gary got discount travel agents' rates at their hotel in New York, he insisted that Loeb's investment in Lin-Tex not include the money-losing travel agency Jim and Gary had bought; Jim and Gary agreed and promised to repay $47,000 the agency had drawn out of Lin-Tex.

Also settled was the question of Jim and Gary's compensation: they would receive annual salaries of $100,000 (an immediate $22,000 raise) plus quarterly bonuses if Lin-Tex made good profits.

When the New York meeting had ended, Jim was satisfied. "When will the papers be ready?" he asked.

In a couple of weeks, Lev had said.

"How about tomorrow?" asked Jim.

Lev said that might be a problem; the following evening was the start of Rosh Hashanah.

"They need the money," Dixon had said.

Lev called his secretary and told her to come in at 6:30 a.m.

Even so, two weeks had passed from that meeting to this one, and Lin-Tex needed the money more than ever. Its Austin supplier was desperate to be paid. Gary was putting him off day by day.

As the parties gathered now in the Lin-Tex conference room, the major issues outstanding had to do with Lin-Tex's balance sheet. They were addressed by the final participant in the meeting, Lin-Tex's accountant, a prim and efficient woman named Marcia.

When Joe Waldon Enterprises had metamorphosed into Lin-Tex Marketing, Marcia explained, its debts and accounts receivable had been carried over to the new corporation. This was convenient but improper; Lin-Tex should have started with a clean slate.

Joe Waldon Enterprises had been a partnership of Jim, Gary, and Joe Waldon; Jim put up the money, Gary did the work, and Waldon drew the armadillo cartoons. Some of the money Jim had put into the business—$19,000—had been considered a loan from Jim to the partnership. Meanwhile, Gary had augmented his small salary by drawing out "loans"—a total of $47,000.

Lin-Tex had thus been created owing Jim $19,000 and owed $47,000 by Gary, Marcia explained. But Lin-Tex had no obligation to pay Jim the money, she said. He should write it off as a bad debt, which would at least give him a tax break.

Jim pretended to fall out of his chair (and actually did fall out partway). "Something is going to work *for* me with the IRS?" he exclaimed. "I don't believe it!"

As for Gary, Marcia said, he could keep the $47,000, but he would have to declare it as income and pay taxes. At the same time, all of Lin-Tex's tax returns would have to be amended and Lin-Tex would have to pay Social Security tax on the $47,000. This was "an accounting nightmare," she said, but she would do it.

Dixon and Lev nodded sympathetically. Jim, bored, trimmed his cuticles with a nail clipper.

"What was the big buildup in accounts receivable from Gary in 1986–87?" Dixon asked.

This was the final problem. During the Lin-Tex years, both Gary and Jim had taken money out of the company beyond their salaries. As before, Gary had drawn out some "loans" to augment his pay. ("What was my salary that year, eighteen thousand?" Gary asked Marcia—twice—as she explained this, in case anybody was getting the idea that he had been overpaid even with the "loans.") Some company money had paid for personal items for Gary and Jim. Some had gone to legitimate business expenses which Gary and Jim had never gotten around to documenting with receipts. Some had gone to purposes lost in the mists of time.

Marcia reported that she had pored over old records for hours and concluded that Jim owed Lin-Tex $64,361 and Gary owed $94,927. Since Loeb Partners was about to buy ownership of approximately one third of the company, it naturally wanted that money repaid.

"What do you want to do about it that won't wreak havoc with Jim and Gary's lives?" Lev asked Dixon.

"We're going to have to take a hickey and pay taxes on that," Gary put in, somewhat irrelevantly, "but I feel that our liability to you, in good consciousness, is one third of that amount."

"Our concern," Dixon replied, "is to make it as easy as possible for your company to grow without doing damage to the way you live. It's in your interest more than ours to get this cash back into the company."

Gary parried. "I think it's common knowledge that we both have about everything we own wrapped up in the company."

Jim, still bored, interrupted. "I'm kind of a bottom-line guy," he said to Dixon. "What do you want to do?"

"I'm asking what *you* could do, what you'd be comfortable with."

"We could pay it on a quarterly basis," Gary said, "as we review our bonuses."

"We recognize that this is the only source of income you have," Dixon said.

"We pay back fifty percent of our bonuses," said Gary. "Is that fair?"

"If that's comfortable for you," Dixon said, "that's fine."

Jim sat up. "Okay!" he said. "It's a deal!"

"Shall we sign," asked Lev, "so we can go have lunch?"

The contract and supporting documents were passed around and signed. Then Gary called for Mitch Tucker, the Lin-Tex sales manager, to come in with his camera and record the moment.

"Why don't we get a shot with the check?" Jim asked.

"Oh," said Lev, pretending he had forgotten. "The check."

Jim and Gary and Dixon posed in the entrance to the showroom and Mitch snapped the picture. It shows Gary handing Dixon a certificate for shares of stock in Lin-Tex Marketing.

Dixon is handing Jim a check for $500,000.

Everyone is smiling.


Three hours later Dixon and Lev were on their way back to New York. At Lin-Tex, the celebration was about to begin.

Gary sat at his desk gazing at a photocopy of the check (the original was in the safe). Lin-Tex's senior male employees were sitting on the office couches guzzling drinks. Jim was at his desk thinking about a new business. He'd recently been at a miniature golf course in Ohio unlike any other he'd ever seen. The holes were elaborate and gigantic; you couldn't even see one hole from another. It cost $3.75 to play, and the public loved it. On a weekday evening, Jim had been number twenty-four in a line to tee off.

After T-shirts, he was thinking, miniature golf. . . .

Gary dialed a limousine service and got a young woman on the line. He was calling to book a limo for the evening but that naturally did not prevent him from launching into a long discussion of the T-shirt business. It was a fun business, he told the woman. Did she ever read the comics?

Eventually, Gary arranged for the limo.

Jim was not much interested in celebrating. He was pleased by the Loeb deal, of course, but one more night out with the boys, after all the years and all the nights out with the boys, held little appeal.

Still, he went through the motions. At a country music bar on the Sixth Street strip, he sent a drink to the singer, an Austin regular named Rusty Wier who was performing his classic, "I Hear You Been Layin' My Old Lady." At a nearby sex shop, he bought Gary a package of "Recycled Condoms—For Cheap Fuckers." As the Lin-Tex party rode away from Sixth Street in their hired limousine, Jim stood up through the sunroof and called out to two women in a car driving in the next lane until one of them stood up through her sunroof and shook hands with Jim as the cars sped down the street side by side.

At the Yellow Rose, however, Jim became engrossed in a conversation with the manager and paid no attention at all to the strippers, not even the plain-looking one who came over to the table and started out telling the guys how shy she was and ended up picking up their drink glasses with her breasts.

The next day was more interesting. Jim and Gary drove over to Lamar Savings, the troubled financial institution that held Lin-Tex's $440,000 loan.

"So you hit the home run," their banker said.

Gary showed him the check.

"I think I'd better touch that," said the banker.

"I'll let you touch it," Gary said, "but I'll hold onto the other side." And he did.

Gary explained their plans for the money: they wanted to buy $500,000 worth of certificates of deposit and keep them intact. They would borrow against them for cash to pay Lin-Tex's bills and to finance more growth.

"I want to be candid with you," the banker said. "You're in a great position now. The money opens up a number of doors that were closed before."

Gary said they wanted the interest rate lowered on their $440,000 loan.

"That definitely can be looked at by the committee," the banker assured him.

Gary said they wanted a line of credit equal to 100 percent of the value of their new CDs, even though 90 percent was customary. The banker said he would take that request to the committee as well. "As far as I'm concerned," he said, "it's a slam-dunk."

Before any of this could happen, however, Jim and Gary had to deposit the check and buy the CDs. And this turned out to pose a problem. Federal deposit insurance covered only $100,000 per depositor. There was no way Jim and Gary were going to put more than $100,000 in any one name in any kind of account with Lamar Savings, which everyone knew was in terrible financial shape. "I can tell you we'll be here in thirty days," the banker said, "but I understand."

For more than an hour, Jim, Gary, and the banker wrangled over a way to get their money into the bank without risking losing it if the bank happened to fail while the check was clearing. (Gary had hoped Dixon would bring down the money in five $100,000 checks for just this reason.) After several false starts, the banker finally exchanged the check—with no wait for it to clear—for five $100,000 CDs, one each in the names of Jim, Gary, and Rudi, and two in the name of Lin-Tex Marketing. The next day Lin-Tex would borrow at least $100,000 against the CDs in its name; if Lamar then folded, Lin-Tex's net position would be less than $100,000 and thus fully insured. Jim and Gary were willing to take the risk that Lamar would survive overnight.


That night Jim did what he wanted to do: he went home early.

He greeted Frances and Frances's dog and three other dogs belonging to one of Frances's girlfriends that were temporarily living in his yard. Then, with more enthusiasm, he greeted his son, J Carroll, now ten months old. J.C., as his parents called him, had the sturdy build and tough-looking face of a miniature prize-fighter. Jim picked him up and tossed him into a pile of pillows. J.C. laughed and came back for more.

Frances went out to get some groceries. A minute later the phone rang. It was Frances, calling on the car phone from Jim's car in the driveway. She wanted him to come out and call the dogs out of her way.

J.C. was trying to walk, and Jim helped him. They walked around the house together, hand in hand—past the crap table, which had been moved into a corner and was piled high with Frances's paints. Past the pool table.

J.C. held himself up against a coffee table and tore through the pages of a couple of Frances's art books while Jim watched. J.C. grunted that he wanted Jim's beer, and Jim gave him a sip.

The phone rang.

"Hello, Frances," Jim said.

It was Frances, back from the store, calling on the car phone from the driveway. She wanted Jim to come out and help her carry the groceries.

Jim gave J.C. a bath, and he thought about his son's future. With the Loeb Partners investment, Lin-Tex was finally secure. Loeb Partners had intimated it would help out with more financing as Lin-Tex needed it. Nothing would prevent the company from growing now. Jim couldn't imagine what Lin-Tex would be selling in twenty years, but it was a safe bet that it would be selling something.

There would be a place in the business for his son.

Jim changed into a pair of tight red running shorts that made him look fat and a "Momma" T-shirt. He tossed a bag of popcorn into the microwave.

"It's time for the Cosbys," he announced. He turned on the large-screen TV and sat down to watch with his son, just like tens of millions of his fellow Americans on a typical Thursday night.

# The End

IN EARLY NOVEMBER, the telephone company disconnected service to Hopes Creek Ranch. Pete had decided he could afford only one phone bill, and he kept the phone at the store.

On November 18, the payments on the ranch were due. Not having raised $250,000 for his aquaculture scheme, Pete didn't make the payment on the back 358 acres.

He didn't make the payment on the front 185 acres either. He didn't have the money.

He did make the $510 payment on the house and surrounding fifteen acres. He wanted to continue living there, even without the ranch, and he was still planning on getting into catfish farming, only with three acres of ponds instead of one hundred.

Two Argentineans showed up at the house one afternoon and asked what Pete would charge for five hundred Senepol embryos. Two hundred fifty thousand dollars, he said, minus a volume discount. The Argentineans said they'd be back at 1:00 p.m. the next day. They never returned.

At Christmas, the Binions gave friends and relatives rocks that Becky and the kids had painted themselves.

The original lienholder, J. S. Mogford, formally foreclosed on all of Hopes Creek Ranch except for the house and surrounding fifteen acres. Pete made plans to move the cattle to Billie's ranch in Burnet and Dr. McCall's ranch in Fayette County, where there was plenty of room for them. He was still counting on having a Senepol auction in the spring to raise cash.

Then the bank came after the cattle.

On January 25, the $33,000 operating loan that Pete had renewed the previous summer was due at First Bank & Trust in Bryan.

On January 27, the bank notified Pete that unless the loan was paid by 10:00 a.m. on January 29, it would come to Hopes Creek Ranch and seize any cattle it found there.

On January 28, Pete met with his banker and asked for extra time. The banker said that if Pete paid $2333 in interest and legal fees by 10:00 a.m. the next morning, the bank would renew his note for thirty days. Pete asked for an extension until 5:00 p.m., and it was granted.

On January 29, Pete drove to Burnet with ten Senepol heifers and sold them to John Hoover, who had expressed interest in buying Senepols several months before. Pete's original asking price had been $2000 apiece; now, pressed, he sold the ten for $10,000. Hoover gave Pete a check. Pete drove to Bryan and deposited $3000 in his own account and wrote the bank a check for $2333. He deposited the other $7000 in a Universal I partnership account, from which he would soon be drawing to make a payment on the partnership's loan from the bank. The day's transactions, Pete said later, made him feel "happy as a lark." In exchange for his $2333 check, the bank had extended his loan for thirty days, which seemed to him like "a lifetime." As part of the loan agreement, Pete promised that none of his cattle would "be removed from its location, transferred, sold, or otherwise disposed of without the prior written consent of First Bank."

On February 2, Pete's banker learned from a banker in Burnet that Pete had sold the ten heifers to Hoover. Pete's banker, worried that Pete might be using the proceeds for purposes other than repaying his debt (and unaware that all the money had been deposited in the bank), telephoned Hoover and told him the sale might be illegal since the bank had a lien on Pete's cattle. Hoover responded by stopping payment on his check to Pete. "I have enough problems in my life," he explained to Billie Pratt. In consequence, Pete's check to the bank bounced.

On February 8, Pete got a letter from the bank saying it was coming to take his cattle on February 10.

On February 9, a cattle hauler hired by Pete trucked all the cattle on Hopes Creek Ranch except for fourteen calves to Dr. McCall's ranch.

At 6:00 a.m. on February 10, Pete, Wendell, and Bryan hauled the calves to a friend's ranch in Edge.

At 10:00 a.m. on February 10, three big trucks arrived at Hopes Creek Ranch with sheriff's deputies and cowboys. They couldn't find any cattle to seize. Nobody was home except Aleta.

At 11:00 a.m. on February 10, Pete's banker called Pete at the feed store and told him the bank might press criminal charges against him.


Five days later, Pete sat at his desk in the feed store filling out bankruptcy documents. He didn't like the idea of going bankrupt but it seemed to be the only thing to do. The bank's talk of criminal charges was so far just bluster—although Pete still expected he might be arrested at any moment—but the bank had sued for repayment of his debt. So had another bank to which he owed $7000 for ranch equipment. So had the man who cut and baled Pete's hay. So had the man who did embryo transfers on Pete's Senepols. Pete owed $6800 in old payroll taxes. He had a $300 bill for moving the cattle in Guatemala from Roberto's cousin's dairy farm to another ranch. He owed a lot of other debts as well. The feed store was grossing about $5000 a month, enough for Pete and Becky to draw out some living expenses but nothing more. The feed store owed $10,000 to Purina.

Pete had consulted a lawyer about bankruptcy and picked up a form called "Statement of Financial Affairs for Debtor Engaged in Business," which would have to be filed with his bankruptcy papers. He was looking it over carefully and writing in answers to its questions:


Q: When was the last inventory of your property taken?
A: *Feb 88*

Q: By whom or under whose supervision was the inventory taken?

A: *Wendell Binion under Pete Binion*

Six feet away, at the feed-store counter, this very inventory was being conducted; Wendell was leaning over a list of ranch tools.

"Mark out the things we don't have any more," Pete told him, "and give the others a price. Low. What a pawnshop would give."

*1 Crescent wrench,* Wendell entered: 10 cents. *2 Phillips head screwdrivers:* 10 cents. *2 Clutch alignment tools:* 4 cents.

The lawyer had told Pete to inventory all his possessions, including his cattle, which were obviously his most important asset. Between Fayette County, Burnet, and Edge, the dispersed Hopes Creek Ranch herd comprised some 120 Senepols. But the question of who owned which was not a simple one. Some were owned by the Universal I partnership (of which Pete was a member). Others were owned by Annaly Farms, which had sent them to Hopes Creek Ranch on consignment. Still others were owned by Pete in partnership with Annaly Farms, or Pete in partnership with Dr. McCall. One belonged to Keith. A handful belonged to Pete outright.

Pete's cattle records were not up to date, so he was tackling the easy stuff first. While Wendell toiled over the list of ranch tools, Pete made a list of personal and office goods: *Hat rack:* $25. *Desk* (the one he was sitting at): $30. *Briefcase* (a Christmas gift from Becky two years before): $10. *5 rugs* (souvenirs of Guatemala): $50. *Beta Max (old and broke):* $15.

In the margin next to the entries for his Apple II computer ($800) and Minolta copier ($600), Pete wrote: "These items are mortgaged to Apple Credit. I want to keep them after bankruptcy and pay them off if possible."

A customer came in and bought a sack of corn for his fighting cocks.

The store was looking good. Wendell had built display racks for nails and sacks of feed, and a new wall separated the front from the storage area in the rear. A refrigerator and microwave oven had been installed behind the counter, and the front of the counter was now a neighborhood bulletin board, lending the place a homey feel. New inventory items included Hamster Chow, Guinea Pig Chow, parrot seed, and Texas A&M onion seedlings. Out back, there were twenty chickens in a pen; Wade was raising them to augment the family's food supply. Bryan was digging a garden and had already planted potatoes. By the side of the building Pete had erected a thirty-foot pole. He wanted to put a windmill on it to generate electricity and save on the store's power bill. He had a book about windmills on his desk.

A customer walked in. A Houstonian on a hunting trip, he asked about deer corn. Pete sold him the most expensive, least dusty kind. That's what he sold to people "if they look like they watch a lot of TV and work in a clean place," he explained after the customer had gone.

Wendell looked up from his list. "What about the branding irons?" he asked.

"Not worth much," Pete said.

"The whole set two dollars?"

"No," said Pete. "The numbered ones are worth something." The ones that branded numbers could be used on any ranch.

Wendell wrote:

*10 Branding irons 0-9*: $15.
*1 Branding iron HCR*: 50 cents.


Around midday, Pete set aside his inventory list and leaned over and polished his boots ("*Boots*: $40").

He started to peel off layers of clothes. He was wearing, above the waist, a blue parka, a sweater, a white shirt, a thermal undershirt, and a T-shirt. The temperature was 50 degrees (a few days earlier it had been in the twenties), and the store's only heat came from a small kerosene heater. Pete generally came to work wearing two pairs of long johns. It was cold at the house, too. Pete hadn't run the furnace in two years and now, since the ranch had been foreclosed, he had as a matter of principle stopped going on it to cut wood for the fireplace. He was building fires with wood from elsewhere, and the kids were sleeping in front of them.

Stripped down to his T-shirt, Pete relayered without the thermal undershirt. He tied a tie on his thigh, transferred it to his collar, and combed his hair in a mirror stuck on a wall above a pile of scratch grains. He drove to the local television station to arrange for some ads in support of an upcoming school bond referendum for a swimming pool that would be used by the Binion kids' swimming program. Pete felt strongly about the issue. On behalf of the pro-swimming pool committee (and with its money), he bought six prime-time commercials for $600.

Becky, meanwhile, was setting out to walk from Hopes Creek Ranch to the feed store, six miles away. She was supposed to be spending the day at home, but Mollie was crying with a bad earache and Becky was worried about her. There was no phone on the ranch and no vehicle either. Pete had been unable to keep up the payments on the Blazer and the pickup Keith used to drive, and he had surrendered them both to the finance company. The family's transportation needs—kids to school, kids to swimming, kids to soccer, kids to basketball, girls to ballet lessons, Pete to feed store, Becky to feed store, Bryan on errands for feed store, Pete and Becky shopping, Pete on business trips—were now tightly orchestrated around one 1976 Ford pickup with 130,000 miles on it. Becky also owned a 1982 Buick, but it had gone into the shop for repairs and could not be picked up until a $238 bill was paid.

Becky wanted to take Mollie to the doctor, so she started walking to the store to get the truck (the nearest pay phone was five miles from the ranch, nearly as far as the store). A passing telephone repairman gave her a lift.

By the time Pete got back to the store, Mollie was there (a friend had fetched her) and feeling better, and Becky was at the computer typing in Pete's inventory list.

"What watch is this?" Becky asked him. "Mine or yours?"

"What's it say it's worth?" Pete asked.

"Ten dollars. My watch is worth ten dollars."

"How much is mine worth?"

"Ten dollars."

The issue was still unresolved when Wendell handed Pete his completed inventory of ranch equipment. The total was only $300, which struck Pete as low. It turned out that Wendell had forgotten the Buick. He entered it now as " '82 Buick Century (family car) not running."

"What price are you putting on it?" Pete asked.

"Five hundred, and you'd have to talk me into that."

Pete didn't try. He picked up the phone and called his sister Mollie in Houston, who recommended another lawyer. Pete called the lawyer and left a message.

"Three hundred paperback books at twenty-five cents each?" asked Becky, still typing the inventory. "You only paid five cents each for a hundred of those."

"Okay," said Pete, "call 'em five cents."

"What's five cents times three hundred?" asked Becky. She got up to find the calculator.

"Fifteen dollars," said Pete. "What's wrong with you people? You look like candidates for bankruptcy to me."

Becky looked at the next item on the list. "Christmas ornaments? Boo-hoo-hoo. Mollie's little hands?"

She typed them in.

Keith walked through the door. Pete hadn't seen him for months. Keith wanted to know when he could get the Senepol calf he'd been promised as part of his pay. He wanted to take it "before the bank gets it." Pete told him the calf had gone with some others to Dr. McCall's ranch, where, after a bad storm, one calf had been found dead in the trough. It might have been Keith's. Pete promised to check the records and let him know.

A friend dropped off Pauline and Wade, their school day done. Pauline immediately set to work on a book report. Wade lounged on the floor atop a worn orange rug depicting Mayan gods that Pete had brought back from Guatemala. He set a box of Lucky Charms on the rug beside him and picked out the marshmallows and stacked them in a pile.

A woman came in to buy a bag of horse feed.

"Howdy," said Pete.

"How ya doin'?" she asked.

"Everything is great!" Pete exclaimed with a tight-faced grin.

It was, in fact, a record day for the store. Three hundred eight dollars in the till—the most ever for a Monday. After closing up, Pete coached Wade's basketball team in a league game, and they won. On their way home, the family stopped at K Mart, where Becky bought some medicine for Mollie's ear. It was near closing time, so sandwiches from the K Mart deli, normally $1.39, were being cleared out at twenty-five cents apiece. Becky bought half a dozen to freeze and take to the store for lunches. She did this a couple of nights a week. Wendell didn't like the sandwiches—they got mushy when he defrosted them in the microwave—but the Binions couldn't afford to pass up the bargain.

That was about the bottom.

Over the next couple of weeks, Pete's attitude changed. He started thinking less about going bankrupt and more about fighting back. He'd gone broke. But he felt aggrieved.

Billie advised him to start suing.

It seemed to Pete he had a couple of strong claims against First Bank & Trust. If the banker hadn't called John Hoover and raised a stink about his purchase of ten Senepols, Hoover wouldn't have stopped payment on his check, and Pete's check to the bank would have cleared, and Pete would have had thirty more days to pay off his note. And who could say—for sure—that he wouldn't have been able to raise the $33,000 and save his herd and stay in business and prosper?

"The bank messed me up real bad," Pete declared.

Even before that, the bank, apparently confusing Pete's personal loan with the Universal I partnership loan Pete had taken out with four other people, had sent a letter to Pete's partners informing them that Pete was in default. This, Pete maintained, had hurt his good name with his business associates.

Pete met with a lawyer who agreed with him. "We're looking at going after maybe about a million and settling for maybe half of that," Pete reported after the meeting. "This sounds kind of corny, but since I haven't had any beer to drink I mean it: this is what the patriotic business is all about. This is the law working for me. It's been my philosophy of life—sticking up for the little guy and standing up for America."

While the lawyer decided whether or not he wanted to stand up for Pete on a contingency-fee basis, Pete was falling out with Dr. McCall. McCall had backed Pete's Senepol venture—he had even backed the feed store—but now, as Pete's finances foundered, so did their relationship. McCall felt that Pete had mismanaged the business and he expressed puzzlement as to where some of the money he'd put into it had gone. Pete thought McCall had more money than he needed and was overreacting to what were for him minor losses. "I'm riding in the back of a truck," Pete said. "He never went a day without riding in his Mercedes." Faced with the prospect of First Bank & Trust seizing any cattle it could find to which Pete was linked—as full or part owner—McCall was worried that cattle in which he or the Universal I partnership had an interest might get swept up in the dragnet. His interests and Pete's were diverging fast.

Meanwhile:

Billie suggested that Pete, Wendell, and Bryan apply for food stamps as separate families, to maximize the benefits.

Pete had a meeting with the co-coach of Wade's soccer team and plotted strategy.

The swimming pool bond issue won by forty-five votes.

Wade's teacher asked if she could bring the class to Hopes Creek Ranch to see what a ranch was like. Pete said sure.

He made plans to have some cattle trucked in for the day.

On a rainy Monday afternoon, Wendell drove Pete to Houston in the old Ford pickup, dropped him off at their sister Mollie's office, and turned right around to try to get back to College Station in time to drive Pauline to soccer practice.

Pete had seven days remaining before the legal deadline to respond to First Bank & Trust's lawsuit against him. He had come to Houston to settle on his course. He would consult with his family, meet with Dr. McCall, find a lawyer if he could, and either go bankrupt or launch his counterattack.

The lawyer who'd met with Pete about suing the bank for a

million dollars had agreed to take his case on a contingency basis—plus $2500 upfront. In the meantime, Pete had talked on the phone to another lawyer he liked even more. But this lawyer told Pete not to bother coming to see him unless he walked in the door with $3500 cash.

"I'll need to borrow five thousand dollars," Pete said to Mollie. She nodded noncommittally. Mollie was a plain-spoken and capable woman who supported her brother any way she could, but she had just opened her own accounting practice with another female CPA in Houston's Galleria district. She and her partner worked at their computers in a single room in their office suite. The receptionist's desk out front lacked a receptionist.

An hour later, Pete borrowed twenty dollars from his sister Gretchen; he needed a little walking-around money while the big decisions were pending, and he had come to Houston broke. At the suburban home of Gretchen and her husband, Brother, Pete prepared for the week's first challenge—an evening meeting with Dr. McCall. Pete showered, slicked down his hair, and donned a blue blazer Becky had bought him at a yard sale for two dollars (which was what he had valued it at on his bankruptcy inventory). Then, to gather evidence in case he ended up in a legal battle with Dr. McCall, Pete borrowed a small tape recorder and practiced concealing it so he could secretly tape his meeting with his partner.

Brother and Gretchen stood with Pete in their kitchen as he experimented with the recorder in his inside jacket pocket. Then his outside jacket pocket. "Why not put it under some papers in your briefcase and leave the briefcase open?" Gretchen suggested.

Pete tried it. He liked it.

Then he wondered how to mask the click the recorder would make after sixty minutes, when the tape came to the end of a side. "You'd better check your watch," Brother advised. "Hold your keys and jingle them when it clicks," Gretchen said. "I'm going to do this," Pete said. He did a little tap dance on the kitchen floor. He was holding up well under the pressure of the past months. Sometimes it looked like he was about to cry, but it was probably only his farmer's squint.

Pete and Dr. McCall had several issues to discuss. McCall wanted to know the status of the Universal I herd, which Pete put at about sixty animals. McCall wanted Pete to resign his general partnership in Universal I. And they had to settle which animals belonged to whom.

A few days before, Pete had met with Hans Lawaetz, who had flown in from St. Croix for the Houston Livestock Show, and they had sorted out which animals belonged to Annaly Farms. As a maintenance fee, Pete was entitled to half the calves that had been born to the Annaly Farms cattle in his care. Hans signed a document assigning ownership of ten young cattle to Hopes Creek Ranch. Pete was pleased with that outcome, but it was not entirely unambiguous. An argument could be made that Pete had made his deal with Annaly Farms as an agent of Universal I and that the ten animals therefore belonged to the partnership.

It was Dr. McCall's position that Pete should claim ownership of as few cattle as possible. Why claim a bunch of animals just to turn around and give them up to the bank? If Universal I owned them, the bank might not get them. McCall argued that Pete should declare he owned a single Senepol cow—and that it was in Guatemala.

Pete saw the logic of McCall's argument, but he didn't see any way he was going to end up with any Senepols if he followed it. His goal, at the moment, was to emerge from his troubles with ten Senepols and the feed store. As a bargaining chip, he was considering claiming ownership of every animal in sight.

The issue was hashed out—but not resolved—at the meeting, a partial tape of which Pete played afterward in Brother and Gretchen's driveway as he and Brother drank Canadian Club and Seven-Up.

The tape opened with a long silence. Pete narrated: "Here's where we went out to the coffee machine to get a cup of coffee."

Then Dr. McCall's voice was heard: "I think it's dumb for you to have *any* cattle."

Late that night, Pete drove out to Dr. McCall's ranch; he had to be there in the morning to meet some cowboys coming to pick up the Annaly Farms cattle. The ranch house was cute, painted white with red trim and decorated inside with a duck motif; there were duck-adorned pictures, salt and pepper shakers, napkin holders, hot mitts, and more. Pete arrived at 2:00 a.m., starving. He found some eggs in the refrigerator, hard-boiled them, and ate seven.

He awoke cheerful. The issues with McCall were clear if unresolved. He thought he might not go bankrupt but instead pay off all his debts—at ten dollars a month. He sang a verse of "Everybody Loves Somebody Sometime," then telephoned the feed store to consult with Becky on the status of the phone bill. They had bounced a check and the phone had been shut off for several days. They got it back on, but they had just written another check to pay a new bill, and it was not certain that it would not bounce.

The hostess at the restaurant where he went for breakfast asked Pete if he wanted the smoking or non-smoking section. "Wherever the fun people sit," he said.

The cowboys showed up with rancher Jim Stinson, who was a friend of Hans Lawaetz and a partner of Texas baseball legend Nolan Ryan in the Beefmaster business. Stinson was going to board the Annaly Farms Senepols. "Wait till you see these cattle," Pete told him.

Stinson had heard about Senepols. "They're gentle as dogs, aren't they?"

Pete helped Stinson's men round up thirty Senepols that Pete had been caring for.

"They look good for just coming off of winter," Stinson said.

"A worming and one month of good grass," said Pete, "and they'll slick off and look great."

Stinson's men loaded the cattle onto two trucks and two trailers, and Pete watched them drive away. If he had been able to sell these Senepols he would have collected a healthy commission and been in better financial shape. But he hadn't. Now, he knew, Lawaetz was already trying to sell them on his own. Another competitor on Pete's home ground.

But it wasn't clear if that mattered any more.

———

Back at Mollie's office, Pete wrestled with the lawyer issue. His choices were still the $2500 lawyer or the $3500 lawyer; his cash on hand was what was left of the $20 he had borrowed from Gretchen.

He was leaning toward the $3500 lawyer, he told Mollie. Whether he could hire him, he said, "depends on whether Gretchen was serious about the lien on the house."

Mollie said she could let him have $750. Her cash flow was tight since she had gone into business for herself. She and Pete called Gretchen together, and Gretchen said she would see what she could do.

Pete called College Station to check on soccer practice. Then he called Gretchen again.

Pete thought about it some more and decided he definitely wanted the $3500 lawyer. He called Gretchen again. She said she could give him a check for $2500 after work.

Mollie repeated her offer of $750.

That left Pete $250 short.

Pete and Mollie stood silently for a moment, and then they both turned to the third person in the room, a person who'd been watching these deliberations and solicitations all day.

It was me.

For more than a year, I'd been traveling with Pete. I'd been with him at the Houston Livestock Show. I'd been with him on St. Croix. I'd been with him in Guatemala. I'd spent days at the feed store and nights on the ranch. We'd gotten drunk together and watched football games and once, at my suggestion, watched Pee Wee Herman, which Pete didn't like at all. For the past few days in Houston, I'd been chauffeuring Pete around in my rental car—to Gretchen's house, to Fayette County. I'd lent him the tape recorder he'd used to tape Dr. McCall. I'd bought most of our meals. One night, in a highway bar, he'd bet he could beat me ten games in a row at pool and lost only because he sank the eight ball in game six. I'd seen everything he was trying to do with the Senepol. And now I was seeing the end.

"I've got two hundred and fifty dollars," I said.

"You're getting a bargain," said Mollie.


Pete called the $3500 lawyer and made an appointment for the next afternoon, so we had a day to kill.

I told Pete I wanted to stop by the Houston Livestock Show. Pete had been planning on exhibiting there again and also selling some bulls at auction there, but those plans had of course fallen through. I was curious to see the show again anyway. Pete agreed to go with me, but when we got to the Astrohall he stayed outside. "Take all the time you want," he said. "I'll wait."

Like an idiot, I was puzzled, until I got inside.

I walked over to the section where Pete had displayed his cattle the year before. The same Charbray booth was across the aisle, with the same sign: "Charbray—The Cowman's Breed."

The same Braler booth was down the row, with the same people tending it.

Cas Maree was around somewhere.

And there were Senepols again in Pete's old booth. Under a sign that said "Senepol: The Sunbelt Breed" stood two bulls, a heifer, and a cow with her calf. They weren't as sleek as Pete's Senepols. And they weren't from Hopes Creek Ranch. They came from American Senepol Limited in Tennessee. ASL was doing fine; Pete had recently heard they'd sold thirty-five bulls to Mexico. At one end of the booth a video was playing in an endless loop. It showed Senepols grazing on St. Croix, tended by old Frits Lawaetz and a Puerto Rican cowboy; it showed Senepols in Tennessee with John Niceley on a horse. "American Senepol Limited is readily accessible to the vast beef-producing areas of the southern states as well as other countries of the western hemisphere," the narrator said. "American Senepol Limited maintains the largest herd of Senepol breeding stock in the continental United States."

Back outside, I told Pete what I had seen. He nodded and didn't say much. He picked the next stop on our tour.

We drove east along the Houston Ship Channel and into a large park dominated by a 570-foot obelisk with the lone star of

Texas atop it. This was the site of the Battle of San Jacinto, where Texas won its independence from Mexico in 1836. Six weeks after the slaughter at the Alamo, the Texas forces caught Santa Anna's army on the bank of the San Jacinto, killed six hundred Mexicans while suffering only nine dead themselves, and captured Santa Anna attempting to escape in the guise of a common soldier. It was a smashing victory.

Pete told me that Brother, who did stone restoration work, once had a job on the tower. His equipment jammed and he was stuck hanging on the side of the monument, hundreds of feet above the ground. Television crews came out and filmed him sitting there, calmly smoking cigarettes and waiting to be rescued.

On another occasion, Brother took Pete to the tower and let him through the trapdoor at the very top. Pete climbed to the peak and touched the star.


The next day, cash in hand, Pete set off to see the lawyer, declaring, "I've scraped up every penny I could from the poor and the downtrodden to put my future in his hands." They met for more than two hours and Pete emerged tremendously encouraged.

The bank's lawsuit against Pete had been filed prematurely, the lawyer told him, since Pete's note had been renewed for thirty days.

The court order under which the bank had tried to seize Pete's cattle had been granted on insufficient grounds, the lawyer told him.

Pete should not go bankrupt, the lawyer told him, because he had assets to protect: the cattle he got from Annaly Farms and the money he was going to win in a lawsuit against the bank.

Riding back to College Station, Pete found a pair of sunglasses and put them on. "I can be cool again," he said. "I'm not going bankrupt."

It was business as usual at the feed store, with customers dropping in to buy horse feed and hay. Becky had the radio tuned to a gardening show so she and Wendell could learn how to sell gardening supplies. There was a passport application on the counter; Billie was talking about taking Bryan to Yugoslavia and, with the help of Aggies there, finding him a bride.

Bryan himself was outside digging a ditch. It had been intended to be a septic tank but a city inspector had come by and said they couldn't build a septic tank without a permit. So now it was going to be a well. It was ten feet deep and growing deeper, and water was already seeping in the bottom. "We got us a little pump that we stick down in the hole, and it pumps the water toward the garden," Bryan told me. "We're gonna take some PVC pipe. We're gonna punch holes in the pipe so we can like irrigate."

I asked Bryan how he'd been taking the loss of the ranch, and he grew reflective.

"Nothin' comes easy," he said. "You know, times all over, if you're in New York, Chicago, anywhere . . . times is tough, baby. You gotta stick it out. You got yourself into a situation that you don't have any control of, you know you're in trouble. I'm not gonna mention any names, but I tell ya, Pete, he was sky-high. This guy was, he was sky-high. He thought he had everything. He had everything, everything. His thing was all going good, y'know, when all of a sudden, *buh,* the bottom pulled out in front of him. You know? The *bottom* pulled out in front of him, and you know what? That could happen to anybody. . . ."

Inside, Pete was telling Becky about his trip. By mutual agreement, he hadn't been briefing her on the details of his troubles lately. It was less stressful not to know. The pressure was getting to her. Not ordinarily a sarcastic person, she had asked me a few days before, "Have you ever seen a dynasty rise and fall in three years? From five hundred acres to fifteen?"

Displayed on the feed-store counter was a picture painted by one of Wade's classmates after the class trip to the ranch. Despite Pete's best intentions, the only animals present when the children arrived had been one horse and a bunch of cats that lived in the yard. The painting was headed "The Sunnyside Ranch." In green, blue, yellow, and red, the artist had painted the house, the horse, the hammock, a rainbow, and what appeared to be a cat flying a kite. Also, Becky pointed out, some birds circling overhead.

"Buzzards," she said.

Pete was unfazed. "The Sunnyside Ranch!" he exclaimed. "Only ranch in the world with no cattle!"

Pete got in my car and we drove off toward Bryan, stopping first at the post office, where a certified letter was waiting for him. "A new lawsuit letter," Pete said. It was a notice that a long-distance telephone company was suing over an unpaid $1700 bill. "No big deal," Pete said. He tossed it in the back.

Then we drove into Bryan, to the county courthouse. Pete climbed the steps carrying a legal paper the lawyer had given him. It was a formal response to First Bank & Trust's lawsuit denying all the bank's allegations—the opening shot in what the lawyer had cautioned him was going to be a long war.

"This is America in action," Pete declared. He handed the paper to a clerk.

As we drove back to the feed store, I asked about Pete's future with the Senepol. Was this the end?

Not so, he said. He was going to emerge with ten good animals of his own. Using embryo transfers, "I'll build up a massive breeding herd."

Of course, that would take a while, he said. He might miss the Senepol boom that he saw coming soon.

But that would be reward enough. "I accomplished what I set out to do. . . . I lectured to empty rooms, sent out hundreds of mail-outs, printed up brochures, spent two years at Houston, got two speakers to A&M. The Senepol is taught as a breed in the freshman course, with slides. We generated a lot of interest."

In sum, even if he was in no position to cash in on it, the Senepol breed had been launched in Texas, and Pete Binion had done it.

I said I'd come back in twenty years to see how far Senepols had spread.

"Drive down I-10 from El Paso to Beaumont, and look on both sides of the road and see if the cattle are red," Pete told me.

Then he opened a copy of the College Station newspaper and started to look in the want ads for a job.

# EPILOGUE

# Jim

TWELVE DAYS AFTER Lin-Tex Marketing signed its deal with Loeb Partners, the stock market crashed. Retailers, fearing a recession, cut back drastically on their Christmas orders. Lin-Tex had projected December sales of $1 million; they were $280,000. Gary began to feel sick again.

Things turned around in the new year with a million-dollar order from Walden Books for "Bloom County" T-shirts. As usual, Lin-Tex needed to borrow money to produce the product. (The $500,000 it had received on signing with Loeb was long gone, the CDs borrowed against and the money spent.) Loeb had business connections with a relatively healthy Austin bank, and Jim and Gary had indirect connections with the bank's former president. "Jim used to date his wife," Gary told Peter Dixon. "I dated her daughter." Even so, the bank declined to make the loan unless Loeb Partners co-signed. Loeb agreed to do so in exchange for an additional 1 percent of Lin-Tex stock. The bank still declined to make the loan unless Loeb submitted a detailed financial statement, which Loeb, as a matter of general policy, declined to do. Dixon arranged for Loeb to lend Lin-Tex $500,000 for market-rate interest plus 1 percent of the company.

———

Roaming around Jim's living room at the age of eleven months, J.C. came upon an open container of fireplace crystals (which produced colorful flames when tossed into a fire) and he ate some. Frances found him with crystals smeared around his mouth and vomit on the floor. She called for help, and the baby was rushed by ambulance to an Austin hospital, where a doctor told Jim and Frances that if the substance had gotten into J.C.'s system it was likely he would die. Jim broke down in tears. He accompanied J.C. on an air ambulance to Galveston, where the baby was put on an infant dialysis machine. Tests showed that he had not ingested any poison. The doctors called it a miracle.

Gary, split from Dayna, resumed an active social life, dating, among others, a seventeen-year-old student and a thirty-nine-year-old grandmother. Shortly after the consummation of the Loeb deal—when he was working hard, dating often, and still spending substantial amounts of time with his three children in Ohio—he reflected on what he had learned so far:

"You can't get all the money you want, *and* all the sex you want, *and* all the family life, *and* all the excitement. It's not possible."

Lin-Tex repaid the $500,000 loan from Loeb Partners two months ahead of schedule, but, as another Christmas approached, it borrowed $500,000 again. Loeb took another 2 percent of the company.

The continuing collapse of financial institutions in Texas and elsewhere became an urgent national problem. President George Bush proposed, and Congress approved, a bailout for savings and loans that would cost American taxpayers $325 billion.

Lamar Savings, its plan to open an office on the moon un-realized, was closed. Federal regulators sold Lamar property at auction, including several five-foot-tall carved wooden elephants they had been surprised to discover at Lamar headquarters.

The Federal Deposit Insurance Corporation took over the loans owed by Jim to North Central National Bank and United Bank, both of which had failed. While Jim began negotiating to settle the loans for less than the full amount owed, the FDIC sold the collateral held by United—the last of Jim's Wendy's stock, the foundation of all his ventures, which had fallen from twenty dollars a share to five.

In "Bloom County," Opus briefly found work as a male stripper (he did a Phil Donahue impersonation that drove the ladies wild) and Bill the Cat ran for President but faltered in the polls when, his heart broken by Jeane Kirkpatrick, he shot up the neighborhood with a machine gun. The strip continued to be immensely popular, but in 1989 Berke Breathed announced that "a good comic strip is no more eternal than a ripe melon" and quit drawing it (although Opus and Bill survived in a new strip Breathed started called "Outland"). This was not the blow to Lin-Tex it would once have been, because "Bloom County" had by then been supplanted as the company's hottest property by "Mother Goose & Grimm," a transition that had begun with a design showing Grimm the dog humping a human leg. The caption was "Safe Sex."

Lin-Tex acquired the T-shirt rights to "Nancy," "Callahan," "Rose Is Rose," "Eggers," and "Mr. Boffo." It signed a deal with Hershey's to sell shirts picturing the chocolate maker's products and logo. Lin-Tex shirts began to make inroads into the department-store market.

Total sales approached $6 million a year, but profits were skimpy. The money came in, and the money went out.

In the spring of 1989, for no obvious sound business reason, Lin-Tex moved from its modest office/warehouse suite to a mammoth new factory/warehouse/office/showroom facility on the south side of Austin. A big red sign on the side of the building identified it as the "Lin-Tex Center."

The Lin-Tex Center comprised some thirty thousand square feet. The factory area—Lin-Tex's first venture into doing its own production—was equipped with high-speed color T-shirt presses. The executive wing included a bathroom (the sign on the door said "Comic Relief") with a shower and monogrammed Lin-Tex towels. Another wing housed Jim and Gary's money-losing travel agency and two new businesses they had established under the Lin-Tex umbrella—a copy and printing service, and a photo lab and studio. A dry-cleaning plant and catering service were on the drawing board. "By combining key operations required for effective market penetration," a Lin-Tex press release explained, "we offer a total marketing service for not only Comic Strip characters, but all types of licenses—social humor, fashion, corporate logos, gifts, and many, many more!"

Lin-Tex had leased the building at a bargain rate from a desperate landlord, but the cost of establishing the Lin-Tex Center had still been substantial. Somehow it had been put together in the midst of yet another cash-flow crisis. "I don't know how we're doing it," Gary confessed. As the grand opening party—dubbed the "Second, Sometimes Annual Comic Collectibles Cotillion, Barn Raisin', and Brandin' "—approached, Gary hoped Peter Dixon would attend so Gary could describe to him in person his vision of a greater Lin-Tex ("I need a couple of million dollars to do it right"). Jim wasn't so sure inviting Dixon was a good idea, since one casualty of the current cash-flow crisis was Lin-Tex's ability to repay the most recent $500,000 loan from Loeb Partners. Under the circumstances, Jim said, "I can't imagine Peter Dixon being thrilled to come into our office and see our shower and monogrammed towels."

Dixon did not show up, but several of Lin-Tex's cartoonists did fly in at Lin-Tex's expense. Also on hand for the three-day celebration were several live bands, a radio station mobile broadcast booth, a friend of Jim's on a horse, and hundreds of invited guests and members of the general public, all mingling with the employees of Lin-Tex, now numbering forty-five, who were dressed as western sheriffs. A local television station interviewed Jim and Gary in their office. Gary told the story of how he'd met Jim in the third grade. "Act like you're working," the TV reporter said. Jim leaned back in his chair, put his feet up on his desk, and started to read a newspaper.

During the formal opening ceremony in the parking lot, a city councilman told the assembled crowd: "I've known Jim and Gary for a number of years, and these guys really hustle."

The mayor of Austin cut a red ribbon held by Gary's daughter in a Bill the Cat costume. Then he hoisted a glass of beer in the direction of the Lin-Tex Center. "This is why Austin is gonna dust itself off and come back very strong," he declared. "We are for the *real* quality of life, and that's jobs jobs jobs for our citizens. . . . And there ain't nothing wrong with making a profit, folks."

The audience applauded. Jim, standing beside the mayor with his arm around Frances, tipped his cowboy hat to the crowd.

Meanwhile, in the Soviet Union, Mikhail Gorbachev was instituting a number of startling political and economic reforms. One of them was a new policy that state agencies start to pay their own way.

In June 1989, Jim called to tell me that Lin-Tex Marketing had obtained the T-shirt rights to the Soviet space program.

Three days later, I walked through the gates of Le Bourget airfield at the edge of Paris, where the Paris Air Show had just begun. Soviet MiG-29 fighters were staging demonstration flights over the field. The new Russian space shuttle, the Buran, had flown in perched atop the largest airplane in the world and was parked at the head of the display area. In the Soviet pavilion, thousands of visitors trooped by exhibits of Soviet space hardware, including a cosmonaut suit and engines from the biggest Soviet rocket. Hundreds of aircraft components were on display and for sale. At a counter near the front door, Jim was selling T-shirts. "Who's next?" he called to passers-by. "This is the best T-shirt made in America."

Jim was working the counter with four other Texans. One was a friend who owned a chain of quick auto lube shops in Austin and hoped his friends in the John Birch Society back home wouldn't find out how he was spending his summer vacation. The others were investors in Space Commerce Corporation, a start-up Houston company that was the American sales agent for Glavkosmos, the Soviet equivalent of NASA. Jim had gotten his T-shirt rights from Space Commerce, which had its own booth in the pavilion and was offering for sale (besides T-shirts) satellite launches on Soviet rockets, research room on the Soviet space station, and anything else anyone might want to buy or rent from Glavkosmos, including cosmonaut endorsements and advertising on the sides of Soviet rockets. ("I think this is a natural," the Space Commerce salesman told me. "How about on the first manned flight of the Buran the cosmonauts wear Adidas?")

"Step right up," Jim called from behind his counter. "Get your Glavkosmos T-shirts. Help us put a bird into orbit."

"Lin-Tex is selling Soviet space launches now?" I asked.

"We're part of SCC," Jim said. He showed me a Space Commerce Corporation business card with his name (misspelled) and addresses in Houston and Moscow.

"Are they going to improve their thermal control?" asked a bald American who had overheard us.

"I don't know a damn thing about it, pal," Jim snapped. "I sell T-shirts for the Russians."

I spent six days in Paris with Jim, watching him sell T-shirts in four designs that had been produced at the Lin-Tex Center (the most popular pictured a Russian rocket with Soviet and American flags) and also Glavkosmos polo shirts, golf caps (dismal sellers), and embroidered satin jackets of the type usually associated with rock tours. Occasionally, I worked behind the counter myself. "Feel that cotton," I urged one wavering Flemish tourist. "This is the finest T-shirt made."

I began to wonder what I was doing there. I knew why Jim was selling T-shirts for the Russians, but why were the Russians having him do it? If the Soviet Union was counting on T-shirt royalties to reduce its budget deficit, it was in worse trouble than I'd imagined.

Glavkosmos officials at the show set me straight. The T-shirt revenues were "peanuts," one told me. Just enough "to buy slips for our girlfriends."

The senior Glavkosmos official present, a sincere young man named Dmitri Poletayev, explained to me that his top priority was to win reversal of an American government ban on Soviet launches of American satellites, a lucrative business that the Russians were eager to get. The Space Commerce Corporation people had told him that in America T-shirts are like billboards and influence public opinion. (The Space Commerce people were at this time impatient to start selling *something* for the Russians; they hadn't sold anything yet.) "What you can see here," Poletayev told me, "the selling of shirts, the main purpose is not commercialization. The main purpose is publicity of possibility of cooperation between U.S. and USSR. . . . To make influence for public, and then to allow this public relation to make influence for the administration."

In other words, Glavkosmos had authorized Lin-Tex to sell T-shirts to influence the American government to change its mind about Soviet launches of American satellites.

I walked back over to the T-shirt counter, past a video display of MiGs practicing battle maneuvers, and put it to Jim: did he realize he was selling T-shirts to achieve a foreign policy objective? Is this where he'd thought his career would lead him?

"Of course," he said. "What do you think I was born to do?"

In fact, Jim didn't care why anybody thought he was selling T-shirts, as long as the T-shirts were selling. He stood behind the counter, a wad of francs in his hand, pushing shirts on Americans, Frenchmen, Germans, Danes. . . . After twenty-five years of hustling, he was hustling once again, hustling still. For Kentucky Fried Chicken, for Wendy's, for Lin-Tex Marketing, for the Union of Soviet Socialist Republics, it was all the same game, and Jim knew how to play. The world was changing, and it hadn't changed one bit.

"Who's next?" Jim called out. "Step right up. It's a very good gift, for ladies or men. . . . Yes, we'll take a check."

# **P**ete

Dear Ed. . . .

The swimming coach stopped by the feed store the other day and offered all three kids a scholarship for the summer swim program. Pete was reluctant to take it (but did). . . .

He is still looking for employment. Everyday he checks out something. . . .

We've been doing with out AC, dishwasher, & dryer. . . . Trying to keep all bills down as much as possible. . . .

With the drought that has gone on I kid Pete that we have made $ by not growing hay this year. It rained good today and I kidded him again that if we had been haying this year we probably would've cut yesterday. Can you see the humor. (He said No, we would've fertilized!). . . .

Wade received a letter from the school district Sat. It informed him he was eligible and selected to be in an excellerated science class next year (otherwise known as Gifted and Talented). We are so proud of him and he is real excited. I told him now maybe he could find out where the world came from (or was it who made the world?). . . .

The girls were so excited to receive the jean skirts. Pauline decided she wanted to save hers for a special time and Mollie wanted to wear hers, but she said the rules were "No eating chocolate, no drinking Kool Aid, and no swimming in it. . . ."

Bryan has moved back to Burnet to try to go to trade school and live in a halfway house or something. We sure miss him. . . .

Glad to hear the book is coming along. . . .

Take care and come see us.

*Love,*

*Becky*

**A**FTER SEVERAL MONTHS, Pete was hired as a maintenance worker at the College Station Hilton. The pay was low, but as a fringe benefit he got two free nights in a Hilton every month. Before starting work, however, he was offered a better job with the Texas A&M Engineering Extension Service, and he took that one instead. When he told me about it in a long-distance telephone conversation, I reminded him that he'd told me in Houston he didn't want a job with the university. "I don't like the idea of working for the government," he'd said. "That practically makes you a Communist."

I asked him now if he'd changed his mind.

"I've sold my soul," he said.

J. S. Mogford, having repossessed all of Hopes Creek Ranch except the front fifteen acres with the house, tried to get that section too, since a ranch with a house was a more valuable property than a ranch without one. He offered to trade a paid-up house in town.

The decision was Billie Pratt's, since Billie had formally repossessed the ranch house from Pete to protect it from Pete's creditors. Pete wanted to stay on the ranch, and Becky felt even more strongly about it than he did. She acknowledged that living in town would be convenient, but "that cannot compare to the offerings a country atmosphere contributes to our lifestyles," she wrote in a letter to her parents. She was concerned that living in town would expose the children to the "constant bad influences" of "bad neighborhood kids" and cable television. "When we moved from our little 2 bedroom trailer to this 500+ ac. ranch," Becky wrote, "I never felt I was deserving of so much, but I did feel a prayer had been answered & there was a purpose for me (us) in the whole transaction. I just don't think the past 4 years at HCR should be for nothing. . . . Besides, how many Class of 52's have a ranch they can stay at when they come down for football games?"

Billie rejected Mogford's offer.


American Senepol Limited, its herd grown to 550 head, held a Senepol auction in Harrogate, Tennessee, and sold 96 Senepols for $205,000, a respectable total. Things had gone right for American Senepol Limited. It was adequately financed, which bought it time to be patient. By the time of its auction (which turned out to be the first in an annual series), the cattle business had come out of its years-long slump into prosperity, and enterprising ranchers were willing to consider investing in what appeared to be a promising new breed. Buyers at the auction included the Niceley brothers, who still had their own Senepol business, and ranchers from Virginia, Kentucky, Tennessee, Louisiana, Georgia, and North Carolina. There were three buyers from Texas, one of them a big Gulf Coast rancher whose family had been among the first in the state to breed Brahmans.

Slowly but steadily, the Senepol was spreading.


Pete and Dr. McCall parted ways, but Pete did retain ownership of a dozen Senepols of his own.

The bank took them.

Pete had said he might extract and freeze embryos from the cattle before giving them up so he could build a new herd, but he dropped the idea. His unpaid bills, he concluded, had caused "too much damage in the credibility" of his Senepol business to get people to trust him again. "It might not be irreparable, but the wonderment is there."

The bank sold the cattle it had taken from Pete. Billie bought several of the best ones.

The lawsuits against Pete entered a dormant phase, at least in part because you can't get blood out of a stone. Pete had no assets for creditors to gain. The cattle were gone, the feed store was in debt (and Pete had assigned his ownership share to his sister Mollie), and the house belonged to Billie.

Pete's lawyer advised him to hold off suing the bank.

Before he got around to doing it, the bank failed.

Pete wanted to put everything behind him. He decided to go back to school.

At first he thought about finishing the master's degree in animal breeding he'd been working on when he first got interested in Senepols, but he decided to drop that and move on to something new. At the age of thirty-eight, he enrolled at Texas A&M as an undergraduate in ocean engineering. When Becky asked why he was giving up all his years of experience with animals, he replied, "There are animals in the ocean, too."

Pete had always loved the ocean, he told me in one of our phone conversations. He said he figured he could get his bachelor's degree in two and a half years if he went to school summers. Then he would go for a job in ocean construction or maybe undersea mining. He thought he might end up working in the Gulf of Mexico and commuting home weekends, and that was all right with him.

If things went well, he figured he could earn a good income from engineering and pursue his agricultural interests with his own money on the side. I asked if those interests would include the Senepol.

"Very likely," he said.

But he would do it on his own this time, with no partners, limited or otherwise. Just Pete Binion, gentleman rancher. "Like George Washington or Thomas Jefferson," he told me. "I think one of them was an engineer and had his own farm, too."

That was the last time I talked to Pete for a while. The next time I called the feed store, the phone had been disconnected.

Eight months passed. Then I stopped off in College Station on my way home from yet another encounter with the killer bees, which had become well established as my journalistic specialty. The news hook this time was that the bees were less than a year away from flying across the Rio Grande into the United States. A magazine had sent me to Mexico, to the killer bees' front line, to see how they were behaving. They were behaving badly. Two of the little fuckers stung me in the head— *through* my pith helmet—and I was not sorry to bid them *hasta la vista* and fly off to Houston, where I rented a car at the airport and drove directly to Hopes Creek Ranch.

There was no one home when I arrived, so I took a walk around. A trailer was parked in front of the house with a green canoe and a white cat inside it. By the side of the house, the frame Wendell had built to grow decorative shrubs for the feed store had collapsed. I thought I saw Wendell and Aleta in the distance, on the far side of the tank and walking away. There were no cattle in sight, not anywhere, and that seemed very strange.

I walked toward the tank and a breeze caught me, breaking through the humidity of the late afternoon. The light was fading quickly. I looked out across the empty pastures, refreshingly green after the yellow hillsides of Mexico. Without the moaning of cattle, it was perfectly quiet. I could hear the rustling of wind over grass. The trees, just budding, stood in silhouette against the sky. It was peaceful and soothing to be there. I could see why Pete and Becky had fought to stay.

As I walked back toward the house the Binions appeared, honking a greeting, in a Chevrolet Suburban wagon. The old blue truck was gone; the Suburban was a gift from Billie (and, to be creditor-proof, held in his name). The family was returning from a swim meet; Wade was wearing nothing but a bathing suit. He hadn't finished above fifth in any event, Becky reported, "but he bettered all his times except one," and that was the important thing.

Pete looked trim and relaxed, and the house was neater than I'd ever seen it, and emptier. Bryan was gone, living with his parents in Burnet and working in a rock quarry. Wendell and Aleta had moved out to the house Keith used to live in. Aleta still tended the main house while Becky drove the kids to school and their extracurricular activities and while Becky attended school herself. She was going to junior college and hoped to transfer to A&M and get a degree in parks and recreation administration. She told me she was thinking of applying what she was learning by building a three-hole golf course on Hopes Creek Ranch—or what was left of it—for the family's own enjoyment and to increase the property's value.

We sat down to visit on the patio, where we had sat on my very first visit years before. There were no blender drinks this time. There was one beer in the house, and we split it three ways. Pete showed me a vegetable garden growing next to the patio. "We're going to get a lot out of that," he said. Mollie came outside with some tomato seedlings, and he helped her plant them. Becky made spaghetti for dinner, and we ate it at the dining-room table surrounded by little green planters filled with young tomatoes, cucumbers, and beans.

In the morning I went to work with Pete. His place of employment, conveniently located on the road between the ranch and town, was marked by a sign that said "Emergency Response Training Area." He worked for HAZMAT, the oil and hazardous materials section of a training center for emergency workers run by the A&M extension service. His job consisted mainly of setting up "scenarios," simulated emergencies for the HAZMAT students to respond to.

The HAZMAT grounds were covered with realistic settings for these scenarios. There were concrete buildings and scorched steel towers, tractor trailers, railway tank cars, and smashed automobiles—props for almost any kind of disaster. It would have made a wonderful playground for children.

Pete's office was a large workshop. In a nearby building, a class of trainees was watching a movie about chemical fires.

Pete's first task of the day was to drive into town and buy donuts for the class's coffee break.

That accomplished, we walked over to a small room in a concrete building where a tank was labeled $H_2SO_4$ (sulfuric acid). Pete ran a hose to the tank, which was empty, and started to fill it with water. This took a while, so we wandered outside to watch a class of firemen in yellow coats spraying water at blazing kerosene. The flames shot up hot and drove us back, but the firemen stood their ground. We watched for a few minutes; it was a pleasant way to pass part of the morning. Pete was smiling. "Government job," he said.

When the bogus acid tank was full of water, Pete adjusted a tap on the bottom to make it leak slowly. Later trainees would come in and find a spreading puddle of "sulfuric acid" on the floor. The first thing they were likely to do was try to close the tap. Pete adjusted it so that, if anyone touched it, it would fall off in his hand and a flood of "sulfuric acid" would burst out.

Pete set up another scenario and was building a shelf when the clock hit noon, his quitting time. I asked if this had been a typical day's work—two scenarios and part of a shelf.

"And we got the donuts," Pete reminded me.

I followed him over to A&M, which Pete, as a Texas veteran, was entitled to attend for free. He had a calculus class that afternoon. He was taking the course—a prerequisite for the engineering curriculum—for the second time; he'd had trouble with it in the fall but was doing well this time around. The professor was a few years younger than Pete. The students were mostly twenty years younger. The professor lectured about functions, and I listened as long as I could, then dozed. Pete took notes on every single thing the professor said.

That night we had a double date, Pete and Becky and I and a woman Becky fixed me up with. Becky checked the free events listings in the newspaper, and we went to a concert by a jazz band from Texas Christian University. Afterward, my date, who was an English teacher, told me her first love had been biology but a guidance counselor had steered her away from studying science because science was not a fit career for a woman. She was still bitter about this. Who knows, she said to me, if she had studied biology she might have found a cure to the common cold by now.

I wondered if there was something in the water in Brazos County that made people dream beyond their means.

The next afternoon—my last in Texas—I stopped by the feed store. It wasn't called Texsen Feed and Supply any more. Creditors had been sniffing around it, looking for seizable assets, to an irritating degree, so Pete had sold the store to a friend in exchange for his taking over its debts. The new owner worked nights at the post office, so Wendell ran the store as his employee. Wendell still enjoyed retailing, and the store was doing well; enough money came in to keep up inventory now that no one was raiding the till for living expenses. Opening a feed store on this site had been a good idea; Pete could have made it work if he hadn't been broke.

I was supposed to meet Pete in the A&M library, where he was going to be working from 5:00 to 7:00 p.m. on some overdue engineering drawings. He had fallen behind on them a couple of weeks before when his lawyer called one morning and told him they had a trial that afternoon. Pete had dropped everything—and missed an engineering drawing lab—to get to the courthouse, where the plaintiff, the man who had done the embryo transfer work on Pete's Senepols, was awarded a $14,000 judgment after a short trial. This so distracted Pete that he got a bad grade on a geology test three days later. And he was still trying to catch up on the drawings.

I got to the library at 5:45 but didn't see Pete, so I went off to photocopy some references on time travel for an article I was writing. At 6:15 Pete still wasn't around, but I found his drafting paper and stencils on an unoccupied table. He came in at 6:30 and said there was a problem. Becky had been on her way to pick up Pauline at ballet class at 5:00 when the Suburban had come to a halt. Becky restarted it, drove seventy-five yards, and it halted again. She did this again and again and finally reached the library and found Pete. They picked up Pauline an hour late and then came back for me.

The car was parked on a campus road with Becky up front and Pauline sitting patiently in the back reading newspaper comics. "It's the transmission," Pete told me. The car had had a thousand-dollar transmission job eight months before in Burnet, but the transmission had apparently failed again. It would drive a little way and then slip completely. After a short rest, it would drive a little way again.

Pete asked me to get in my rental car and follow them out to HAZMAT. He would leave his car there and, in the morning, call the mechanic in Burnet to see if the transmission was under warranty. If it wasn't, he would get to the library somehow and find a book on auto repair and try to fix it himself.

We drove from the campus to HAZMAT in stages. Pete drove skillfully, building up speed to coast through the transmission failures, and the Suburban came to a stop only five times. Pete turned in at the sign, "Emergency Response Training Area," and started up a small hill. The car came to a stop for the sixth time.

As soon as it moved again, Pete would get it into the parking lot and I would drive the family back to the ranch. In the morning, Pete would have to get to work and to school (and to the library to find a book on transmission repair), and he still had his engineering drawings to do. Becky had to get to her junior college for a political science test. The kids had school and dance lessons and swimming. And they would all be sitting eight miles from town with no phone and, now, no car.

I got out of my rental car and walked over to the Suburban. Pete was standing there staring at it.

"Dead?" I asked.

He shook his head ruefully. "It wasn't even 'I think I can.' "

"*You* can," I said encouragingly.

Pete raised a hand and pointed at the sky and replied, without a trace of uncertainty, "We *will*!"

# Postscript

I N FEBRUARY 1990, Jim and Frances separated and started the
process of getting divorced.

Later that month, an Austin bank that had lent Lin-Tex
Marketing $1.15 million nine months earlier for yet another bout
of optimistic expansion grew nervous about the loan. Lin-Tex was
still selling $5 million worth of T-shirts a year, but it had debts of
over $2 million and negligible profits. The bank seized the cash
in the company's checking accounts. Loeb Partners declined to
pump any more money into the company. Lin-Tex Marketing filed
for bankruptcy and went out of business.

While Jim prepared to file personal bankruptcy as well, his
Mercedes was repossessed and he began receiving unemployment
benefits of $217 a week. Before getting his first check, he attended
an orientation session where a counselor advised those new to
unemployment to stress their professional backgrounds on the
forms they filled out so they would not be forced to apply for "dead-
end jobs at places like Wendy's."

But Jim already had other plans. He was thinking of joining
a friend in starting a mobile home park for the homeless. With
city and federal funds available to subsidize such a project, Jim
thought it looked like a way to "make real good money."

In College Station, Pete had become a full-time employee of
the hazardous materials training center and a part-time graduate
student. He had switched his field from Ocean Engineering to

Industrial Hygiene. He was headed toward a career in hazardous waste management.

In the meantime, he enjoyed his work and was earning a decent wage. "Things here are on an even keel," he wrote in a letter, "and all people, family, pets, and friends are healthy and doing well." He was grateful every day that he no longer had the burden of a failing business on his shoulders. He didn't have to worry any more. "Life is a joy," he said. "I'm living in Heaven."